DALIT THEOLOGY

DALIT THEOLOGY

History, Context, Text, and Whole Salvation

JAMES MASSEY

MANOHAR
2014

First published 2014

ISBN 978-93-5098-027-9 (Hb)
ISBN 978-93-5098-033-0 (Pb)

Published by
Ajay Kumar Jain *for*
Manohar Publishers & Distributors
4753/23 Ansari Road, Daryaganj,
New Delhi 110 002

Printed at
Salasar Imaging Systems
Delhi 110 035

To KALA *(my wife)*

Who shares with me my birthday (11 *May) and*

has travelled with me for 42 *years and*

intends to journey for many more years of our active life.

Contents

PART 3: CONTEXT

PART 4: MULTI-RELIGIOUS APPROACH

PART 5: BIBLICAL MODELS OF LIBERATION

Preface

Dalits were forced to adopt the 'culture of silence' for centuries by the so-called upper caste people, but today they have broken their silence. Behind this breaking-up of the culture of silence, there have been many liberative forces working for a long time. It visibly began with the revolts of Lord Mahavira (540 BC-468 BC) and Lord Buddha (563 BC-483 BC) against the supremacy of the Brahmins who were the creators of the caste system in India. The efforts continued all through the history since then, and was upheld and sustained by many including various Hindu Bhakti movements, Christian and missionary movements, Muslim Sufi movement and teachings of Sikh Gurus till it reached the present times under the leadership of Dr. B.R. Ambedkar, himself a Dalit. Dr. Ambedkar (1891-1956) was indeed the first representative voice of the Dalits and helped in giving a positive shape to the movement. Today thousands of Dalits and non-Dalits are keenly involved in this movement. This book on 'Dalit theology' is part of the same liberative process.

Inspite of all these efforts the Dalits till date do not have a common 'ideology' or a 'theology' from their perspective ('Dalit theology'), which can become a basis of the struggle for their total liberation. The common ideology or Dalit theology can be the binding force and can bring about a solidarity among various groups of Dalits, which certainly they need for their improvement to carry on their struggle for liberation. This book is part of the effort to fill this gap.

The book itself in the present form is result of, almost three decades of the reflective experience of the author. He entered into the process of doing theology from the Dalit perspective from the mid 1980s onwards. He had the privilege to be part of the first generation theologians and even their collective experience is also in spirit as part of this book. Beside working with the Dalit Christians at different levels, the author took active part in the multi-faith struggle of the Dalits which include: Dalit Hindus, Dalit Muslims, Dalit Christians, Dalit Sikhs and Dalit Buddhists.

Therefore this book is rooted in the historical experience of all Dalits including Dalit Christians (see for history in general chapters 1-3) and Dalit Christians (chapters 4 and 5). The same way this book in depth deals with the past context of Dalits in general (see chapter 6), and has discussions on the existing caste based social order as well on the added contextual factor globalization and its impact on the Dalits (see chapter 6). Besides the general context, the specific context of Dalit Christians and their civil rights are also part of the discussion in this work (see chapter 7). The text includes multi-religious approaches (see chapter 8) to the whole issue of Dalits. In depth reflection is included in the discussion of this book on the issues of 'peace, reconciliation and justice' from the perspective of the Dalits (see chapter 9), which is the core of Dalit theology.

The 'text' which is the third key foundation of Dalit theology, not only offers models (see chapters 10, 11, 12 and 13), but also offers tests for any authentic expression of theology including 'Dalit theology' is dealt equally in this book (see for tests chapter 10.7).

In the last section, this book deals with the 'vision, nature and role' of 'Dalit theology' (see chapter 14) and also calls for a paradigm shift in the whole theological education system (see chapter 15). The last chapter deals with the most important aspect of 'Dalit theology', which is not only the end goal of it, but also the very essence. It is the 'Dalit combat spirituality' which enables the Dalits to achieve 'whole salvation' for which they are waiting for the last 3500 years. This whole salvation includes personal transformation as well as the societal, which leads to the establishment of 'just society' in which every human being enjoys a full redeemed humanity. This is what this book is about.

This book is the result of the encouragement and help from many individuals and organizations to whom I would like to express my gratitude. I am specially thankful to the Centre for Dalit/Subaltern Studies, New Delhi for sponsoring this project on 'Dalit theology' as part of its programme. I am specially thankful to Deepak Seth, a close friend whose immense knowledge and sound judgement I highly regard. I am grateful to my colleagues Nungsang Jamir and Imti Jamir, who have helped in putting and arranging the material very carefully through its many stages. I am indebted to my publisher Ramesh Jain, his son Ajay Jain, their editor Siddharth Chowdhury for their valuable suggestions and keen interest in this publication.

I am also grateful to my family members, specially my wife Kala, for patiently bearing up with my pre-occupations while working on this volume.

Above all I am thankful to God Almighty for giving me the strength to complete this work, which I believe will provide the necessary support to people of different faiths and ideologies.

11 May 2013 JAMES MASSEY

PART 1

DALIT HISTORY

CHAPTER 1

Ancient Roots of the Term 'Dalit'

1.1. Relationship of the Semitic and the Indo-Germanic

The term 'dalit' is perhaps one of the most ancient terms which has not only survived till date, but it is also shared by a few of the world's oldest languages. For example, Hebrew and Sanskrit, though they differ in their grammatical structure and in their lexicographical connotation, yet share the term 'dalit' almost with the same root and sense. One basis of such agreements among different families of languages is stated by German scholar E. Kautzsch in these words:

> A considerable number of Semitic roots and stems agreed in sound with synonyms in the Indo-Germanic family. But apart from expressions actually borrowed.... The real similarity may be reduced to imitative words (onomatopoetica), and to those in which one and the same idea is represented by similar sounds in consequence of a formative instinct common to the most varied families of language.[1]

E. Kautzsch's observation helps us in understanding the possibility of a journey of words and terms from one language to another, through time and space.

One may raise a question about the term 'dalit', how it travelled either from Sanskrit to Hebrew or from Hebrew to Sanskrit. Because these two languages belong to two different families of language, namely, Semitic and Indo-Germanic. But our problem can be solved by looking into the history of the root of this term in Hebrew. The Hebrew root of the term, *dall* has a relationship with the Akkadian term *dalulu* (be weak)[2] and close to that is the Assyrian *dalulu* (be weak or humble.)[3] Hebrew is part of the North-West Semitic group of languages and Assyrian, along with Babylonian, forms from the East Semitic group classed as Akkadian.[4] Now a possible answer to our question regarding the relationship between Sanskrit and Hebrew can be established by looking into the relationship which existed between two ancient civilizations, Indus and Babylonian. There are enough archeological evidences to prove such a relationship. For example, C.J. Gadd and Sydney Smith make an important observation about such an ancient relationship when they say:

> The most important objects in this respect are the seals from Harappa, which appear to be exactly similar in shape to square stamp seals which are commonly found at and on Babylonian sites of the early period. ... These close resemblances of the Harappa seals to the products of Babylonian civilization cannot be accidental. The people who made these seals must have been in very close contact with Sumerian civilization, and have barrowed their artistic style and the basis of their writing from the Sumerians.[5]

A number of other authorities also agree with the above view.[6] From other sources we also know that the written form of Sanskrit (its first ancient document is the *Rigveda*) was composed between 1500-2000 BC.[7] And of course, today's Sanskrit which falls under the 'classic' category, belongs to a much later period. Around the same period Hebrew and other Semitic writings also developed.[8] Now as the discussion on establishing the linguistic relationship of Hebrew and Sanskrit does not fall directly within the scope of this work, but if we accept the above observations, both historical and linguistic, for our purpose, then one point which becomes clear is that the Hebrew root *dall* and Sanskrit root *dal*, which resemble both in sense (idea) and sound through the Akkadian relationship with *dalulu*, have their roots prior to both present classical Sanskrit and Hebrew. There is a real possibility of 'Dalit' or *daluth* belonging either to the language used by people of the Babylonian or the people of the Indus civilization.

1.2. Hebrew use of the Term 'Dalit'

As mentioned earlier, the biblical root of the word 'Dalit' is *dall*. The word *dall* is a verb and it means to hang down, to be languid, be awaken, be low, be feeble. It has been used in the Old Testament Hebrew in its various forms.[9] Examples are: in perfect form *dalote*, it has been used in Pslams 116:6, 142:7 and others and an imperfect verb form *y-dal* used in Isaiah 17:4. In the Bible it has been used more often as object in order to denote the state of certain groups of people. Its basic adjective form is *dal*, masculine plural is *dalem*, and feminine plural *dalot*, feminine singular is *dalah*. As an adjective it has been translated commonly in English as low, weak or poor. Examples of such references in the Bible are: Genesis 41:19, Exodus 23:3, Leviticus 14:21, Judges 6:15, Isaiah 11:4, Jeremiah 40:7, Amos 2:7, Ruth 3:10, 2 Samuel 13:4, Job 5:15, Psalms 41:1, Proverbs 10:15, Zephaniah 3:12, and others. Special note should be made of the collective use of the feminine plural constructed from the *dalat* and *dalot* in II kings 24:14, 25:12, Jeremiah 40:7, 52:15, 16, where it has been translated in the New Revised Standard Version as 'the poorest people of the land' and 'the poorest of the people'. Almost all the English translations, including in Indian languages, have followed the same English sense and meaning.

But what actually is the meaning of this Hebrew word or term *dall?* Does it mean 'poor' as it has been understood by the English translators of the Bible, or does it mean such more than that? At least a few scholars have made an attempt to understand its meaning. For Example, Elsa Tamez, a liberation theologian, while listing the major Hebrew terms used for 'poor', has also included *dal*. According to her *dal* is used in two senses: it may refer either to physical weakness or to a lowly, insignificant position in society'.[10] C.U. Wolf in his essay on the term 'poor' which he contributed to *The Interpreter's Dictionary of the Bible* makes the Hebrew meaning of *dall* more clear. While referring to those people for whom the term *dal* or *dalah* or *dalot* has been used in the Hebrew Bible, Wolf says:

> They are those whose prosperity and social status have been reduced. In this respect they are the opposite of the rich (Exodus 23:3, 30:15, Leviticus 14:21, Proverbs 22:16, others). In physical strength, in psychological ability, they are also impaired and helpless. (Job 34:28; Psalms 82:3, Jeremiah 40:7; 52:16, and others)[11]

In this observation an important point to be noted is that *dal* or *dalot* people are not only economically or physically poor or weak, they are also poor in their 'psychological ability' and their being has been 'impaired' to such a state that they have become 'helpless'. So in other words, this Hebrew term denotes a much deeper side of the state of the people known as *dalot*, which cannot be covered by a simplistic English term 'poor'.

Till this point we have tried to answer our question about the meaning of the term 'dalit' in Hebrew, either on the basis of what Hebrew lexicon tells or what a few interpreters have said. It may be good to determine the meaning or sense of 'dalit' in Hebrew ourselves by analysing the use of this term in the Bible. But before doing so, we need to keep in mind that this effort is also going to be made *via* the English language, as our basic knowledge of biblical languages, Hebrew, Aramaic and Greek, is only through English. And all that we find in English is to some extent contextual, that is based on the experience of the English people, it is still a challenge to the African, Asian and Indian biblical scholars to come forward with some biblical study material based directly on our knowledge of Hebrew or Greek through Tamil or Hindi or Panjabi. Anyhow, our brief analysis under the different sub-themes of the selected verses where the term 'dalit' has been used in the Hebrew text may still be useful for our present purpose. The English versions of these verses are found in the New Revised Standard Version.[12] Here below some examples are given of the use of expression of 'Dalit', where it has been used in different senses.

1.2.1. *Existence of Dalits is Recognized*

In this sub-section are listed three verses in order to show that the existence of Dalits and their problems were part and parcel of the life of the biblical Hebrew people in the ancient time. Below are listed a few examples which prove the existence of Dalits in biblical society:

(a) The rich shall not give more and *weha-dal* (the poor) shall not give less than the half shekel, when you bring this offering to the Lord to make atonement for your lives (Exodus 30:15).
(b) If I have withheld anything that *dalim* (the poor) desired or have caused the eyes of the widow to fail (Job 31:16).
(c) Give justice to the *dal* (the weak) and the orphan; maintain the right of the lowly and the destitute. Rescue *dal* (the weak) and the needy; deliver them from the hand of the wicked (Psalms 82:34).

1.2.2. *Physical, Economic, Political, Judicial and Religious Sense*

Here a few verses are quoted to show how the Dalit concern was part of every aspect of human life. The passages listed below also throw light on the different shades of meanings in which the term 'dalit' has been used in the Hebrew language.

(a) Then seven other cows came up after them *dalot* (poor), very ugly and thin. Never had I seen such ugly ones in all the land of Egypt (Genesis 40:19).
(b) He said, 'May you be blessed by the Lord, my daughters; this last instance, your loyalty is better than the first; you have not gone after young men, whether *dal* (poor) or rich (Ruth 3:10).
(c) There was a long war between the house of Saul and the house of David. David grew stronger and stronger, the house of Saul became *w-dalim* (weaker and weaker) (II Samuel 3:1).
(d) If a king judges *dalim* (the poor) with equity, his throne will be established forever (Proverbs 29:14).
(e) For you have been a refuge to *la-dal* (the poor), a refuge to the needy in their distress, a shelter from the rain-storm and a shade from the hat (Isaiah 25:4).

These five verses are sufficient to show how the term 'dalit' in the Hebrew text of the Bible has been used to link various aspects of a Dalit's life. In these five passages, it is clear that in the passage in Genesis 40:19, the term *dalot* has been used in its literal sense. In another instance, it has been used to show the physical weakness of a human being. For example, in II Samuel 13:4, the term *dal* has been used for King David's son Amnon when his friend Jonadab asked him, 'O Son the King, why are you so *dal* (haggard) morning after morning?' Number two taken from the book of Ruth (3:10) uses the term *dal* in the economic sense as opposite to rich or richness (wealth). Number three quotes verses from II Samuel (3:1) and shows how the same term (*w-dalim*) is used to make a comparison of two political powers. There are other passages where one finds a still stronger use of the term to show its deeper link with the political power. Two such examples are in Proverbs 28:2 (*dalim*) and 15 (*dal*) where an oppressive ruler's relationship has been expressed with the

Dalits. Number four from the Book of Proverbs (29:14) tells us how the qualification of a just ruler is dependent on the justice received by the *dalim* (Dalits or poor). Number five from the Book of Isaiah (25:4) establishes a direct relationship between God and the Dalits (*dal*). This verse is a part of prophet Isaiah's song of praise, which he sang on the wonderful works of his Lord, the God. Similar experiences we find of King David, when he blesses those people who show concern for the Dalits (*dal*). He says in his Psalm 41:9, 'Happy are those who consider *dal* (the poor); the Lord delivers them in the day of trouble.'

1.2.3. *Process and Deeper Sense*

There are also a number of passages in the Hebrew Old testament, which not only deal with the different aspects of Dalits' concern but there are also other passages which go into the deeper meaning of 'dalit' in Hebrew and how or by which process the people for whom this expression has been used, turned into or were brought into the sate of 'dalitness'. In fact, theses passages are in the form of tragic songs, which are sung on behalf of the Dalits. Here a few passages are given below from these Hebrew Dalit songs as examples:

(a) They will give back the fruit of their toil and will not swallow it down; from the profit of their trading, they will get no enjoyment. For they have crushed and abandoned the *dalim* (the poor), they have seized a house that they did not build (Job 20:18, 19).

(b) Do not remember against us the iniquities of our ancestors; let your compassion come speedily to meet us, for we are *dalonu* (brought very low) (Psalm 79:8).

(c) Those who oppress *dal* (the poor), insult their Maker, but those who are kind to the needy honour Him (Proverbs 14:31).

(d) O Lord, do your eyes not look for truth? You have struck them but they felt no anguish;
you have consumed them,
but they have refused to turn back.
Then I said, 'These are only *dalim* (the poor),
they have no sense;
for they do not know the way of the Lord,
the law of their God' (Jeremiah 5:34).

In this work, we are especially concerned with a section of the people of the biblical Hebrew world, to whom is given the collective name *dal* or *dalot*. Our biblical references are limited to such passages or verses in which this name has occurred. But besides these references, there are many incidents and stories of people which have been recorded in the Bible, which reveal to us the process by which certain sections of people have been reduced to the state of *dalitness*. Therefore, in order to draw a vivid picture, we refer to a few of these incidents or stories, before we offer our observations on the passages quoted above.

Perhaps the first direct reference regarding the evil of untouchability or considering one lower than the other, we find in Genesis 46:34, when Joseph tells his brothers how all shepherds are abhorrent to the Egyptians. Then of course, Exodus 1:8 onwards tells the story of how the Egyptians tried to turn the shepherd community into a community of non-entities by forcing on them 'every kind of field labour' (Exodus 1:13).

Later on, when under Moses' leadership, God liberated this untouchable shepherd community, they treated other communities more ruthlessly, turning them into a state of *dalitness*. A number of stories are available in the Old Testament. For example, in Joshua (9:3-27), we find how the Gideon community was turned into this state by Joshua by force to be 'hewers of wood and drawers of water' for the Israelites (Joshua 9:27). We find in Judges 1, the more popular methods of reducing defeated people to the state of *dalitness*. According to this, the Israelites defeated a number of communities as the Canaanites and the Amorites and reduced them to 'forced labour' for themselves (Judges 1:28, 30 and 35).

The passages which are quoted above further testify to the ongoing oppression of the Dalits. The first passage from Book of Job 20:18, 19 is part of a longer narrative, in which one of Job's friends Zapher makes some observations about the wickedness of the powerful oppressors and their methods of oppressing others including *dalim*. In verse 19, a special reference is made to the oppression, which is perpetrated on the Dalits. The Dalits are left home alone after being crushed and even their houses are taken by their oppressors. In the book of Amos, the prophet has even named the oppressors. About the people of Israel, he says that they 'trample the head of the *dalim* (the poor) into the dust of the earth' (Amos 2:7). In Amos

4:1, even rich women perform the role of oppressors against *dalim*. The prophet speaks on behalf of the Dalits to their oppressors very forcefully in his disclosure as follows:

Hear this, you that trample on the needy,
and bring to ruin the poor (*ani*) of the land,
saying, 'When the new moon be over so that
we may sell grain;
and the Sabbath,
so that we may offer wheat for sale?
We will make ephah small and the shekel great,
And practice deceit with false balances
Buying *dalim* (the poor) for silver
and the needy for a pair of sandals,
and selling the sweepings of wheat.' (Amos 8: 4-6)

In this passage, we see how the Dalits have reached the lowest level in prophet Amos's days. One could buy and sell the Dalits like commodities for a few silver coins.

In passage two quoted above from Psalms 79:8, the Psalmist addresses his whole community as *Dalit*. This is like saying, 'The whole of the Indian Christian community is composed of Dalits' or 'The Indian Church as a whole is the Dalit'. Of course, the Psalmist says his community's lowest state of dalitness is because of the past collective sins of their ancestors. He uses a verb *dalonu* with the meaning 'brought very low'. The next passage is clear: here the Creator God is being equated with the Dalits. According to this, to oppose the *dal* (poor) as a community means insulting or oppressing God himself (Proverbs 14: 31).

In the last passage quoted above, the prophet Jeremiah describes the state of *dalitness*. One may even beat them but it does not give them pain; changing their *dalit* state perhaps is the most difficult. They themselves have become completely unconscious of their *dalit* state, so no correction is needed, there is no way they can go back–after all, according to Jeremiah, 'these are only *dalim*, they have no sense' (Jeremiah 5:4). Is this not the state of the majority of the Dalits in India today?

1.3. Indian use of the Term 'Dalit'

At the beginning of this chapter, a reference has been made to the Sanskrit root *dal* of the term 'dalit' and also its possible historical relationship with the Hebrew root *dall*. Some European friends and also Indian Christian scholars, have raised questions about this relationship. Some have even gone to the extent of saying that it is just a 'coincidence' that these two Hebrew and Sanskrit terms resemble each other. Others have raised the question that if it is found in the Hebrew language and has been used in the Old Testament, then why did biblical scholars and interpreters till date have not taken note of it. Of course, the answer to this is simple. All the biblical interpretations and translations have been contextual in nature and those mostly have the background of an English-speaking context. Even the Indian biblical scholars have been trained in the European or English context, or their concern has been limited to a context, what till now has been considered the greater Indian religious traditions. Both these approaches till date have ignored the context of the masses. On the other hand, Dalit concern is part of the reality of the Indian masses, because they are a majority in the Indian population and includes besides Dalits, the indigenous communities and the Other Backward Classes (OBC).

The term 'dalit' in the Indian context has been used from ancient times, but not very much. In reality, the history of this term started only three decades ago. The term itself has today become part of the vocabulary of all north Indian languages. It has been accepted in Sanskrit also with the root *dal*, which means to crack, split, be broken or torn asunder, trodden down, scattered, crushed, destroyed. As a noun and adjective, 'dalit' can be used for all these genders, masculine, feminine and neuter.[13] Some of the regional languages, including Hindi dictionaries, have included in the list of meanings a special meaning, which also refers to a section of our Indian people, who have suffered oppression throughout history because of the accepted religious and social norms of our social order. For example, the famous *Bhasha-Shabad Kosh* in Hindi has given a special explanatory meaning, along with the above meaning according to which, 'dalit' describes 'an undeveloped or backward section of people like Hindu untouchables (*achut*) or *shudra* (forth serving caste) group (*jati*).'[14] In Panjabi, Bhai Kahan Singh in his *Mahan Kos* defines a Dalit, as one who belongs to the lowest caste (*hini jati*) and has been trampled or broken under the feet (*pairan heth dalia gia ho*) of the upper caste (*uchi jatan*).[15]

But 'dalit', more as a concept and in its present use, has its seed in the writings of two great Indian personalities; one, a nineteenth century Marathi reformer and revolutionary Mahatma Jyotiba Phule, and second, an intellectual writer and revolutionary Dr Babasaheb Ambedkar. Mahatma Jyotiba Phule in his writings uses the title *Shudra-Atishudra* for Dalits. According to his definition, *shudras* are *schuta pichari jatian* (touchable backward castes) and *atishudra* means *achuta pichari jatian* (untouchable backward castes). *Shudras* are the last in *varna* (caste) system, but *atishudras* are outside the *varna* system. According to Mahatma Phule, both the *shudras* and *atishudras* are indigenous people (*mula nivasi*, means original settlers). According to him, in order to make both *shudras* and *atishudras* their slaves, the priestly caste (Brahmin) divided them into two castes or classes.[16] Dr Ambedkar deals in detail; with shudras and the untouchables (*Achutas*) in his two works, *Who Were the Shudras*? (1947) and *The Untouchables* (1948).[17] For the Dalit, he uses the title, 'Untouchable' (*achuta*) in his writings. But of course, for him, shudras are also Aryan[18] and 'there is no racial difference between the Hindus and the untouchables'.[19] So in this way, all are racially the same.

But in a real sense, both the use of the term 'dalit' as well as a broad meaning (concept) behind it has been worked out by the Dalit Panther Movement of Maharashtra. The following quotation from the manifesto (Bombay, 1973) of the Dalit Panthers makes their concern for the Dalits clear:

> We must pay attention to the objective process of social development and make an historical analysis of the power that imprisons that Dalit and which has succeeded in making him tie his own hands. The Hindu feudal rule can be a hundred times ruthless today in oppressing the Dalits than it was in the Muslim period or the British period. Because the Hindu feudal rule has in its hand all the arteries of production, bureaucracy, judiciary, army and police forces, in the shape of feudal landlords, capitalists and religious leaders who stand behind and enable these instruments to strive. Hence, the problem of untouchability of the Dalits is no more of mere mental

slavery. Untouchability is the most violent form of exploitation on the face of the earth, which survives the ever- changing forms of the power structure. Today, it is necessary to seek its soil, its root causes. If we understand them, we can definitely strike at the heart of this exploitation…Truly speaking, the problem of the Dalits or Scheduled Castes and Tribes, have become a broad problem; the Dalit is no longer merely an untouchable outside the village walls and the Scripture. He is untouchable and he is a Dalit, but he is also a worker, a landless labourer, a proletarian.[20]

Dalit Panthers' Manifesto has answered a question, 'Who is a Dalit?' It says:

Members of Scheduled Castes and Tribes, neo-Buddhists, the working people, the landless and the poor peasants, women and all those who are being exploited politically, economically and in the name of religion.[21]

Besides other points, one point that needs to be noted is that 'dalit' is a title which Dalits have given to themselves. This is the reason why this term is used and has become popular among Dalit people of different protest movements in our country.

Besides its common use, the term 'dalit' today is especially being used for those people who, on the basis of caste distinctions, have been considered 'outcastes'. They were 'outcaste', because they were not, according to the architect of the system, fit to be included in the fourfold graded caste structure of our society.[22] On the basis of this status, they were made to bear extreme forms of degradation and oppression for centuries, which made them almost lose their humanness, and finally, they reached the state of being 'no-people'. Many Dalits today prefer to be called Dalits, because this term is not a mere name or title for them; it has in fact, become an expression of hope for them in recovering their past self-identity. Because of these 'outcastes' and their struggle, the term 'dalit' has acquired a new connotation, which has a more positive meaning.[23]

The Dalits in our country are known by many other names, which to them, were/are given by others, mostly to despise them or to show contempt.These include: *Dasa*, *Dasyu*, *Raksasa*, *Asura*, *Avarna*, *Nisada*, *Panchama*, *Mleccha*, *Svapaca*, *Chandala*, *Achuta*, Exterior Castes, Depressed classes, Scheduled Castes, Harijan, Untouchables and so on. Besides these names, there are a number of other titles or names which have been given to them in regional languages.

For example, *Churas* in Panjabi (North-West India); *Bhangi* or *Lal-Beghi* in Hindi (North India); *Mala* in Telugu, *Paraiyan* in Tamil, and *Pulayan* in Malayalam (South India).

In the early sixties, Yesu Das Tewari in his New Testament translation has used the term 'dalit' in Hindi for the Greek term *Tethrausmenoi* (downtrodden). This is to me, the most correct rendering of the Greek term and it is most suitable in the context in which it has been used. The context is the Nazareth manifesto of Jesus Christ which He declared in the beginning of His movement for the liberation of *din jano* (the poor), *bandion* (the captive), *andhon* (blind) and *daliton* (downtrodden or oppressed or broken into pieces).[24] Besides being used in Hindi New Testament the term 'dalit', is also used today by almost all the Christian groups who are fighting for the rights of Dalits both within the Christian community and outside it.[25]

1.4. Conclusion

From the discussion of this chapter, the following main points emerge:

From ancient root of the term Dalit in Akkadian and Assyrian groups of Semitic languages and their possible historical link with the ancient people of India through the existing relationship of Babylon and Indus Civilizations, the first point that emerges is that the problem of Dalits existed in the history of human beings from ancient times. This fact is also made clear by the use of the same expression in the later Hebrew and Sanskrit. So it seems the term 'dalit' itself is ancient and was in use in the era of both Hebrew and Sanskrit.

Both from the biblical use of the term 'dalit' for the 'poorest people of the land', and what Indians use in Panjabi and Hindi, we have seen its use for the people considered as 'untouchables' (*achut*) or 'the lowest caste' (*hin jati*), which means those who were/are outside the caste structures of society. This proves that the term 'dalit' had/has a special use for indigenous or earlier (settlers) people of a particular land or country.

The third main point is that the basic meaning of the term 'dalit' is not 'poor' (economically) or 'caste; it really denotes the state to which a certain section of people of a particular society have been reduced through a long systematic process of trampling them down. It refers to the broken or trodden-down state of the people.

NOTES

1. E. Kautzsch, *Gesenius, Hebrew Grammar*, translated into English by A.E. Cowley, Clarendon Press, Oxford, 1910 (rpt. edn. 1946 and 1949), p. 4.
2. *The Interpreter's Dictionary of the Bible: An Illustrated Encyclopedia*, vol. 3, Abingdon Press, Nashville, 16th print, 1996, p. 883.
3. S.V. 'dall', Francis, Brown, *Hebrew and English Lexicon of the Old Testament*, Clarendon Press, Oxford, 1957 (rpt.), p. 195.
4. E.T. Ryder, 'The Language of the Old Testament', in Peake's *Commentary on the Bible*, ed. Mathew Black, Thomas Nelson and Sons Ltd., London, 1963, p. 66.
5. C.J. Gadd and Sidney Smith, 'The New Links between Indian and Babylonian Civilizations', in *Ancient Cities of the Indus*, ed. Gregory L. Possehl, Vikas, New Delhi, 1979, p. 109.
6. See Samuel N. Kramer, 'The Indus Civilizations, and Dilmun: The Sumerian Paradise Land', in *Ancient Cities of the Indus*, ed. Gregory L. Possehl, Vikas, New Delhi, 1979, pp. 168-73.
7. Basham, A.L., 'The Aryan Problem', in *The History and Culture of the Indian People: The Vedic Age*, ed. R.C. Majumder and H.D. Pasalkar, University Press, London, 1951, p. 204.
8. Ryder, op. cit., p. 541.
9. See for all the occurrences of Hebrew usage of term 'dall': Robert Young: *Analytical Concordance* to the *Holy Bible*, Butterworth Press, Guildford and London, 1975, pp. 761-2.
10. Elsa Tamez, *Bible of the Oppressed*, Orbis Books, Maryknoll, New York, 1982, p. 20.
11. C.U. Wolf, 'Poor', in *The Interpreter's Dictionary of the Bible: An Illustrated Encyclopedia*, op. cit., p. 843.
12. *The Harper Collins Study Bible* (New Revised Standard Version), Harper Colins Publishers, London, 1993 (for further references used as (NRSV).
13. S.V. 'dal' and 'dalit'. A *Sanskrit-English Dictionary* by Sir Monier Monier-Williams, Motilal Banarsidass, Delhi, 1988 (rpt.), p. 471 and also *The Practical Sanskrit-English Dictionary* by Vaman Shivam Apte, Motilal Banarsidass, Delhi, 1989 (rpt.), p. 493.

14. See Ramsankar Sukal Rasal, *Bhasa-Sabad Kos* (in Hindi), Allahabad, 1971, pp. 778, 779.
15. Bhai Kahan Singh, *Mahan Kosh* (in Punjabi), Bhasa-Vibhag Punjabi University, Patiala, 1981 (rpt.), pp. 325, 624.
16. D.K. Khapde, *Mahatma Jyotiba Phule* (in Hindi), New Delhi, 1990, pp. 119, 120.
17. Vasant Moon (ed.), *Dr Babasaheb Ambedkar's Writings and Speeches*, vol. 7, The Education Department, Govt. of Maharashtra, Bombay, 1990, pp. 1- 227 (reprint of '*Who are the Shudras*'), pp. 228- 382 (reprint of '*The Untouchables*').
18. Ibid., p. 11.
19. Ibid., p. 242.
20. 'Dalit Panthers Manifesto' (English translation of the text) in *Untouchables: Voice of the Dalit Liberation Movement* by Barbara R. Joshi, Select Book Service Syndicate, New Delhi, pp. 141-2.
21. Ibid, p. 145.
22. 'Four-folded Caste Structure' included in priestly (Brahmin), Warrior (Kshatriyas), Traders (Vaishya), and Serving Caste (Shudras).
23. See Joshi, Barbara, op. cit., p. 3.
24. *Naya Niyam*, The New Testament in Hindi (revised with references), The Bible Society of India, Bangalore, 1967, p. 113.
25. *Nai Hindi Bible*, The Bible Society of India, Bangalore, 1985, p. 102 and also see *Pavitra Bible- Naya Niyam* (in Hindi), India Bible Publishers, New Delhi, 1978, 1982, p. 89.

CHAPTER 2

Ancient Sources of 'Dalit Identity'

2.1. THE *RIGVEDA*

The *Rigveda* is the earliest written literary source of the ancient history of India. A large part of the text has been addressed to Lord Indra, which narrates a fierce war having taken place among different groups. Two opposing forces may be seen in the *Rigveda*—*first*, on whose behalf the hymns of the *Rigveda* are addressed to different gods and, *second*, against whom the same are addressed. Ramprasad Chanda has made this important observation: 'These hymns revealed two hostile peoples in the land of the Seven Rivers now called the Panjab—the deva worshipping Arya and deva-less and the riteless Dasyu or Dasa.'[1] To know more about these two opposing groups, a few of the relevant verses from the hymns of the *Rigveda* are examined below. These verses are listed in seven sets and then brief comments are offered on them:

2.1.1 (a) *vi janihayaran ye ch dasyvo …*[2]
You (Indra) know well Aryas and Dasyus …
(b) *…hatavi dusyun prarya vaarnamavata.*[3]
…he (Indra) Killed the Dasyus and protected the Aryan race (colour).

2.1.2 (a) *Indra panch Kachhatinama.*[4]
Indra is the ruler of the five (races).
(b) *Tadindragni Yadus Turvasesu yad*
Druhyus pavanusu purusus sath.[5]
O Indra- Agni, you live among (the people of) the Yadus, Turvasas, Druhyus, Anus Purus.
(c) *par yet samudramati sur parshi*
paraya turvasa Yadu svasita.[6]
O hero (Indra)! When you came over the sea, you Brought over it Turvasa and Yadu.

1.1.3 (a) *vadhihi dasyu dhanini...*[7]
You (Indra) killed rich Dasyu ...
(b) *akarma dasyurabhi no amanturanya-varto amanus.*[8]
All around us are ritualless Dasyu, inhuman, who are following alien laws.
(c) *anaso dasyu ...*[9]
Noseless Dasyu ...

2.1.4 (a) *sa jatubharma chhadsdsdhana ojo.*
puro vimindannacharada vidasi.
vidana vajirna dasyuve hetimasnarya
Saho vadhrya sumnamindar ...
dasyu hatyaya.[10]
Armed with his thunderbolt, Indra went about
destroying the forts of Dasas.
O Indra, throw your thunderbolt at Dasyus,
increase the power and glory of Aryas.
(b) *yo hatavahimarinata sapat sindhuna*
Yo ga udajadapadha valasaya,
Yo asamanorantargina jajana
savivak sa janam Indra.[11]
One who killed the Dragon and freed the Seven Rivers (*Sapatsindhu*):
He who drove the cows from the vala,
One who created fire between stones,
and had beaten the warriors in the battle.
He, O people, is Indra
(c) *sa vartrahendra Karsunayoni*
purandaro dasirariyada vi ...
hatavi dasyuna pura ayasinin tarita.[12]
Indra the Vartra-killer, fort-destroyer,
scattered the dasa,
who dwelt in darkness ...
he killed the Dasyu
and broke the forts made of iron.

2.1.5 (a) *dasa cha vartra hatamayrani cha*
Sudasmindravrunavasavatama.[13]
Indra and Varuna killed the Dasa and Arya,
who were Sudas' enemies and helped him with favour

(b) *yo no dasa ayro vapurustutadeva*
Indra yudhve chiketati.[14]
O Most respected Indra, the godless people, whether
Dasa or Arya, who want war with us.

2.1.6 (a) *yatha deva asureshu sadramugaresu chakirre*[15].
Even the gods kept faith in the mighty Asuras.
(b) *hatyaya deva asurana* ...[16]
When the gods killed Asuras ...

2.1.7 (a) a*pasedhana raksaso yatudhanansthadad deva:* ...[17]
Driving off raksasa and Yatudhanas, the god
is present ...
(b) *jahi nyatrina pani varko hisa*[18]
You (Soma) kill Pani. He is like a wolf.

2.1.8. *Reflection*

The main point of the first set of two verses of hymn 51 of Mandala book one, and hymn 34 of Mandala three is that the *Rigveda* definitely deals with two different groups of people. These are the Aryans and the Dasyus. *The Aryas* in hymn 3.34.9 are addressed as *varna* (races). According to to the authors of *Vedic Index of Names and Subjects*, 'Arya is the normal designation in Vedic literature from the *Rigveda* onwards of an Aryan, a member of the three upper classes, Brahman, Ksatriya, or Vaisya ... the Arya stands in opposition to the Dasa, but also to the Sudra.'[19] Regarding the Dasyu, the authors of the 'Vedic Index' on the basis of some passages of the *Rigveda* (1.51.8, 103.3; 2.18.19; 3.34.9, etc.), see the possibility of their being indigenous people, who are addressed in the *Rigveda* with special negative traits, which are nowhere applied in the same text to Aryas. The Dasyu according to the *Rigveda* are: *anaso* (without face), *anas* (noseless), etc.[20] The distinction between the Aryas and the Dasyu is affirmed by V.S. Apte also.[21]

The second set of verses of the *Rigveda* 1.7.9; 1.108.8 and 6.20.2 make a few important points about Aryas. Verse 1.7.9 makes the point that Indra was the ruler of the five races. Who are these five races (*panch*)? A number of views are offered to answer this question.[22] Two main views are that *panch* here refers to the four *varna* (castes) and the fifth indigenous known as *Nisadas*. According to the second view, the *panch* here refers to the five main tribes of Arya people,

Yadu, Turvasa, Druhyu, Anu and *Puru*. On the basis of the various testimonies available from the text of other hymns of the *Rigveda*, particularly the hymn from the second verse of the second set quoted 1.108.8, the second view can be supported more easily that the *panch* here refers to the Aryas' five main tribes. Also when the hymns of the *Rigveda* such as 1.7.9 were composed such as caste distinction did not exist.[23] The third verse, 6.20.2 of this set, hints at the Arya people coming across the sea. Ramprasad Chanda strongly supports this possibility and says:

> According to some scholars *samudra* in the *Rigveda* does not mean sea, for the Aryas had not yet reached the sea, but only the lower course of the Indus. This interpretation of *samudra* may be traced to the preconceived notion that the *Rigveda* Aryas were homogeneous body of men who came from the north-west. But once this notion is dimissed from the mind, there is nothing left to prevent us from accepting *samudra* in its usual sense. The sea that lies the nearest to the country of the *Rigveda* Aryas is the Arabian sea. So if we are to attach any value to this Vedic tradition, we are forced to assume that the Yadus and the Turasas came across the Arabian Sea. The evidences contained in the later Vedic and Epic literature relating to the Indian home of one of these two folks, the Yadus, lend support to this hypothesis.[24]

The third set of verses 1.38.4; 10.22.8 and 5.38.10 lists some of the examples of allusions to the Dasyu in the *Rigveda*; they also highlight some traits of the Dasyu, which separate them from the Aryas both racially and culturally. A number of hymns of the *Rigveda* tell that the Dasyu were rich and well to do (10.22.38); they also lived in well-fortified houses and cities.[25] They are also contemptuously said to be ritualless, inhuman, following alien laws (verse 10.22-38). The Dasyu had their own religious and social customs and rites, which were alien to the Aryas but not to them. The Dasyu are also described as 'noseless' (verse 5.38.10), which means the appearance of their face is different from that of Aryas. In other hymns of the *Rigveda* their skin colour is described as dark.[26]

The verses in set four and other references in the *Rigveda* described how under the command of Lord Indra, the Aryas defeated, destroyed, scattered and looted the Dasyu or Dasas. A large part of the *Rigveda* glorifies Lord Indra for his capacity for war against his and the Aryas' enemy (*sataru*). Thus Indra fought with the Dasas

(Dasyu) and destroyed their forts (verse 1.103.4, 4.). Indra's war efforts increased the power and glory of the Aryas. Hymn 2.12.3 refers (it seems) to one of the main victories of Lord Indra, in which he killed his chief enemy (*sapat* which means Dragon) and freed (the land of) seven rivers (*Sapat-Sindhu*), which means the land from river Sindh to Sarasvati (almost the whole of north India, part of which now in Pakistan). In hymn 2.207, 8 again Lord Indra is shown as the killer of *Vartra* (a common name used in the *Rigveda* for Indra's powerful enemies), destroyer of forts, killer of the Dasyu (or the Dasas) and also scattering them all over. In hymn 2.12.4 Indra is further shown chasing, defeating, and looting his enemy's riches. In 7.5.3 the author describes how the dark-skinned races fled, scattered abroad and left behind their possessions.

The two verses in set five (78.3.1 and 10.38.3) bring to light new information about the war affairs of Lord Indra. Here he is shown fighting both with his Dasa and his Aryan enemies (7.83.1). On the basis of such verses some scholars, particularly Ambedkar, have tried to work out a theory that both the opposing forces in these verses are Aryan.[27] How he has arrived at this conclusion is not clear; neither has he offered incontrovertible evidence to prove his thesis. The *Rigveda* itself offers clear assistance in the matter. For example hymn 18 of Mandala 7 of the *Rigveda* narrates a major event, the battle of ten tribes. In this war, ten tribes were onone side, that is *Puru*, *Yadu*, *Yurvasa*, *Anu* and *Dhaahyu* assisted by five smaller tribes *Alina*, *Pakthas*, *Bhalana*, *Siva* and *Visanin*.

It is seen from verses listed in set two that the first five tribes were Aryan. The five other smaller tribes *Paktha*, *Bhalana*, *Alina*, *Siva* and *Visanin*. It seems were non-Aryan. Griffith has labelled all the ten tribes as 'the Non-Aryan confederacy'.[28] K.P. Chattopadhyaya's observation on this issue are also notable. According to him:

The *Rigveda* tribes were not homogeneous. It has been pointed out by Vedic scholars that the battle of ten kings mentioned in the *Rigveda* was probably between two groups who differed in language. The Purus who led the ten tribes were called *mrdhvavacan*, i.e. speakers of incorrect or corrupt speech (*Rigveda* VIII 18-13). Their opponents the Bharatas under Sudas were speakers of correct speech ... the leadership of the antagonists of Sudas and the Bharatas was, therefore, partly of Asura descent. ... This Asura character of the Purus would explain their speakers of a somewhat different speeches.[29]

These observations and the above quoted verses from the *Rigveda* help in understanding the complixity of Indra fighting both his Dasa and Arya enemies, but certainly they are not the same, though there is real possibility of the existence of mixed racial groups, particularly during the later Vedic period.

The last two sets (six and seven) of verses indicate the existence of other non-Aryan people with whom also the Aryans waged war. These included the Asuras (10.151.3; 10.157.4), the Raksasas (1.35.1) and the Pani (6.51.14).

2.2. The Archaeologists

Archaeological sources are a great help in reaching the historical roots of the Dalits. Archaeological literature, certainly, has not been written keeping the Dalit in mind but it throws much light on the ancient people of India. The 'Ancient Cities of the Indus'[30] edited by Gregory L. Possehl is superb work of reference, for our purpose. It includes the main research papers written between 1924 and 1979 and contains, among others, the works of the famous pioneer archaeologist John Marshall, Ernest Mackay, Mortimer Wheeler and the well known Indian archaeologists S.R. Rao, Gurdip Singh, C. Ramasamy, Iravatham Mahadevan and B.M. Pandey. The other works referred to are the *Early Indus Civilization* by Ernest Mackay[31] and *The Indus Civilization* by Mortimer Wheeler.[32] Given below are brief relevant extracts from the works of various authorities in the field of archaeology on the nature of the Indus Valley Civilization. Four aspects are covered, namely, that it was a well-established civilization, the nature of the people, the date of the civilization and how it met with its end.

2.2.1. *Well-Established Civilization*

In the field of exploration, it is natural this year to give the premier place to the remarkable discoveries made by the Department in Sindh and the South West Panjab...Hitherto India has almost universally been regarded as one of the younger countries of the world...Now, at a single bound, we have taken back our knowledge of Indian civilization some 3000 years earlier and have established the fact that in the 3rd millennium before Christ, and even before that, the people of Panjab and Sindh were living in well-built cities and were in possession of a relatively mature culture with a high standard of art and craftsmanship and developed a system of pictorial writing. The sites where these discoveries have been made are at Harappa in the Montgomery district of the Panjab and Mohenjodaro, more than 400 miles away, in the Larkana District of Sindh.[33]

John Marshall, 1923-4

The Indus Valley Culture of Harappa Culture as it is called after the name of the village occupying the site.... The known remains of their culture, with all its ramifications, occupy a broad triangular area in North-West and West Pakistan, extending from the foot of the Himalayas to the Makram Coast, Gujarat, Bahawalpur and North-West Rajasthan, covering nearly 1000 miles from Sutkagu Dor near the foot of Sivaliks in the extreme north-west. Further explorations have now pushed the limit of this culture from Cambay in the south of the Jamuna Basin, about 30 miles north of Delhi. The Harappa culture is essentially a riverine culture....[34]

Gurdip Singh, 1971

It does suggest that the Indus Valley Civilization was an indigenous development that arose out of the evaluation of developed village cultures in a favourable environment. It emphasizes the subcontinental roots and the consequent 'style' which gives the civilization its uniqueness.[35]

Walter A. Fairservis, Jr., 1967

2.2.2. *The People*

Who were those people who built Mohenjodaro and Harappa? No definite answer can be given at present to this question, though it is certain that they were a pre-Aryan race, for their cities were flourishing some thousand years before any Aryan-speaking people had entered India, which took place, according to modern ruling, about 1500 BC.[36]

Ernest Mackay, 1935

If, it seems likely, it is permissible to take the custom worn by the clay figurines of the Mother Goddess as representative of the normal attire of the feminine population of Mohenjodaro and Harappa...as nearly the same costume is worn by many of the women of Southern India, the view may provisionally be accepted that the dress of the figurines was the usual feminine attire of the Harappa period, especially as there is strong reason to believe that the climate of north-west India has altered considerably since the middle of the third millennium BC.[37]

Ernest Mackay, 1935

Without identifying the symmetry of the people with any particular racial stock, the late Dr. Guha had said that the skulls from Stratum II belonged to a large-headed dolicocephalic type with well-developed supra-orbital ridges and high cranial roof, long face and prominent nose. These features, according to him, showed a continuity of the Indus people of Harappa and Mohenjodaro. However, in the pot burials of Stratum I, Guha had observed an element of small, low-headed people, and this, Vats thought, indicated 'a definite admixture' which might be due to racial or cultural upheaval brought about by the immigration of a foreign people into this district of the Panjab.[38]

H.D. Sankalia, 1972-3

There is now incontrovertible archaeological evidence that the major population shift was to the south-east into the area of the Kathiawar peninsula north of Bombay. Here the Harappas mingled with other indigenous populations and gradually, there was complete absorption and transformation of the remnants of the formerly great Harappan culture into what we are coming to recognize as a distinctive chalcolithic culture of Central India.[39]

George F. Dales, 1964

2.2.3. *Date*

Thus, of the twelve seals for which any sort of dating can be postulated, seven may be Sargonid, one pre-Sargonid and four of the Larsa or later periods. On current dating, the maximum period required to cover these possibilities would be 2500-1500 BC, with a strong focus on 2550 BC.[40]

Mortimer Wheeler, 1953

Now that general archaeological opinion is in favour of dating the uppermost levels of Mohenjodaro to the seventeenth century....[41]

Ernest Mackay, 1935

2.2.4. *End*

In the course of excavations of Mohenjodaro in 1925-26, several groups of skeletons were found.... Excavation elsewhere in the city has laid bare other groups of skeletons, one being of special interest. In this group, the remains of some members of the party lay at the foot of a staircase leading down from a street to a well, while one, a woman, had nearly climbed up to the level of the street, but had succumbed on the top step (P1.1, 2). It was thought at first that an epidemic disease must have been responsible for these deaths, but this theory was refuted by the later discovery of two more groups.... It now seems certain that Mohenjodaro was attacked by enemies during, at least, one period of its later history....

The subsidence of walls and well-livings at two distinct levels of the city, one much lower than the other, proves that it was flooded early in the history of Mohenjodaro and that another marked the beginning of its decline.[42]

Ernest Mackay, 1935

Tentatively, the evidence suggests that Mohenjodaro and much of the lower Indus Valley suffered from a series of severe and extensive floods which eventually forced most of the population to abandon the area, possible around 1800 or 1700 BC.[43]

George F. Dales, 1966

2.2.5 *Reflection*

Among the four sets of extracts from the works of various authorities on the archaeological findings on Mohenjodaro and Harappa, the first set establishes that there was a well established civilization on our country even before 3000 years. John Marshall's findings quoted above are still the best possible summary of the description of this ancient civilization. His comment is notable where he writes, 'In the 3rd millennium BC and even before that, the people of the Panjab and Sindh were living in well-built cities and were in possession of a relatively mature culture with a high standard of art and craftsmanship and a developed system of pictorial writing.' John Marshall's contention has been supported by a number of other authorities.[44] Samuel N. Kramer in his essay, 'The Indus Civilization and Dilmun: The Sumerian Paradise Land' says:

To be sure the Indus people did have a well-developed system of writing consisting of some four hundred pictorial signs....One of the most striking and impressive features of the Indus cities and towns ... was water and cleanliness seems to have played an important role in the life of the people, as is evident from the extraordinary number of wells and baths in both public and private buildings, as well as the carefully planned network of covered drains built of kiln-baked bricks.[45]

The second point from the first set of extracts is that the Indus Valley culture was basically a 'riverine culture' which covered the whole of old Panjab, starting almost from Iran's border and spreading beyond Delhi. These two points are confirmed by Gurdip Singh in his essay 'The Indus Valley Culture'. It is also confirmed by Mortimer Wheeler in his work, *The Indus Civilization*. He even said, 'For what such claims are worth, the Indus Civilization can thus claim a larger area than any other of the known pre-classical civilizations.'[46]

The third point is that 'the Indus Valley Civilization was an indigenous development' and it has its roots in the Indian sub-continent itself.

The second set of extracts on 'The People' raises a number of important points with regard to the kind of people who were living in various ancient cities and towns of the Indus. They were pre-Aryan, (extract 'a'); resemblance to these pre-Aryan people is still found in India, particularly in southern India (extract 'b'). The clothes which small idols of a female goddess wear include a small dhoti (half sari, which goes from the waist to the knee only). This kind of clothes and similar style of hair of these female idols are still found in some parts of the western coast of Tamil Nadu. There is further support to this truth from the fact that during the middle of the third millennium, the climate of north-west India was the same as is common to the western coast of Tamil Nadu and because of the warm climate, heavy clothing was not needed.[47]

The third extract adds a further element about the possible race of people who were living at the site of Mohenjodaro or Harappa. Though Ernest Mackay is clear that they were Aryan, H.D. Sankalia points out possible racial admixture, because of the immigration of a foreign people into the Panjab of that time. But before H.D. Sankalia, Mortimer Wheeler had made more detailed observation on the issue of the people. Besides the skeleton found in a grave at Harappa, he has considered the skeleton remains of people who were massacred in the streets Mohenjodaro. He has identified four racial groups including the proto-Australoids, who, according to him were: '... a small folk with long, narrow skulls, a somewhat broad nose. ... These features are at home in India, Ceylon ...'. In modern language, these folk may be classed as the 'aboriginal' element in the population.[48] Wheeler also means to say that there was one race already living in these ancient cities. What needs to be remembered here is that most of the these archeological findings belong to the upper layers, because still archeologists have not arrived at virgin soil and one does not know how many layers they will find.[49] The last extract from George F. Dales' essay talks about the movement of Harappa's people toward the south-east and also how these migrated people influenced the culture of central India. The idea of mixed population also gets support from this extract.

The third set of extracts deal with the date of the Indus Valley Civilization. On this issue, all the leading archeologists agree more or less, that well civilized people were living in the cities of Harappa and Mohenjodaro before 1500 BC.[50] Wheeler has tried to fix the period of these people on the basis of twelve seals which were found during the excavations, and has concluded that it should be around 2500-1500 BC. But these dates only refer to the time when these seals were made. They cannot help us about the exact time of the beginning or how far back the roots of the Indus Valley Civilization go. Archaeologists have not yet unearthed the lowest level upon which the first foundations of the cities were laid.[51] Therefore, Ernest Mackay rightly talks about the date of the uppermost levels of Mohenjodaro being the seventeenth century BC. On the basis of some evidence found outside India, he has also suggested to shifting the date of the end of the Harappa cities into the sixteenth century BC.[52] Taking into account the views of these well-known archaeologists, one may safely say that the people who were part of the Indus Valley Civilization were living in the cities of the Indus prior to 1500 BC.

As far as the date of the destruction of the cities of the Indus is concerned, it is more or less settled above. But the other vital question regarding the Indus Valley Civilization or destruction of its cities and the cause of this destruction are still to be considered. There are three different theories about this issue put forward by experts. One traditional and popular theory is the invasion theory, based on the position of some skeletons found during the excavations at Mohenjodaro (see first extract of group IV above).[53] The second theory, put forward more recently, is that this destruction was due to a series of severe and extensive floods (see extract second of group IV above). There is not much support to this theory.[54] A middle path theory put forward by an archaeologist like Gurdip Singh is:

The extinction of the Indus culture may have thus been initiated through gradual decline as a result of climatic change, but the process may yet have been completed by successive invasions, from the North-West by the Aryans.[55]

Gurdip Singh expressed this view in 1971. A similar view had been put forward earlier in 1961 by A. Fairservis, Jr.[56]

The third extract of group IV is closer to the first view. Only it adds a new insight to the possibility of the destruction of Harappa by Aryan invasion. Even this view sees the influence of the flood factor in the destruction of Indus cities. It seems that the middle path theory expressed by Gurdip Singh is closer to probability.

2.3. The *Rigveda* and the Archaeologists

A number of attempts have been made to co-relate the informations based upon the *Rigveda* and the archaeological works. These attempts have been made by historians like N.N. Bhattacharyya;[57] the authorities on the Vedic age or the Prehistoric Age, which include H.D. Sankalia, S.K. Chatterji, A.D. Pusalkar,[58] and K.P. Chattopadhyaya[59] and a number of archaeologists such as Mortimer Wheeler[60] and Arlene R.K. Zide.[61] Historians and archaeologists have been able to fix the dates only approximately. N.N. Bhattacharyya in his work on *Ancient Indian History and Civilization* has rejected Wheeler's view that the Aryans first destroyed the Harappans and then erected their settlement on the same site. On that basis, later scholars have fixed the date of Harappa civilization as 1750 BC, not 1500 BC[62] but then B.K Ghosh has discussed in his essay on 'The Aryan Problem' in *The Vedic Age* and has rightly pointed out that on the basis of the language of the *Rigveda*, an approximate date of the composition can be fixed around 1000 BC. He also confirms that the Mohenjodaro culture is of about 2500 BC and possibly, that is the time when the first invasion of Aryans took place. The discussion above on dates also points towards such possibility. Therefore, where the period and date are concerned, one may more or less agree with Zide's view:

The chronology of the indo-Aryan civilization in India on the other hand, has its upper limit the date 1200 BC, but recent examination of the literary evidence of the *Rigveda* and the Athara Veda would place the limit more probably around 1100 BC. The archaeological evidences as well point to such a conclusion, and to a definite break between the Indus Valley Civilization and the advent of the Aryan invaders.[63]

The second point is that both the literary (*Rigveda*) and the archaeological sources deal with two groups of people. On one hand, there is an already settled group; on the other hand, is the intruder or invaders' group and the violence which took place between these groups (see section on the *Rigveda* and the Archaeologists). The *Rigveda* names these people as the Aryans and the Dasyus or the Dasas. There are other names of the Aryan tribes as well as the non-Aryan tribes. The Aryan enemies are also addressed as Asura, Raksasa, Pani, etc. Archaeologists, particularly Mortimer Wheeler, have also identified four different groups of people (mention has been made earlier) and one of them is very close to the Dasa or the Dasyus with narrow skulls, and broad nose (whom the *Rigveda* alluded to as 'without face', 'noseless', etc).

Wheeler has even tried to establish a direct relationship with the cities of the Indus civilization and the names of places found in the *Rigveda*. For example, the Rigvedic name Hari-Yuppuya, he sees as today's name for Harappa where he argues, possibly Vircivants was defeated by Abyavartin Cayamana. The Vircivants tribe according to him 'may be connected with Varcin, who was a foe of Indra and, therefore, non-Aryans'.[64] Wheeler has also discussed, in detail, the discovery of fortified citadels at Harapppa and Mohenjodaro, and forts and citadels mentioned in the *Rigveda* as being destroyed by Indra. According to him these citadels are the same.[65] A.D. Pusalkar discusses in detail the people of the Indus Civilization and the Rigvedic people.[66] K.P. Chattopadhyaya too has identified the people of Mohenjodaro and Harappa with the Asuras of the *Rigveda*.[67]

2.4. Conclusion

Once the identity of the people of the *Rigveda* and Indus Civilization has been agreed upon, other questions related to the destruction and uprooting of different groups of people are easily dealt with. But first, in the light of the discussion above, we may conclude as follows:

➢ The groups of people mentioned in the *Rigveda* are the same as those established by the archeological findings at places like

Mohenjodaro and Harappa. Basically they belonged to two groups; one already settled at these places and the other invaders.

- Both the *Rigveda* and the archeological findings testify to the fact that calamity stuck the people and their cities in the form of floods, climatic changes, and in a major way, invasions.
- The conflict between the two major groups of people took place around the middle of the second millennium (1500 BC). This possibly is the point or moment in history from which the history of the people known as Dalit problem developed.
- Finally, both 'the *Rigveda*' and the findings of 'the Archeologist', leads to the conclusion that they were certainly once normal human beings and this identity is core subject of the 'Dalit Theology'.

NOTES

1. Ramaprasad Chanda, *The Indo-Aryan Races: A Study of the Origin of Indo-Aryan People and Institution*, Asiatic Society, Calcutta, 1969, p. 3.
2. *Rigveda* 1.51.8. (All the *Rigveda's* Sanskrit verses texts is taken from *Rigveda* in Devanagari Script edited by Shriram Sharma Acharya and published in four volumes by Sanskrit Sansthan, Bareilly, 1985).
3. *Rigveda* 3.34.9.
4. *Rigveda* 1.7.9.
5. *Rigveda* 1.108.8.
6. *Rigveda* 6.20.12
7. *Rigveda* 1.33.4.
8. *Rigveda* 10.22.8.
9. *Rigveda* 5.38.10.
10. *Rigveda* 1.103.3, 4.
11. *Rigveda* 2.12.3.
12. *Rigveda* 2, 20, 7, 8.
13. *Rigveda* 7.83.1.
14. *Rigveda* 10.38.3.
15. *Rigveda* 10.151.3.
16. *Rigveda* 10.157.4.
17. *Rigveda* 1.35.10
18. *Rigveda* 6.51.14.
19. Arthur Anthony Macdonell and Arthur Berriedall Keith (in future reference Macdonell and Keith are only given): *Vedic Index of Names and Subjects*, vol. I, Murray, London, 1912, p. 64.

20. Ibid., p. 347.
21. S.V. 'Arya' and 'Dasyu', Vaman Shivram Apte, pp. 229, 494.
22. Macdonell and Keith, op. cit., pp. 466-7.
23. Cf. Ralph T.H. Griffith, *The Hymns of the Rigveda*, Motilal Banarsidass, Delhi, 1986 (rpt.), p. 5 (fn. 9).
24. Chanda, op. cit., p. 15.
25. *Rigveda* 1.32.6, 1.51.5; 2.146, 6.314, etc.
26. *Rigveda* 1.133.8, 7.5.3, etc.
27. Dr. Babasaheb Ambedkar, *Writings and Speeches*, vol. 7, Education Department, Government of Maharasthra, Bombay, 1990 (ed. Vasant Moon), pp. 86-100.
28. Griffith, op. cit., 342 (fn. 7)
29. K.P. Chattopadhyaya, *The Indian Culture Contacts and Migration*, Asiatic Society, Calcutta, 1970, pp. 7, 8.
30. Gregory L. Possehl (ed.), *Ancient Cities of the Indus*, Vikas, New Delhi, 1979.
31. Ernest Mackay (second edition revised and enlarged by Dorothy Mackay), *Early Indus Civilization*, Eastern Book House, Patna, 1989 (rpt.).
32. Sir Mortimer Wheeler, *The Cambridge History of India: Supplementary Volume, The Indus Civilization*, Cambridge, Cambridge University Press, 1953.
33. Marshall, 'Harappa and Mohenjodaro' in *Ancient Cities of the Indus*, op. cit., p. 181.
34. Gurdip Singh: 'The Indus Valley Culture', in *Ancient Cities of the Indus*, op. cit., p. 234.
35. Fairservis, Jr., 'The Origin, Character and Decline of an Early Civilization', in *Ancient Cities of the Indus*, op. cit., p. 79.
36. Mackay, op. cit., p. 10.
37. Ibid., p. 77.
38. H.D. Sankalia, 'The "Cemetery H" Culture', in *Ancient Cities of the Indus*, op. cit., 324.
39. George F. Dales, 'The Mythical Massacre at Mohen-jodaro', in *Ancient Cities of the Indus*, op. cit., p. 296.
40. Wheeler, op. cit., p. 86.
41. Mackay, op. cit., p. 148.
42. Ibid., pp. 13, 14.
43. George F. Dales, 'New Investigations at Mohenjo-daro', in *Ancient Cities of the Indus*, op. cit., p. 194.
44. George F. Dales, 'The Decline of the Harappans' in *Ancient Cities of the Indus*, op. cit., p. 311.

45. Samuel N. Kramer, 'The Indus Civilization and Dilmun: The Samarian Paradise Land' in *Ancient Cities of the Indus*, op. cit., pp. 168-9.
46. Wheeler, op. cit., p. 2.
47. See Kapur Singh, op. cit., pp. 170, 171.
48. Wheeler, op. cit., p. 51.
49. Mackay, op. cit., p. 4.
50. See for detail and more views about the date:
    (a) Kramer: op. cit., p. 171.
    (b) B.K. Thapar, 'Kalibangan: A Harappan Metropolis the Indus Valley', in *Ancient Cities of the Indus*, op. cit., p. 202.
    (c) Gurdip Singh, op. cit., p. 235.
    (d) Arlene R.K. Zide, 'A Brief Survey of Work to Date on the Indus Script', in *Ancient Cities of the Indus*, op. cit., p. 257.
    (e) Robert L. Raikes, 'The End of the Ancient', in *Ancient Cities of the Indus*, op. cit., p. 297.
51. See for details anaylsis:
    Kapur Singh, op. cit., pp. 146-7.
    a) Mackay, op. cit., p. 4.
52. Mackay, Ernest, op. cit., p. 157.
53. See Kapur Singh, op. cit., p. 227.
    Wheeler, op. cit., pp. 91, 92.
54. Raikes, op. cit., p. 301.
55. Gurdip Singh, op. cit., p. 242.
56. Walter A. Fairservis, Jr., The Harappa Civilization, 'New Evidence and More Theory', in *Ancient City of the Indus*, op. cit., p. 50.
57. N.N. Bhattacharyya, *Ancient Indian History and Civilization: Trends and Perspectives*, New Delhi, 1988, op. cit., pp. 1-26.
58. R.C. Majumdar, and A.D. Pusalkar (eds), *The History and Culture of the Indian People: The Vedic Age*, University Press, London, 1951, pp. 123-200.
59. Chattopadhyaya, op. cit., pp. 43-6.
60. Wheeler, op. cit., pp. 18, 90-2.
61. Zide, op. cit., pp. 256-60.
62. Bhattacharyya, op. cit., p. 23.
63. Zide, op. cit., p. 257.
64. Wheeler, op. cit., p. 18.
65. Ibid., pp. 90-3.
66. Pusalkar, 'The Indus Valley Civilization', in *The Vedic Age*, op. cit., p. 179.
67. Chattopadhyaya, op. cit., p. 44.

CHAPTER 3

Historical Development of the Dalit Problem

3.1. Early Development

The history of the Dalits began almost 3500 years ago. H.G. Wells tells how at that point of history, one group (nomad folk) defeated the other groups (the settled folk) and how as a result, the history of both the groups was completely changed. He wrote:

> Down pour the united nomads on the unwarlike unarmed plains; there ensues a war of conquest. Instead of carrying off the booty, the conquerors settle down on the conquered land which becomes all booty for them; the villagers and townsmen are reduced to servitude and tribute-paying, they become hewers of wood and drawers of wood and drawers of water, and the leaders of the nomads become kings and princes, masters and aristocrats.[1]

A number of other writers have also made the same point.[2] The Dalits have been reduced to their present state 'by centuries of exploitation and servility'.[3] This is corroborated, besides, the *Rigveda*, by other later literary sources, A few references are given below to show this development.

In the *Rigveda*, which is supposed to be the oldest literary source available to us, the famous *Purusasukta* hymn mentions the existence of four castes when it says: 'The Brahman was his mouth, of both his arms was the Rajanya (Ksatriya) made, His thighs became the Vaishya, from his feet the Sudra was produced.'[4]

On the basis of this hymn, orthodox people believe that the four-fold division of Indian society exists from the earliest times; but according to some scholars, this hymn was composed at a later time and therefore, does not represent the state of the Rigvedic period.[5] This may be true, but it is also true that the Dalit problem took root right in the *Rigveda* times as a result of the conflict between two hostile peoples. The next *Rigveda* pre-dates 1000 BC which is followed by Upanishadic period, which begins around 800 BC and also closes towards the end of the sixth century BC.[6] There are references and testimony in the text of the *Upanishads* that by the time these texts came into existence, the problem of the Dalits was getting entrenched. For example, the *Chandogya Upanishad*, not only refers to the three upper castes, but also compares Chandala (outcaste) with a dog or a swine. In the tenth *Khanda*, verse seven reads as follows:

> Accordingly, those who are of pleasant conduct here … the present is, indeed, that they will enter a pleasant womb, either the womb of a Brahman, or the womb of a ksatriya, or the womb of a Vaisya. But those who are of stinking conduct here … the prospect is, indeed, that they will enter a stinking womb … either the womb of dog, or the womb of a swine or the womb of an outcaste (*chandala*).[7]

This verse testifies not only to the existence of caste but also, in the way an outcaste is compared to a dog or a swine or the manner in which the 'womb' of the upper caste is addressed as a 'pleasant' one and the womb of an outcaste as 'a stinking' one, to the further degradation of the Dalits. It also makes clear that from now onwards the caste status also depends upon one's conduct in one's previous birth.

The two great epics *Ramayana* and *Mahabharata* explicity tell us how far the condition of the Dalits had deteriorated by the time these were composed. The period of composition of the *Ramayana* scholars have fixed around fifth century BC.[8] The period of the *Mahabharata* too, scholars have prescribed, according to different stages.

Leaving out at the early stage, the second and the third stage, with which this discussion is concerned, is the stage of the Pandu heroes and of the divine hero Krishna. The period of Pandu stage is between 600 BC and 200 BC and Krishna stage 200 BC to AD 500.[9]

Valmiki, in his text of the *Ramayana* tells through a story, how much the Sudras, the fourth caste, had become degraded (not to speak of the Dalit or outcaste). According to this story, in Lord Rama's time only three upper castes were allowed to do *tapasya* (penance and meditation). Yet a Sudra undertook penance in order to attain divinity, as a result of which, a Brahman boy of 15 years died. The bereaved father complained to Lord Rama, who after learning the cause of the death, went in search of the Sudra. On meeting him, Lord Rama said to him:

> You are indeed blessed. Tell me in which caste you have been born. I am Rama, son of Dasaratha. Out of curiosity I have asked you this question. Tell me the truth. Are you a Brahman, Ksatriya or a Sudra?
>
> The ascetic replied, 'O King! I am born of Sudra caste. I want to attain divinity by such penance. When, I want to attain divinity, I won't tell lies. I am a Sudra by caste, and my name is Samvuka.'
>
> As soon as the ascetic uttered those words, Rama drew forth his sword and severed Samvuka's head.[10]

In the continuing narrative it is said that Lord Rama asked gods to restore the Brahman boy to life and he was told that he had already been revived the moment the Sudra ascetic was killed.

In the *Mahabharata* also there is a reference to the degraded state of the Dalits. The story of Ekalavya, an indigenous boy, tells how he had to lose his 'right hand thumb', because he had learned archery and was in no way inferior to Arjuna in his skill. Again the main point of the story is how at the time of *Mahabharata*, low castes or the Dalits did not have the right to education.[11]

Srimadbhagavada Gita also not only affirms faith in the four castes (*chaturvarnyam*), but also tells these had been created by lord Krishna himself.[12] It also advises members of each caste to follow faithfully the duties prescribed for them on the basis of their caste.[13] The only difference one finds in the *Bhagavada Gita* is that by taking refuge in Lord Krishna, the outcastes, women, Vaisyas and also Sudras can attain the highest goal.[14]

Among the literary sources which throw light on the degraded state of the Dalits is the *Manusmriti* (the ordinances of Manu), which was possibly composed during the period AD 1-700.[15] It is the author(s) of *Manusmriti*, who now onward removed even the human identity of the Dalits. Till then the Dalits were considered outside the pale of the *chaturvarnyam*, but at least their existence was recognized. The *Manusmriti* accepts only the twice-born three castes: Brahman, Ksatriya and Vaisya, but the fourth, Sudra has only one birth. It says, 'there is no fifth (caste).'[16] To explain the existence of those who were not of the four castes, *Manusmriti* put forward the concept of 'mixed castes' which included those who were born out of inter-caste marriages. The main divisions of such unions were named *anuloma*, where the male partner belong to the upper caste and the female to the lower caste; and *pratiloma*, were considered degraded.[17]

According to *Manusmriti*, the most hated groups were *Chandal* and *Sapaka*, who were the offsprings of a Sudra male from a Brahman woman, and *Chandala* male and *Pukkasa* female respectively.[18] The *Manusmriti* 10.51.52 narrates the real degraded non-human state of these groups in the following words:

> The dwelling of Chandals and Cavpacas (spaka)(should be) outside the village; they should be deprived of dishes (apapatra) their property (consists of) dogs and asses. Their clothes (should be) the garments of the dead, and their ornaments (should be) of iron, and their food (should be) in broken dishes; and they must constantly wander about.[19]

By the time the *Manusmriti*'s composition was complete (around AD 700), the negative development of the Dalit state had reached its climax.

Against the supremacy of Brahmans, the revolt of Mahavira (540-468 BC) and Gautama Buddha (563-483 BC), the founders of Jainism and Buddhism, more or less failed.[20] About Gautama Buddha a French scholar Louis Dumont says, 'the Buddha himself, if he transcended caste, did not attack or reform it'.[21] According to G.S. Ghurye 'The Buddha is represented as being inclined to accept the divisions, basing them only in the individual's actions and not on his birth'.[22]

There is no doubt that Jainism and Buddhism were the first attacks or revolts in general against the caste system, and Dumont observed in this context that 'a sect cannot survive on Indian soil if it denies castes.'[23] It was because of this phenomenon, according to Dumont, that Buddhism could not survive as a force beyond the fourteenth century. The Jain strategy to deal with the Hindu influence, according to Marcus Banks, 'was to Hindu-ize Jainism. Jinasena (a Digambara scholar ascetic) not only rewrote Hindu mythological history, he also included all the major Hindu *samakaras* (life-cycle rituals) within the Jain ritual system by giving them a Jain gloss.' In fact 'Jinasena created the notion of a Jain caste-system, which he legitimated as an institution of Rishabhas.'[24] In other words, even Jainism ultimately could not divest itself from the influence of the Hindu caste system. In Gujarat, even to-day two groups of Jains known as Visa and Dasa will not inter-marry.[25] With such caste distinction Jainism could contribute little to ameliorate the problem of the Dalits.

Buddhism faced a different kind of problem, because by the time of the *Manusmriti*, the followers of Gautama Buddha were also considered untouchables.[26] By and by Buddhism also got influenced by the caste system.[27] In the post-Independence era of India, hundreds of thousands of Mahar Dalits of Maharashtra became Buddhists, and their progeny are known as Bauddh, which in Marathi has become a synonym for Mahar (untouchable).[28] Thus the protest of Jainism and Buddhism against Brahmanism or the caste system was in course of time diluted.

3.2 Later Developments

The period with which the discussion here is concerned (from AD 700 till date) can be divided broadly into three parts:

Muslim Period AD 700 to 1700
British Period AD 1700 to 1947
Post-Independence Period 1947 till date

3.2.1. *Muslim Period*

As seen above by the time the *Manusmriti* (AD 700) reached its final literary form with its strict social religious discipline to govern the graded Indian society, the religion of Prophet Muhammad also came into existence in the Arab world. The first conquest of Sind by the Arabs was in AD 712, but only in AD 1206 the Slave Dynasty established its rule in Delhi. The Muslim invaders continued to come and go with their leaders like Sultan Mahmud of Ghazni and Muhammad Ghori. After the Slave Dynasty, India was ruled by different Muslim rulers and dynasties, Khiljis, Sayyids, Suris, Moghuls till the death of the last Moghul King Bahadur Shah in AD 1862.[29] During this long period of Muslim domination in India, one would have expected some changes in the lot of Dalits, as Islam upholds the principle of equality of all human beings.[30] But after going over the social and religious conditions of Muslim period, one sees more or less that the state of the Dalits continued as before. Al-Beruni, writing on his visit to India around AD 1030, describes the treatment received by the Dalits as follows:

The people called Hadi, Doma (Domba), Chandala, and Badhatau [*sic*] are not reckoned amongst any caste or guild. They are occupied with dirty work, like the cleaning of the villages and other services. They are considered like as one sole class, and distinguished only by their occupations. In fact, they are considered like illegitimate children; for according to general opinion they descended from a Sudra father and a Brahmani mother as the children of fornication; therefore they are degraded outcastes.[31]

More to the point, a number of well known research works have confirmed that Muslim society itself was divided into a number of different grades/classes, though not exactly like the Hindu caste system. The highest grade, which was/is comparable to the Hindu 'twice-born' upper castes were Ashrafs (meaning honourable), Shaikhs (chiefs) and Mughals and Pathans (corresponding to the Hindu Ksatriyas). The middle group was made up of those who have clean occupations. The last group included the converts from the untouchables, who do scavenging, sweeping and other menial tasks.[32] This division among the Muslims was confirmed by later historians and scholars like J.S. Grewal.[33] Grewal has also observed that the differences:

... on the basis of religion or race or occupation were reflected in the morphology of cities and towns. Urban centre were divided into separate quarters for the various social groups. On the outskirts of town generally lived the scavengers, the leather dressers and the poor beggars.... The respectable social groups among Muslims lived apart from the common populace...[34]

Why did caste distinctions continue during the Muslim period in India and no change came even in the case of those Dalits who had embraced Islam? 'Acculturative influence of Hinduism' can be one reason. The other possible reasons 'are those elements in Islam itself which support such distinctions'. Imtiaz Ahmad, in the introduction to his edited work *Caste and Social Stratification among the Muslims*, has summarized these elements (based upon traditions) in these words:

- An Arab was superior to a non-Arab,
- Among Arabs, all Quraishities were of equal social standing in a class by themselves, and all other Arabs were equal irrespective of their tribes.

- Among non-Arabs, a man was by birth the equal of Arabs, if both his father and grandfather were Muslims, but only if he were sufficiently wealthy to provide an adequate *mahr* (endowment),
- A learned non-Arab was equal to an ignorant Arab, even if he was a descendant of Ali, 'for the worth of learning is greater than the worth of family' and
- a Muslim Kazi or theologian ranked higher than a merchant, and a merchant higher than a tradesman.[35]

From the above work it become also clear thay have shown how even at present, social distinctions among the Muslims continue in Bombay, Rajasthan, Haryana, Tamil Nadu, Uttar Pradesh and West Bengal.

Besides Islam, during the Muslim period, there were other religions practiced in India. The religions which came from outside India included Christianity, Judaism and Zoroastrianism. Christianity had already arrived before the Muslim presence got established here, and Judaism and Zoroastrianism came around the same time when Islam entered India. The indigenous religions which came into existence during the Muslim period were Lingayatism and Sikhism. Baha'i religion, which originated in Iran with its founder Baha'u'llah (1819-92), is to be found in the Malwa region of Central India.

Where Judaism is concerned, there have been two ancient settlements of Jews, one in Cochin (in south India in the state of Kerala) and the other in and around Bombay in the state of Maharashtra of western India. Historically their presence in India is confirmed from AD 1020 onwards. This date is known from the date inscribed on a set of copper plates which were given to a Jewish leader named Joseph Rabban by a Hindu king. These copper plates had inscribed on them 72 privileges which he granted to the Jewish community. These included: 'the right to ride an elephant, to be carried in a litter, to be preceded by drums and trumpets, to have a crier call out before their approach so that the lowly might withdraw from the streets.'[36] Similar privileges were granted to a group of Syrian Christians by the same Hindu king, which thus gave both the communities the status of caste Hindus. Jewish scholars Shalva Weil, says about this phenomenon:

> In terms of the larger order of ranking, both these groups individually have had to internalize caste perceptions in order to provide legitimation for their

ascribed status. As intermediaries in ranked order of things between the local king and inferior castes, they have both, individually, shared what Fuller (1976) has termed a common 'orthopraxy' with Hindus, while at the same retaining theoretical adherence to the equalitarianism of the Judeo-Christian tradition.[37]

Jews, both of Cochin and Bombay are divided into two main castes or *jatis* (groups) known as *Gora* (white) Jews and *Kala* (black) Jews. According to David G. Mandelbaum, these two groups of Jews, 'did not inter-dine or inter-marry, though they did worship in the same synagogues. Those of the higher jati claimed poorer Jewish ancestry. The lower, they alleged, was of mixed origins.'[38] These facts were also confirmed during a visit to the Cochin Jewish community by the author. [39] Shalva Weil also has confirmed that till 1950 there was a sizeable Jewish community in Cochin, but as most of these have migrated to Israel, their number now is very small.[40]

The other religious community which needs mention here, are the Parsees, whose members are followers of Zoroastrianism. Their ancestors emigrated from Persia during seventh century AD.[41] Eckehard Kulke has pointed out in his work *The Parsees in India* that Parsees before they came to India, were divided into four classes in the pattern of the Hindu caste system which were as follows:

Clergy (Athravans = Guardians of the fire)
—corresponding to the Brahmans among the Hindus.
Warriors (Rathaeshtars = He who is standing on a war-chariot).
—corresponding to the Ksatriyas
Peasants (Vactrya = He who cultivates the land).
—corresponding to the Vaisyas
Artisans (Huiti = Someone who produces objects)
—corresponding to the Sudras.[42]

The forefather of the Parsees, when they emigrated to India were allowed by the local king Sanjan Jadi Rana to settle in a place named Sanjan in Gujarat under certain strict conditions, which they accepted.[43] since the Parsees of course did not believe in conversion,[44] there was very little chance for them to influence the social order in India based on the caste system. So Parsees or Zoroastrianism may be considered to be more or less unconcerned with the problem of the Dalits.

Lingayatism or Veerasaivism as it is better known is a religious sect whose heartland is northern Mysore in the state of Karnataka. Lingayatism is an egalitarian religion and the Lingayats treated everyone, including women as equal. Lingayats worship the Shiva and according to their rule all members must always wear the Shiva emblem, the lingam. But according to Mandelbaum, Lingayats' *jatis* or groups are similar to those of Hindus. He says: 'Despite the explicit rejection of caste-ordering in Lingayats' scripture, Lingayats group themselves into ranked jatis. The highest are the Jangamas, hereditary priests and teachers.'[45]

In any case, as Lingayatism was limited to a small part of one state, Karnataka in the south, and also since its followers were not free from the *jati* distinctions, their role in the area of the Dalit problem is also limited.

The other religion which came into existence during the Muslim period was the Sikh religion, which also upholds the concept of egalitarianism.[46] The founder of Sikh religion Guru Nanak 'did away altogether with caste distinctions and ceremonials'.[47] But there are a number of testimonies available which show that by the time of the first half of the nineteenth century, the caste hierarchy among the Sikhs was well established.[48] While summing up the discussion on caste hierarchy among Sikhs, Ethne K. Marenco says:

> To sum up, therefore from the evidence of the Sikh Empire period, the many sources show that the Sikhs maintained caste practices, despite the fact that their religious dogma was against caste.... The original conversion to Sikhism was striving for upward mobility, particularly when the lower Hindu caste converted. This type of corporate caste mobility, where whole groups convert to a religion that promises them an escape from their low caste position, has occurred more than once in India, and it was the phenomenon which was involved in the original conversion of Jat Hindus or Chuhra and Chamar Hindus or Chuhra Muslims (Mazhabis) to Sikhism.[49]

Marenco finally has observed that to some extent there is upward mobility among the Sikh Dalits, but it was not due to the fact that they embraced Sikhism: 'For the most part, their advance in Sikh society was because they held with the British, on whose side they had fought during the Sepoy Mutiny.'[50]

An egalitarian religion which came from outside is Baha'i. Its members are limited to Malwa villages in central India and also it has got indigenized fully under the influence of Hindus. Therefore Baha'i egalitarian religion made very little contribution. A quotation from the work of W. Garlington will be helpful to clarify this point further:

> Therefore, by presenting Baha'u'llah as an avatar who has come to revitalize Hinduism rather than denounce it, Baha'i teachers do not make declarants forsake their Hindu heritage, and in effect they can psychologically remain Hindus: they are Hindus who believe in the Yugavatar, Baha'u'llah.[51]

Garlington also adds:

> On the normative level the Baha'i Faith is an egalitarian religion, all believers are considered equal in the eyes of God, and therefore they all assume a similar status- that of God's servant. This ideal is in direct contrast to the traditional Hindu view as practised in Malva villages, whereby an individual is ranked according to his status group (caste)....[52]

3.2.2 *British Period*

The next important period of Indian history is the British. Technically this period began with the inauguration of the East India Company (London) in AD 1599.[53] But for the first 150 years, the East India Company showed interest only in business and trade. It was only from AD 1744 onward that Lord Robert Clive turned into a military power.[54] In 1857 for the first time a major revolt took place in the Indian (British) army dominated mainly by upper class which some of the historians see as the main reason for this revolt as it was a threat to the caste system and its practices. After crashing the revolt, the British with a proclamation of Queen Victoria in 1858 transferred political authority from the Company to the English Crown.[55]

During the British period a number of events took place, which finally led the country into freedom in 1947. As far as the religious and social practices were concerned, the British maintained the status quo and followed a policy of non-interference, 'actively upholding and supporting the caste order'.[56] 'Even the protection of caste was decreed by an Act of Parliament'. In an order, it was declared, 'due regard may be had to the civil and religious usages of the natives...'.[57]

The work of Christian missionaries in many ways has influenced the situation in India, particularly in challenging the various religious traditions to evaluate and rethink their approach to the poor and various Dalit groups.[58] But they also upheld the Varna system. They even accepted it in the Christian Church.[59] When this was the case with both the British rulers and the Christian missionaries in general, one could expect very little from them which could be of help to the Dalits.

There was, however, one positive note. During the British period a number of small movements came into being, which showed concern for the Dalits. Before the British, during the Muslim period, the Bhakti movement helped the cause of the Dalits, particularly in the spiritual sphere. This happened mostly through the Bhakti saints, who either were non-Brahmans or themselves were Dalits.[60] The efforts of most of these movements during the British period were limited to reform rather than aimed at total change.[61] But there were some personalities who were involved directly in the struggle either for change or reform and they deserve mention here because they certainly left their impact on the present Dalit movements. They include Jotiba Phule, Ambedkar and Gandhi. Among these, the first two were for the total uplift of the Dalits, Gandhi's work was limited to certain reforms, more within the framework of the Hindu society.

Ambedkar dedicated his work *Who Were the Sudras* to Phule with these words:

Inscribed to the memory of Mahatma Jotiba Phule (1827-1890)

The Greatest Sudra of Modern India who made the lower classes among Hindus conscious of their slavery to the higher classes who preached the gospel that for India social democracy was more vital than independence from foreign rule.[62]

These words of Ambedkar are true to the spirit of Phule's pioneering work. The important phrase to be noted is 'who made the lower classes of Hindus conscious of the slavery'.

Phule belonged to the Mali caste, and had little education. In 1873 he started an association named Satyashodhak Samaj with the definite purpose of 'asserting the worth of man irrespective of caste'. He encouraged through his writings a revolt against 'the tyranny of the caste-system'. His revolt was 'against caste in so far as caste denied ordinary human rights to all'. In 1851 he started a primary school for the so-called untouchables in Poona.[63] He criticized the

Manusmriti because he realized that it was the greatest stumbling block in the way of social change.[64] Phule 'made efforts to unite all the non-Brahmin',[65] which specially included Shudra and Ati-Shudra (fourth service caste and outcaste Dalits).

The efforts Ambedkar and Gandhi made with regard to the Dalits during the British period are also important. In a real sense they were opposing one another in this struggle. This is known through the different approaches they adopted in dealing with the British on the question of the Dalits. This well-known struggle of theirs was another glaring example of the Dalits' problems and it had an impact on the history of the Dalits for years to come.

As mentioned earlier, a number of reform movements including those by Christian missionaries[66] were at work for the betterment of the Dalits, which ultimately also influenced the British Government to do something in this regard. During this period new titles and phrases were coined to denote the Dalits. For example, for the first time the existence of the 'Depressed classes' was recognized in the text of the Act of 1919.[67] In 1931, the Census Superintendent of Assam made a suggestion to change this title 'the Depressed classes' to the 'Exterior Castes'. The argument for this suggestion was that it is a broader title, because its connotation does not limit itself to 'outcaste' people (which mean people who are outside the caste system). On the other hand, Exterior Castes would include those who had been caste out, because of some breach of caste rules.[68] More pertinent to our discussion, and the struggle of the Dalits, is the term 'Scheduled Castes', which was first coined by the Simon Commission (appointed by the British government) and embodied in the Government of India Act, 1935, in Section 305.[69]

Prior to this coinage, the term 'Depressed Classes' was used in government circles and also by the members of various reform movements. But till 1932 the latter expression was used more or less for all kinds of 'depressed' people, including the 'untouchables'. Also till then no effort was made to define this term on a religious basis. It was in 1932 that for the first time the expression the 'Depressed Classes' was used only for people with an Untouchable background. The British Government, which was at that time also trying to help all other minor communities such as Muslims, Christians, Anglo-Indians, and so on, excluded them from the definition of Depressed

Classes, while bestowing on them special benefits, such as giving them separate communal electorates. In 1931 a special committee was also set up to draw a 'Schedule' of the castes and classes covered under the Depressed Classes. Also at that time in 1931, the Round Table Conference was called in London.

At the Round Table Conference, Gandhi and Ambedkar were the key members. Ambedkar demanded a separate electorate for the Depressed Classes, whom he always referred to as the 'Untouchables'. At this Conference, he also proposed that the Untouchables be called 'Protestant Hindus' or 'Non-conformist Hindus'.[70] But Gandhi objected to Ambedkar's demand for a separate electorate. By that time, of course, Gandhi had also introduced his favourite term 'Harijan' to be used in place of Untouchable, which was not accepted or liked by the untouchables themselves.[71] As Gandhi and Ambedkar did not agree with each other at the Round Table Conference, no final decision was taken.

Finally, the whole matter of a separate communal electorate was left to the chairman of the Conference, Prime Minister Ramsay Macdonald, who in 1932 issued the Communal Award. In this he also replaced the expression 'Depressed Classes' with 'Scheduled Castes' (from then on the Untouchables of India were known as 'Scheduled Castes'). Later the same expression was included in the Government of India (Scheduled Castes) Order, 1936.[72] Gandhi opposed the Communal Award in the case of the Scheduled Castes because of the fear of their getting separated from Hindu society in general.[73] Therefore he went on a fast unto death for which nobody was willing to take the responsibility. Even Ambedkar had to bow and agree to alter the Communal Award in a manner satisfactory to Gandhi.[74] According to this agreement in place of the 'separate' electorate; 'joint' electorate for the Scheduled Castes with the caste Hindu majority was accepted. This according to Upendra Baxi was a defeat for a political liberal like Ambedkar by his shrewd opponent Gandhi. 'Gandhi gambled on Ambedkar's self-restraint and won' says Baxi and 'the costs of the victory would have to be recorded by Untouchable historians of future India.'[75] in this way one more chance of effective liberation and freedom was lost by the Dalits. But Ambedkar at least got a larger number of seats for the Dalits, which of course was an achievement.[76]

3.2.3 *Post-Independence Period*

The problem of the Dalits and the struggle for liberation is continuing in the post-Independence period with equal fervour, because even India's political freedom in 1947 was not able to help in getting them out of their condition. Prior to Independence, the British rulers used the policy of 'non-interference' in local, cultural and religious practices, in order to rule the people of India, and for that they even created a new vocabulary. The new rulers of the Independent India have continued to use the same vocabulary and expressions which in no way have helped the masses, particularly the Dalits.

This was perhaps the reason why most of the Dalit movements and their leaders were not supportive of the freedom movement led by upper castes under the Indian National Congress.[77] While piloting the Constitution of Independent India on 4 November 1948 Ambedkar did say it was 'workable' and flexible but even this character of the Constitution has been used only to maintain the *status quo* of the set rules of life in Indian society because it has only gone in favour of the powerful, not the mass of powerless people. The Constitution itself, as Ambedkar said, is not 'bad', it is the use of its flexibility, which has proved bad. It is because of this truth, that the condition of the Dalits, even after Independence, has not improved.

We will not discuss here in detail about the condition of the Dalits in the post-Independent era, as this is going to be dealt in chapters six and seven which deals with the context of the Dalits as well as Dalit Christian in full. But still before concluding this chapter, we answer one very important question: 'Are Dalits Indigenous People?'

3.3. Are Dalits Indigenous People?

Who are the indigenous people? The report of the first Commissioner for Scheduled Castes and Scheduled Tribes, L.M. Shrikant gave three main characteristics, which according to him are applicable to all the Scheduled Tribes of India:

(a) Primitive way of living,
(b) Habitation in remote and less easily accessible areas,
(c) Nomadic habits and love for drink and dance.[78]

Besides this above view, he also invited comments in order to establish some definite criteria for identifying the Scheduled Tribes. After receiving the comments from the states, he fixed the following criteria without any explanation:

(a) Tribal origin
(b) Primitive way of life and habitation in remote, less easily accessible areas, and general backwardness in all respects.[79]

It would have been better if Shrikant could have gone back to the history of the origin of these people for the above purpose. Then he could have also understood why they are still living in remote areas and why they are backward in all respects. Answers to these questions could have helped also in establishing the relationship between indigenous people and the Dalits. This information, at the same time, could have helped in defining the term 'indigenous', especially its use for a particular group of people in the society. In the absence of such information, one may look into some agreed international views with regard to 'indigenous' people, which will clear the concern whether there exists any relationship between the Dalits of India and the indigenous people of India. Here for the purpose of this study a Report of the Independent Commission on International Humanitarian Issues (ICIHI) on indigenous peoples of the world, which appeared as a printed document in 1987 is being referred to. ICIHI listed the following four major elements in the definition of indigenous people: pre-existence (that the population are descendants of those inhabiting an area prior to the arrival of another population); non-dominance, cultural differences; and self-identification as indigenous. ICIHI also adds: 'The most undisputed criterion is that indigenous people are the descendants of the original inhabitants of the territory taken over through conquest or settlement by aliens.'[80]

It is true, there is no universally accepted definition of indigenous people. But a definition which is being used by the United Nations, (developed by Special Rapporteur on the Problem of Discrimination against Indigenous population for the United Nations Sub-Commission on Prevention of Discrimination and Protection of Minorities) could be of further help in understanding the criterion of identifying the indigenous people in Indian situation. The special

Rapporteur, has included also 'isolated and marginal population' as indigenous, even if they have not suffered conquest or colonization directly.[81] The special Rapporteur, in 1982, while recognizing that the right of defining what and who is indigenous belongs to the indigenous peoples themselves, has proposed the following definition:

> Indigenous communities, peoples and nations are those which, having an historical continuity with pre-invasion and pre-colonial societies that developed on their territories, considered themselves distinct from other sectors of these societies now prevailing in those territories, or part of them. They form at present non-dominant sectors of society and are determined to preserve, develop and transmit to future generations their ancestral territories, and their ethnic identity, as the basis of their continued existence as peoples, in accordance with their own cultural patterns, social institutions and legal systems.[82]

In principle, the Dalits themselves have to decide if they are indigenous or not. But if one looks at the four major elements given above, and the definition of indigenous peoples, these three: pre-existence, non-dominance and cultural differences—are applicable to the Dalits, as also to the indigenous groups (particularly groups in Bihar and central India known as Adivasi). Only the fourth element namely 'self identification as indigenous' may be questioned, but the answer to this question is found in their forgotten history: an attempt has been made to reconstruct it in the previous sections of this pamphlet. At this point another question may be raised about the Dalits being indigenous and their present relationship with land and its natural resources, which are considered divine by indigenous people—'gifts entrusted to them for safe-keeping and for passing on intact to future generations'.[83] It is true that this custodial attitude, as it were, is missing among the Dalits, but here one needs to remember (as pointed out in the earlier sections), that during the last more than 3000 years too many generations have passed to remember that possibly once the land and its natural resources belonged to their ancestors, where now they live landless and resourceless. With this long time gap and the kind of oppression they have undergone or are facing, their attitude not only towards land and natural resources, but also toward themselves (toward their very being) possibly has changed, which they have now accepted 'as a part of the natural order of things' (words of the Mandal Commission) or which now they have accepted 'as a privilege' (words of L.M. Shrikant).

Before taking this point of the discussion further, on this question of the Dalits being indigenous people, it may be worth stating that a number of writers' hint directly or indirectly that the Dalits once were, in real fact a part of the communities of people, who today fall under the category of indigenous. These scholars include Stephen Fuchs,[84] Hugh Kennedy Trevaskis,[85] Romila Thapar,[86] Prabhati Mukherjee,[87] G.S. Ghurye, [8] N.K. Dutt, [9] and Nirharanjan Ray.[90]

Besides the indirect or direct comments of the writers, which help to link the roots of the Dalits with a large number of indigenous groups, known as Adivasis (living in the central part of India) three works of other writers have dealt in detail with the question of 'Dalits being an indigenous people.' These are Ambedkar, Suresh Narain Srivastava and J. Van Troy. But before moving to their work, it should also be mentioned here that the two main sources—the *Rigveda* and the archeological sources also extent support to this contention.

In the hymns of the *Rigveda*, there are a number of references which draw attention to the defeated indigenous groups, and how after their defeat they were either forced to be scattered or they themselves willingly got scattered in different directions. Some of the references in this regard are found in hymns 2.20.7, 4.28.4, 6.25.2, 6.69.6, 3.5.7, etc.[91] Where evidences from the works of archeologists are concerned, this has been quoted already and the works of Ernest Mackay and George F. Dales in earlier sections and which hint at the shift or movement of people from north-west India (Mohenjo-daro and Harappa) to other parts of India.

Coming to the works of the three scholars, Ambedkar has discussed this question in his work *The Untouchables* (1948), with a question: who were they and why did they become untouchables? The first point about Ambedkar's work that needs to be remembered is what he himself has said about it: 'This book may, therefore, be taken as pioneer in the exploration of a field so completely neglected by everybody.[92] So while considering his views here, one need to take these as 'pioneer' in nature, which also demands further work in the field of the history of the untouchables or the Dalits.

Ambedkar's work is based on his thesis that there is no racial difference between the Untouchables (Dalits) and other groups or castes. According to Ambedkar, the divisions in the Indian society began with a primitive society which consisted of many local communities (or tribes). In the beginning, all these communities were nomadic. But with time and because of intra-tribal warfare, they got divided into three groups: a Settled Community, a Raider Community belonging to nomadic tribes, and a Broken Men's Community consisting of defeated people of defeated tribes. The last group is important, because it is these broken men, according to Dr. Ambedkar, who at a later stage, were turned into untouchables or today's Dalits. These 'Broken Men' were the people of defeated tribes, who with their defeat got scattered or broken from their original tribes.[93]

Ambedkar's pioneering effort to deal with the roots of the Dalits (untouchables), is important, because besides throwing light on, how the Dalits have reached their present state, it puts forward another important point in the beginning—today's so called 'Criminal tribes,' 'the Aboriginal Tribes' and 'untouchables' (Dalits) had a common beginning.[94]

Suresh Narain Srivastava's work *Harijans in Indian Society* (1980) adds clarity to this concern of the 'Dalits being indigenous.' Besides considering most of the possible literary sources, he also takes into account the archeological findings concerning Mohenjodaro and Harappa and has come to clear conclusions, which were very helpful in setting up this issue. The following two quotations from Srivastava's work may be sufficient for our purpose:

> The pre-Dravidian settlers were the natives of India.... The Dravidians were the first to have attacked the Aboriginals of India ... they did not make aboriginals their own slaves.... After the Dravidians, another major attack was made by the Aryans.... As the victorious people, the Aryan invaders looked down upon their opponents and called them the Dasa-Dasyus and the Nishadas.[95]

Srivastava in his work further elaborates:

> Therefore, defeated aboriginals were made 'slaves' in their social order.... These slaves have been included in the fold of Hinduism by placing them on the lowest rung of the social ladder.... Those who did not accept the offer of becoming slaves, were driven away into forests and they remained aboriginals with their social, economic and cultural distinctions.... In the course of time, these people were divided into two classes. Some became nomadic tribes and others roaming from place to place. These roaming peoples were

called criminal tribes.... In this way; an ancient Indian society came to be divided into four parts—the Aryans, the non-Aryans, the aboriginals and the nomadic criminal tribes.[96]

In the second quotation, the last two lines make one point clear—while leaving out the first groups of Aryans, the other three groups of people, the non-Aryans (today's Dalits), the aboriginals (today's indigenous people) and the nomadic criminal tribes (today's communities of groups, who will roam around) have the same roots. In other words these later three groups are in real sense the people of indigenous origin, because their forefathers were the same.

The third work is an article included in *Cultural Chotanagpur-Unity in Diversity*, edited by S. Bosu Mullick in 1991, 'Pre-history and Early History of Chotanagpur' by J. Ven Troy to establish a historical relationship between the people of Chotanagpur (indigenous) known as *Kurukh* or *Oraons* with their past history. He has taken into account the archaeological and linguistic evidences. There are two possibilities: first, the forefathers of Oraons were the first descendants of the pre-Harappa people; second, the Oraons came from north-west India. The latter view is based on linguistic evidence.[97] Van Troy's article has not given any final conclusion, but it certainly raises a possibility of establishing a link of the indigenous people of Chotanagapur and those who once lived in the ancient part of India known today as north-west India. This attempt definitely points towards a close relationship between the Dalits and the indigenous people (*adivasis)* and ultimately their having common forefathers.

3.4. Conclusion

Three main points become clear on the historical background of the Dalits of India:

First, the Dalits are the descendents of the earliest settlers of India.

Second, the history of the Dalit's present problem began around 1500 BC and for more than 3500 years they have suffered and continue to suffer multiple oppressions, which have always been supported by religion, directly or indirectly.

Third, and (which is most important) because of the long history of oppression the Dalits have even lost their self-identity as full human beings, which they have now accepted 'as part of the natural order of things' or 'as a privilege' and this is in a real sense the inner capacity of their being from which they need liberation or release and towards this end Dalit theology is supposed to lead them.

NOTES

1. (a) Quoted in *The Land of the Five Rivers* by Hugh Kennedy Trevaskis, Oxford University Press, Oxford, 1927. Also see: (b) S.V. Desikachar, *Caste, Religion and Country*, Orient Longman, New Delhi, 1993, p. 116.
2. (a) Ramprasad Chanda, *The Indo-Aryan Races: A Study of the Origin of Indo-Aryan People and Insitutions*, Varendra Research Society, Calcutta, 1875, p. 3.
   (b) Prabhati Mukherjee, *Beyond the Four Varnas: The Untouchables in India*, Motilal Banarsidass, Delhi, pp. 78, 79.
   (c) Romila Thapar, *From Lineage to State*, Oxford University Press, Bombay, 1990, p. 42.
3. Waskom J. Picket, *Christian Mass Movements in India*, Abingdon Press, New York, 1933, p. 217.
4. Ralph T.H. Griffith, *The Hymns of the Rigveda*, Motilal Banarsidass, Delhi, rpt., 1986, p. 603.
5. N.K. Dutt, *Origin and Growth of Caste System in India*, South Asia Books, Calcutta, p. 25.
6. Fr. Zacharias: *An Outline of Hinduism*, St. Joseph's Apostolic Seminary, Alwaye, 1956, pp. 21 and 117
7. Robert Ernest Hume (tr.), *The Thirteen Principal Upanishads*, Oxford Univerisity Press, Delhi, 1992, p. 233.
8. Fr. Zacharias, op. cit., p. 360.
9. Ibid., pp. 375-6.
10. Makhan Lal Sen (tr.), *Ramayana*, Rupa & Co, Calcutta, 1989, pp. 699-702.
11. Goyandka, Jayadayal (ed.), *Snkhipat Mahabhrate* (Hindi), Gita Press, Gorakhpur, n.d., pp. 69-72.
12. Swami Vireswarananda (tr.), *Srimad Bhagavat-Gita*, Sri Ramakrisna Math, Publication Department, Madras, 1978, p. 128.
13. Ibid., pp. 506-8.
14. Ibid., p. 282.
15. Arthur Coke Burnell (tr.), *The Ordinances of Manu*, Motilal Banarsidass, New Delhi, 1971, p. xxiii (Introduction). Also see Fr. Zacharias: op. cit., p. 323.

16. Ibid., p. 305.
17. See for discussion on 'Anuloma' and 'Pratiloma', Dr. Suresh Narain Srivastava, *Harijans in Indian Soceity*, The Upper India Publishing House, Lucknow, pp. 25-8.
18. Burnell (tr.), op. cit., p. 306 (*Manusmriti* 10.12), p. 310 (*Manusmriti* 10.38).
19. Ibid., p. 312 (*Manusmriti* 10.51, 52).
20. See for detail discussion:
    (a) R. Sangeetha Rao, *Caste System in India: Myth and Reality*, India Publishers and Distributors, Delhi, 1989, pp. 72-80.
    (b) G.S. Ghurye, *Caste and Race in India*, Bombay, Popular Prakashan, 1979, pp. 69-72.
21. Quoted in Duncan B. Forrester, *Caste and Christianity*, Curzon Press, London, 1980, p. 11.
22. Ghurye, op. cit., p. 71.
23. Quoted in Duncan B. Forrester, *Caste and Christianity*, Curzon Press, London, 1979, p. 11.
24. Marcus Banks, *Organizing Jainism in India and England*, Oxford, 1992, p. 27.
25. Ibid., p. 52.
26. Dr. B.R. Ambedkar, 'The Untouchables', in Dr. Babasaheb Ambedkar: Writings and Speeches, vol. 7, Education Department, Government of Maharashtra, Bombay, 1990, p. 315.
27. P. Lakshmi Narasu, *The Essence of Buddhism*, Thacker & Co., Bombay, 1948, p. 98.
28. Eleanor Zelliot, 'The Psychological Dimension of the Buddhist Movement in India', in G.A. Oddie (ed.), *Religion in South Asia-Religious Conversion and Revival Movements in South Asia in Medieval and Modern Times*, Manohar, New Delhi, 1991, p. 204.
29. See for detail of facts and dates in:
    Francis Watson: A *Concise History of India*, Camelot Press Ltd., Southampton, rpt., 1981, pp. 87-124.
30. Imtiaz Ahmed (ed.), *Caste and Social Stratification Among Muslims in India*, Manohar, New Delhi, 1978, p. 204.
31. Al-Beruni: *India* (abridged edition of Dr. Edward C. Sachan's English Translation and edited by Qeyamuddin Ahmed), National Book Trust, New Delhi, 1988 (revised), p. 46.
32. See for detail discussion:
    (a) Louis Dumont, *Homo Hierarchicus: The Caste System and its Implications*, The University of Chicago Press, Chicago, 1970, pp. 205-12.

(b) David G. Mandelbaum, *Society in India*, Popular Prakashan, Bombay, 1990 (rpt.), pp. 246-51.

33. J.S. Grewal, *Guru Nanak in History*, Publication Bureau, Panjab Univerisity, Chandigarh, 1979 (rpt.), p. 61.
34. Ibid., p. 40.
35. Ahmed (ed.), op. cit., 1973, pp. xxx-xi (Introduction).
36. Mandelbaum, op. cit., pp. 560-1.
37. Shalva Weil, 'Symmetry between Christians and Jews in India: The Cananite Christians and the Cochin Jews of Kerala', *Indian Sociology*, vol. 16, no. 2. Paris, 1992, pp. 194-5.
38. Mandelbaum, op. cit., p. 563.
39. On December 3, 1993, I visited in Cochin the locality known as Kochi (Jew Town) and visited the local Synagogue also. During my visit I asked number of questions to local Jews and others. During this visit, I was told that there was separate worship place for the *Kala* (black) Jews, and there is very little social dealings among the two groups.
40. Shalva Weil, op. cit., p. 184.
41. Eckehard Kulke, *The Parsees in India*, Vikas Publishing House, New Delhi, 1993 (rpt.), pp. 13, 26.
42. Ibid., p. 48.
43. (a) B.K. Boman-Behram, 'Social Relationship Between the Communities', in Nancy Singh and Ram Singh (eds.), *The Sugar in the Milk: The Parsis in India*, ISPCK, Delhi, 1986, pp. 53-4.
    (b) Kulke, op. cit., p. 38.
44. Ram Singh, 'The Incredible Community', in *The Sugar in the Milk*, op. cit., p. 3.
45. David G. Mandelbaum, op. cit., p. 537.
46. Ethne K. Marenco, *The Transformation of Sikh Society*, Heritage Publishers, New Delhi, 1976, pp. 26, 298.
47. R.C. Majumdar, 'Evaluation of Religio-Philosophic Culture in India, in Haridas Bhatacharyya (ed.), *The Culture Heritage of India*, vol. IV, The Religions, The Ramakrisna Math, Institute of Culture, Calcutta, 1983 (rpt), p. 61.
48. Ethne K. Marenco, op. cit., pp. 41-2.
49. Ibid., p. 63.
50. Ibid., p. 285.
51. W. Garlington, 'The Baha'i Faith in Malwa', in G.A. Oddie (ed.), *Religion in South Asia*, Manohar, New Delhi, 1991 (second revised and enlarge edition), p. 181.
52. Ibid., p. 182.

53. John Wiliam Kaye, *Christianity in India*, Missions Publisher, London, 1959, p. 38.
54. Watson, op. cit., p. 125.
55. Ibid., pp. 141-4. Also see: *The Untouchable Story*, by D.P. Das, New Delhi, 1985, p. 171.
56. Marc Galanter, *Competing Equalities in Law and the Backward Classes in Media*, Oxford University Press, Delhi, 1984, p. 19.
57. Kaye, op. cit., p. 375.
58. See for details discussion: *Religion and Society*, vol. XXXVI, no. 4, December 1989, pp. 26-8.
59. Kaye, op. cit., pp. 30-3, 352-3.
60. See for details: R. Sangeetha Rao, op. cit., pp. 106-16.
61. Suresh Narain Srivastava, *Harijans in Indian Society*, pp. 247-8.
62. Vasant Moon (ed.), *Dr. Babasaheb Ambedkar's Writings and Speeches*, vol. 7, Education Department, Government of Maharashtra, 1990, reprint of *Who are the Shudras*, vol. 7, op. cit., p. 4.
63. Ghurye, op. cit., pp. 286-87.
64. G.S. Lokhande, *Bhimrao Ramji Ambedkar*, Intellectual Publishing House, New Delhi, 1982, p. 9.
65. A.K. Vakil, *Gandhi—Ambedkar Dispute*, Ashish Publishing House, New Delhi, 1982, p. 47.
66. See for summary of these movements and their work:
Louise Ouwerkerk, *The Untouchables of India*, Oxford University Press, Oxford, 1945, pp. 16-29.
67. Lokhande, op. cit., p. 181.
68. J.H. Hutton, *Caste in India*, Cambridge University Press, Cambridge, 1946, p. 167.
69. Ghurye, op. cit., p. 306.
70. Harold R. Isaacs, *India's Ex-Untouchables*, Asian Publishing House, Bombay, 1965, p. 36.
71. Ibid., pp. 39-41.
72. See for detail discussion: *Bulletin of the Christian Institute for Religious Studies*, vol. 20, no. 1, January 1991, pp. 3-6.
73. A.M. Rajasekhriah, *B.R. Ambedkar: The Quest for Social Justice*, Uppal, New Delhi, 1989, p. 63.
74. Ibid., pp. 66-7. Also see Louise Ouwerkerk, op. cit., p. 306.
75. Upendra Baxi, 'Political Justice, Legislative, Reservation for Scheduled Caste and Social Change' (Dr. Ambedkar Memorial Lectures, 1978), University of Madras, Madras, p. 9.
76. Zelliot, op. cit., p. 188.

77. S.K. Gupta, *The Scheduled Castes in Modern Indian Politics*, Munshiram Mahohar, New Delhi, 1985, pp. 211-12.
78. Shrikant, op. cit., p. 2.
79. Ibid., p. 9.
80. *Indigenous Peoples: A Global Quest for Justice*, a Report for the Independent Commission on International Humanitarian Issues—Foreword by Agha Khan and Hassan Bin Talat (Co-Chairman), Zed Books, London, 1987, p. 6.
81. Ibid., p. 7.
82. Quoted in ibid., p. 8.
83. Ibid., p. 10.
84. (a) Stephen Fuchs, *At the Bottom of Indian Society*, Munshiram Manoharlal, Delhi, 1981, p. 25.
    (b) Also see Fuchs' other work, *The Aboriginal Tribes of India*, The Macmillan Press, London, 1983, pp. 12f.
85. Hugh Kennedy Trevaski, *The Land of Five Rivers*, Oxford University Press, Oxford, 1928, p. 29.
86. Romila Thapar, *From Lineage to State*, p. 28.
87. Prabhati Mukherjee, *Beyond Four Varnas: The Untouchables in India*, pp. 28, 91.
88. Ghurye, op. cit., p. 52.
89. N.K. Dutt, *Origin and Growth of Caste System in India*, pp. 70, 71.
90. Niharranjan Ray, Introductory Address, in K. Suresh Singh (ed.), *The Tribal Situation in India*, Indian Institute of Advanced Study, Shimla, 1986 (rpt.), pp. 10, 11, 14, etc.
91. Ralph T.H. Griffith (tr.), op. cit., pp. 143, 220, 300, 322, 336.
92. Dr. B.R. Ambedkar, *The Untouchables*, op. cit., p. 241.
93. Ibid., pp. 271-7.
94. Ibid., p. 239.
95. Srivastava, op. cit., p. 3.
96. Ibid., pp. 9, 10.
97. J. Van Troy, 'Pre-history and early History of Chotanagpur', in S. Bosu Mullick (ed.), *Cultural Chotanagpur: Unity in Diversity*, Uppal, New Delhi, 1991, pp. 34-5.

PART 2

DALIT CHRISTIAN HISTORY

CHAPTER 4

Historical Background of Dalit Christians

4.1. Why Dalit Christians?

The basic question addressed here is: Why Dalit Christians? Why Dalits even after becoming Christians, particularly when the Christian religion upholds the principle of equality?[1] Why are the conditions of Dalit Christians still unchanged? This problem as it stands today is well recognized in some circles both among Church Christians as well as outside. But the whole blame is put on the caste system in Indian society. For example, in October 1992, the Synod of the Church of North India, while recognizing the problem of Christian Dalits said, 'The Synod of the CNI recognizes the problem of the caste Christians and Dalits within the Church and outside it.'[2] Nirad C. Chaudhuri, a well known author and by faith, a Hindu has long time back stated the same fact in his book *The Continent of Circe*.[3] It is true that in general, the caste system is the root cause of the problems of Dalits in India. But is it true of Christian Dalits also? Or is their problem more deeply based or rooted in some particular religious understanding (of the Christian faith)? Besides addressing this question, the discussion here covers questions of missionaries' methods, missionaries' response to the problems of the Christian Dalit, and later dwells on how Indian Christians/ Church responded to the same issue.

The history of the Dalit Christians in India began mainly with the coming of Western missionaries. Prior to that, the only Christian tradition existing in India was Syrian, which has its base in Kerala (south India) and these Christians right from the beginning were made a part of the caste structured Hindu society through a charter of seventy two privileges offered to them by a Hindu king.[4] A brief survey of the historical data with an analysis is given here.

4.2. Some Cases of Missionaries

4.2.1. Francis Xavier and Roberto de Nobili

The first Western missionary was a Roman Catholic Jesuit, Francis Xavier, who arrived in India in October 1542. On his arrival, he adopted a simple method of preaching. He did translations of the Apostles' Creed, the Lord's Supper and the Ten Commandments in Tamil. Then he took a bell in His hand and went around ringing it, first in the streets of Goa and then from village to village on the western coast among the fishermen. It is believed he baptized 700,000 people belonging to different caste groups but the majority of his converts came from people known as pariah (outcastes).[5]

The next well-known missionary who played an important role in the history of Christian Dalits was another Jesuit missionary Roberto de Nobili. He arrived in Madurai (south India) in AD 1606. He found that the Christian religion was successful only among the people considered as low caste, and that it was because of the Portuguese who were known as *Paranghis*. These *Paranghis* ate beef, drank liquor and lived unclean without bathing and had contact with the low-caste people. Therefore, de Nobili wanted to change this. Kaye says:

> Rejecting the example of Xavier, whose warm heart expanded towards the poor and the oppressed, and whose ready limbs had ever borne him amongst them, Roberto de Nobili, his associate and his successor, addressed themselves to the dominant class and sought their converts among the Brahmins.[6]

Roberto de Nobili, in order to gain converts from so-called upper castes, declared himself a high caste *Raja* (King). He said he was not a *Paranghi*, but a royal person from Rome. Later on, he, along with his colleagues, declared that they were the 'new Brahmins' (priests). They made use of a current belief of that time that the original Veda was lost. Roberto de Nobili declared that he had found the true lost Veda and he was teaching from that. He started following the Hindu religious customs. He accepted castes and practiced untouchability. Seeing this, many upper caste Hindus became Christians.[7]

Roberto de Nobili then introduced separate priests for upper and lower caste Christians.[8] These efforts of his brought much fruit, but it proved to be negative: 'A divided Church resulted. On the one hand were Brahmin Christians, on the other hand, Pariah Christians.'[9]

4.2.2. *Ziegenbalg and Plutschau*

Bartholomew Ziegenbalg and Henry Plutschau were the first Protestant missionaries. They studied at the University of Halle, a great centre of evangelical Christianity, under the learned and pious Professor Francke.[10] Therefore, as expected, they were both trained within a tradition of pietism which was highly individualistic.[11]

The pietistic tradition laid special stress on the second or new birth (*Wiedergeburt*). Professor A.H. Francke himself had a dramatic conversion experience in 1686.[12] With this kind of religious background, Ziegenbalg and Plutschau arrived in south India during 1706. On their arrival at Tranquebar, they first mastered the local language and started translating the Scripture. The method of preaching of these Protestant missionaries was different from that of Jesuits, which was based on a set of moral teachings and a mere ceremony of baptism. But as per the pietistic tradition, the work of Ziegenbalg and his colleagues was based on the Bible. Scripture was the basis of their preaching. Their first convert was baptized on 12 May 1707, who was a poor slave (a Dalit). Their later converts were mostly from the low, poor castes.

Besides Ziegenbalg and Plutschau, an important early Lutheran missionary was Christian Frederick Schwartz, who was also trained at the University of Halle. Schwartz did help the poor people, but it was for him a secular work. He considered this kind of work subordinate to spiritual.[13]

A method similar to that of those missionaries was adopted by other Protestant missionaries both in north and other parts of India.[14]

4.2.3. *Bishop Middleton and Bishop Heber*

In 1813, when the British Government passed a bill, it gave more concessions and greater liberty to Christian missions. This also was followed by another decision, to have in India a Bishop of the Church of England. The first Bishop elected was Thomas Franshawe Middleton, whose main interest was classical and Western theology, which he introduced in India by founding a college after his name, Bishop's College in Calcutta.[15] But he was against Indians being made priests.[16]

The bishop who succeeded Bishop Middleton after his death in July 1822 was Bishop R. Heber, who reached India in October 1823. Bishop Heber tried his best to change the situation. He seriously considered the question of caste in the Church. Before his visit to the south in 1826, he wanted to prepare himself to face this problem. He knew that even famous missionaries like Ziegenbalg and Schwartz had accommodated the evil of caste in the Church. At that time, there was a convert in Bishop's College by the name of Christian David, who was a follower of the teachings of Schwartz. Bishop Heber asked the opinion of this native Christian, who gave it in writing. Kaye has summarized Christian David's view in these words:

> First, with regard to the nature of Caste, it was declared by Christian David, that it was among the natives of South India, 'purely a worldly idea'.... From the days of Ziegenbalg downwards, they had wanted to sit at Church in two separate divisions, and had communicated separately at the Lord's Supper, drinking out of the same cup. But high-caste converts drinking first....[17]

Bishop Heber accepted the views of Christian David, which in fact, were the views of early missionaries such as Christian Schwartz. Bishop Heber concluded that in some form, distinctions existed even in Europe.[18]

4.3. Root Causes of the Problem of Dalit Christians

The discussion in the last section gives us hints about both the origin and causes of the development of the problem of the larger section of Christians in India, namely Dalit Christians. One can easily see the basic causes for the unchanged conditions of Dalit Christians even after their embracing the Christian faith for an analysis. These causes can be classified into the following three categories:

- Missionaries' Theological Background
- Missionary Methods and Missionary response to the problem of Dalit Christians
- Indian Churches'/ Christians' Response

4.3.1. *Missionaries' Theological Background*

As far as the early Roman Catholic missionaries (i.e. Francis Xavier) were concerned, their religious teachings were limited to a set of moral teachings based on the Creed, The Lord's Prayer and the Ten Commandments. On the other hand, the early missionaries, viz. Ziegenbalg, Plutschau and Schwartz had a pietistic religious background, which demands a special look into the past history of their theological thoughts, which had roots in the prevailing theological conditions of their time, which is linked with the social and religious conditions of medieval Europe. Here, a brief attempt is made to understand that background, which again, to me, makes it clear why almost all the early European missionaries adopted a common mono-path to preach the Christian Gospel in India. In the remaining part of this section of this chapter, we will first narrate a case of middle ages' German Church and then we will make some more comments basing on the context in which the whole missionary movement was born.

It was in October 1991, when along with some friends, I paid a visit to Germany. While staying in Frankfurt, we were taken by one of the German friends to visit a small, but historic German church in a small town named Idstein. The present name of Idstein's Church is *Unionskirche* (Union Church). The original name, when it was founded in AD 1330 was St. Martin's Church. We were told that this was one of the earliest churches in Germany which was changed from the Roman Catholic Order to Protestant Lutheran Order in AD 1558. The history of the present name of the church goes back to AD 1817, when two Christian traditions, that is the Lutheran and Reformed Churches came together in the area of Nassau. It was 1917 at the time of the celebration of the first centenary of this union that the Church was renamed *Unionskirche*. This small church indeed stands as a testimony to a number of historical truths about the social, religious, political and cultural life of the European people. During our short visit, a number of things were told to us by our host who took us there. Here below, I am sharing some of these notes which I took concerning the pews in the church, which surrounded the formerly empty nave.

These pews are divided into boxes according to the social order (classes) of medieval Germany. In the upper balcony, the box-type pews were for men of different classes. These classes include *Herrschaftsstuhl* (ruling classes), *Ratsstuhl* (bureaucrats) *Sekretarstuhl* (secretaries) *Gerichtsstuhl* (care takers of justice), *Vorstcherstuhl* (managers) and *Burgerstuhl* (ordinary citizens). Each of these classes had opposite titles for women also. Women in those days could not sit along with their husbands or other male members of the families. Women's pews were/are located below, and above them were men's in the gallery. But in both cases, these were divided into boxes according to their social status and at the front of each box, a Bible verse(s) was/is inscribed. These box-type pews in the church reveal what kind of a social order the missionaries came from and this perhaps was the basis on which Bishop Heber came to the conclusion that in some sense, distinctions exist even in Europe. The inner side of the *Idstein Unionskirche* reveals the existence of social distinctions or class system of Europe. The verses inscribed in front of each box also tell us what kind of biblical and theological understanding prevailed in those days with regard to these social systems. It is interesting to quote below a few examples in support of this point. The verses used for first class (ruling class) and the class of ordinary citizens for example were/are:

Herrschaftsstuhl:

Men: ... for he is God's servant for your good. But if you do what is wrong, you should be afraid, for the authority does not bear the sword in vain. It is the servant of God to execute his wrath on the wrong doer (Romans 13:4).

Women: Do not adorn yourselves outwardly by braiding your hair and by wearing gold ornaments or fine clothing; rather, let your adornment be the inner self with the lasting beauty of a gentle spirit, which is very precious in God's sight (I Peter 3: 3-4).

Burgerstuhl:

Men: Let every person be subject to the governing authority; for there is no authority except from God, and these authorities that exist have been instituted by God (Romans 13:1).

Women: Wives, in the same way, accept the authority of your husbands, so that, even if some of them do not obey the Word, they may be won over without a word by their wives' conduct, when they see purity and reverence of your lives (I Peter 3:1-2).

Space does not permit us to quote all the Bible verses inscribed in the front of all the boxes representating various classes, but these verses definitely help us to understand the religious and theological understanding of the medieval German Church (Europe). First, these convey that theology or religious understanding was dominated by the feudal lords and their bourgeois representatives. The overall purpose of such theology was to maintain the status quo of various classes of people.

Already reference has been made to the theological background of the early missionaries, particularly Protestants who include Ziegenbalg, Plutschau and Schwartz. Also reference has been made to how all these missionaries had their theological and missionary training at the University of Halle, the great centre of pietistic and evangelical Christianity. These men were taught by the well-known and pious Professor Francke and his son. Theologically, the main concept in which Prof. Francke, like his predecessor Spencer, believed, was the concept of the second or new birth (*Wiedergeburt*). He himself as mentioned earlier had a dramatic conversion experience in 1686. The basis of Halle theology was infallibility of the Scripture. In this expression, a special emphasis was laid on personal holiness and the concern of another world. Prof Francke's theology of new birth included five main points: realization of men's invalidity and sinfulness; recognition of divine illumination of human will to do the truth; experience of God's act of conversion which includes a struggle against the old nature; assurance of salvation means becoming aware of God's working in one's life, and live a life of newly recreated person which includes a new style of life.[19]

It is also true that pietists believe in doing good works, but these were never considered as a contributory factor for salvation. According to one of the earliest pietist, George Major, they considered good works necessary only to preserve salvation, but these do not contribute to the process of salvation. One of Luther's close associates, Nicholas Amsdorf even claimed that good works are injurious to salvation.[20] It is also true that Prof. Francke and others believed in social work. He even started a comprehensive educational system to help the orphans and other poor children. He also established hospitals, printing presses, book stores, bindery, tailor shop, smithy, carpenter shop and copper shops. All these works were done with the idea that the 'Scripture is not only to be interpreted, but also implemented'.

But the undergirding concept which played a key role was the 'piety of Pietism'.[21] About the meaning of this concept of piety and its final goal, Prof. John Weborg says: 'True piety, the congruence of words, acts, and love, activates the person's will to meaning and prepares the person for the hearing of the Gospel, which is the aim of pietism's social apologetic'.[22]

In a way, these pietistic theological stands make the point clear why a missionary like Schwartz considered helping the poor a secondary level and a secular work as compared to his missionary obligations which means spiritual ones.

One interesting historical point is that the University of Halle's medieval influence was not limited to the German missionary movement of that time, but spread to almost all parts of Europe including England, and also to America. It was also not limited to one Christian denominational tradition, it influenced all the major Christian traditions of that time. For example, John Weborg summarized the story of the influence of Pietism in these words:

> So did Pietism, both the Halle and Herrnhut varieties, spread to the Baltic states and Scandinavia, to England by the enormous influence of Bengal on Wesley, to America by Halle's influence in Muhleherg (the patriarch of American Lutheranism) and by Cotton Mather's correspondence with Francke and by the rise of the missionary movement.[23]

The same happened to Princeton Theology, which was the basis of Presbyterian missionaries in India. Here again, one of the chief exponents of the Princeton School, Charles Hodge (1797- 1878), was a Professor for two years at the University of Halle and was directly influenced.[24] For Hodge, 'Scripture was the ultimate standard' for building a theological expression or helping the evangelists how they should deal with inquiries or to test the sincerity of one's repentance or preparing for foreign missionary work.[25]

The point about Halle's deep influence on various missionaries we need to remember is that, *first*, it influenced those (missionaries) who were trained there; *second*, it influenced their disciples like Christian David; and *third*, its influence spread from generation to generation and even bishops like Heber were not spared. Now, what is wrong with Halle's theological influence or what relationship one has with the problem of the Christian Dalits in India? To answer this, we have to peep into the context into which Pietistic theology was born.

Any living theological expression has to be noted in the actual experiences of believers in a particular historical setting.[26] This was true with Pietistic theology also. In the background of this theological expression was a war, which is known in Europe history as 'The Thirty Years' War', which ended in 1648. This war was followed by three French invasions of Germany. The Thirty Years' War and these invasions not only reduced the population of Germany by one third, they also created chaos in all spheres of people's lives. The soldiers used all kinds of inhuman means to achieve their ends, including 'harassing, torturing, raping the citizens'. Prof. Weborg adds, 'so dehumanized had conditions become that the dead were found with grass in their mouths and cannibalism was not unknown.'[27] He further says: 'What it all added to was a de-population of the land, dehumanization of people due to sheer need to survive and dissolution of morals and manners.'[28]

On the cultural and religious plane, already a decline had begun, but the Thirty Years' War further accelerated it. Feudal lords from the time of the Middle Ages had already started expanding their power. They had become 'a law unto themselves, including a growing power over the Church'. A rigid class distinction had emerged and it had entered fully into the life of the Church. The interior or Idstein Unionskirche, with classified box-type pews, is a living testimony to this reality.

The worst type of social and religious life of Christians at that time in Germany can be seen through their practicing of the two major Christian sacraments, Holy Communion and Baptism.

> For example, people from the upper classes insisted on receiving the Holy Communion separate from the lower classes, or, if there must be communion together, at least from a separate cup. The same happened with baptism...upper class families would not have their children baptized in the Church, because that would involve the use of water already used by the lower classes.

Prof. Weborg also adds to his summary of observations that:

> This is likewise the era in which the address 'Herr Pastor' became part of formal etiquette. Since the 'lordly' bearing was transferred to the clergy,

it may not be surprising that it is offensive to learn that since duties were clearly differentiated according to class, there was a case of a woman in Wittenberg who had to get the Bishop's permission to give consolation to a sick friend since consolation was the proper function of a pastor.[29]

Now according to Prof. Weborg (and also others), the pietism or the theology of Pietism came into existence in response to the above described life of the Church. It was supposed to re-introduce the priesthood of all believers. The recovery of the person or human being was the key agenda of Pietism. The solution to this Pietism offered was 'the experiential side of Christianity'. As already stated, theological emphasis was laid on the second or new birth (*wiedergeburt*), personal holiness and other-worldliness were part of the same faith. But pietist theologians, though very much believed in charitable and good works, yet they always had to struggle to establish a relationship between 'faith and works.' More or less, all of them believed that 'works' do not 'contribute anything to the substance of salvation'. Pastor Joachim Bealke (1601-66) in his work *Sacrdotium* published during the Thirty Years' War in 1640, wrote the following as the opening words of his work which helps us in the basic concern of pietists:

> All those who have been baptized into Jesus Christ/ and live in his other worldly kingdom/whether they be peasants/burghers, noblemen/ are alike spiritual men and priests/ provided they hold fast to the covenant of baptism/are faithful to their rebirth/ and truly and diligently exercise their office of spiritual priesthood.[30]

In these words, we see Pastor Bealke restating the words of St. Paul in Galatians 3:27-8 according to his context. The sacrament of baptism here is the means of removing all kinds of distinctions among people.

The pietists also followed the idea of the missionary work, which already existed in the Protestant world. This idea was more effectively followed by Prof. Francke and finally his two disciples Ziegenbalg and Plutschau became the first Protestant missionaries and came to India in 1706. Both of them, and later on, others came on their mission armed with theology and a special understanding of Christian faith. But if we see carefully, *first*, the context of Pietism in which this understanding of Christian faith was born and also the theological expression to which it gave birth as stated above and *second*, we also see the application of their theology in the Indian context (ruled by caste system), we finally can understand how much they could succeed in practice. Christian David, a disciple of Christian Schwartz (trained missionary of Halle), testifying to Bishop Heber and it may be worth to quote once again Kaye's summary of Christian David's testimony: 'From the days of Ziegenbalg downwards, they had been wont to sit in Church in two separate divisions and had communicated separately at the Lord's table, drinking out of the cup, but high-caste converts drinking first.'[31]

Christian David also added to his testimony (as has been quoted already) that caste distinction is a 'purely worldly idea'. Once these concepts and practices were formulated by the early missionaries, their influence continued[32] right up to their time among Indian Christians.

In a nutshell, the theological teachings of the early missionaries in India provided only a 'half salvation' to the Christians. It was 'half salvation' because in it, no effort was made to relate to the teachings of the Christian faith to the life of the people, and it dealt only with moral issues, or the personal holiness and other-worldly spirituality. The ordinary Indian Christian, even the most illiterate, today carries this aspect of Christian faith deep inside him. Because this very theological factor is the main one on which Christians in India have been nourished from the beginning. And this factor was/is the main reason which kept the 'dalitness' perpetuated within the inner being of the average convert and to practice caste even after becoming Christians and not to treat as equal the other Christians. This theological understanding of Christian faith, needs radical change and that is where the need of 'Dalit Theology' arose.

4.3.2. *Missionaries' methods and their response to the problem of Dalit Christians*

The first major point with regard to the missionaries' methods is that most of them '...wanted to penetrate India from the top, rather than the bottom'.[33] This is true more or less in the case of all early missionaries as mentioned already, particularly Robert de Nobili and Alexander Duff. One made an attempt to identify himself with the highest caste, Brahmin and became almost a high caste Hindu by disguising himself. On the other hand, Alexander Duff used the instrument of highest culture and science of the West in a Christian setting to reach the high caste Indian.[34] This is also true of the Presbyterian missionaries in Panjab, who at the beginning, made an attempt to convert the people considered upper caste.[35] The first missionary of the United Presbyterian Mission, Andrew Gordon himself admitted in 1886, at the end of his first thirty years of work, that: 'In concluding these remarks about my own evangelistic work in the last decade, I may say briefly that I began with my eyes upon the large towns and cities, but have been led from them to the country villages. I began with the educated classes and people of good social position, but ended among the poor and the lowly.'[36]

The second major point with regard to the missionaries' methods is the way they tried to use the education system. The famous Scottish Presbyterian missionary Alexander Duff's purpose was to introduce a new system of Western education, both to Westernize and Christianize the people belonging to the so called upper caste in India. But what was true with the early missionaries, with regard to the use of education, was also true with the later ones. For example, Robert Clark of the Church Missionary Society, at the end of first thirty years in 1883, tells about the Boys' School at Batala, Panjab and the Alexandra Girls' School, Amritsar, that: 'In Batala, near Amritsar, Mr. Baring had established his Boarding School for the better classes of Native Christian boys.'[37] About the Alexandra Girls' School in Amritsar, he says: 'This school has been established for the children of the higher classes of Native Christians....'[38] But the results of this best education and Christian institutions were more negative than positive, particularly with regard to the Christian Dalits in India, because these educational institutions and systems supported more the values of the oppressors, rather than the oppressed. These gave education mainly to the children of the rich belonging to people considered of the upper classes or caste. Not giving proper opportunities to the children of the poor and people considered low-caste, the missionaries kept them away from the educational institutions.[39]

The third major point, which is also connected with the methodology of the missionaries which a famous missionary and bishop of the Church of South India, Leslie Newbigin, while on his return to England, after retirement, admits and testifies, how from the very beginning of their arrival in India, they were considered as 'Sahibs'

(Lords).[40] Another well known missionary, C.F. Andrews also agrees with this view and says: 'The missionary is not only a Western, but a Sahib'.[41] C.F. Andrews quotes an example to make his point clear. He says that once in north India, he was walking along with an Indian gentleman, and they were discussing the Christian faith. Just then a Sahib drove by in a trap, with a groom seated behind. The crowd scattered before him, and the policemen saluted in military style. 'Look', said the Indian gentleman as he drew me aside, 'there is your Christianity driving along; that Sahib is the missionary of this place and that is his position, and that is how he goes to his work.'[42]

Related to the question of 'Sahibism' among the Western missionaries, the racial superiority complex of Europeans in India as rulers is also equally responsible for the unchanged condition of Christian Dalits in India. For example, Nirad Chaudhuri has compared the Muslim rulers with the British rulers (as Christians) and those low caste people who became Muslims, with those who were converted to Christianity. He says as per his experience in Bengal, he could see that Muslims belonging to low castes could gain a higher status with their fellow Muslims, because the Muslim rulers did identify themselves with all the Muslims. This not only gave a new faith to the low caste Muslims, but also a new political status. But under the British rule in India, on the other hand, the Christians remained as much a subject population as the Hindus.[43]

Already reference has been made to the general education of Indian Christians, which was mainly for the children of the so-called upper castes. Even a missionary educationist like Alexander Duff was not happy when vernacular schools were opened for the children of people considered as low caste.[44]

Among the missionaries, there were two groups: *one*, those who were interested at a later stage to increase the number of converts from the low castes for the sake of numbers; *second*, those who opposed the whole idea of accepting converts from the people considered to be of low caste. These two groups of missionaries existed from the very beginning. Francis Xavier representing the first group and Robert de Nobili, the second. Tyndale Biscoe (a missionary of the Church of England) describes in his autobiography how the first group used to baptize people at sight by filling 'a bowl full of water and sprinkling on the whole crowd sitting in front saying: 'In the name of the father, the Son and the Holy Ghost.'[45] Narrating another example of a

Methodist missionary, Biscoe writes how a senior missionary rebuked a junior missionary for not maintaining an increase in baptisms for fear of losing dollars from America.[46]

The early missionaries as well as later ones had created a myth that a convert belonging to a community considered high-caste had to lose much from the worldly point of view, whereas a convert from people considered to be of low caste had to lose nothing. But it is not true.[47] The fact is that most of the converts from former community almost always gained much more than the convert of latter community even from a worldly point of view. For example, the first Presbyterian convert's family, even today, owns the largest property among Christians in Panjab.[48] All these worldly means were developed with the help of the missionaries, but that cannot be said about the Christians from so called lower castes, except that they got odd employment from the missionaries as gardeners, cooks, sweepers, and so on.[49]

The missionaries in fact, have always felt embarrassed with the converts from the community considered low caste. They made a distinction by referring to them as 'mass movement Christians' or 'simple Christians', but not 'converts'. The title 'convert' they used only for the so called upper caste Christians.[50] Because of this embarrassment, some missionaries were afraid to mention in their reports the caste of the Christians considered low caste. They would address them as 'common villagers' or 'illiterate menials.'[51] Even the famous missionary J.C.R. Ewing, while reporting to his Board of Foreign Missions in the USA referred to low-caste people as 'raking in rubbish into the Church'.[52]

Again missionaries, as their common response to the caste problem, which can be labeled as 'the policy of accommodation,' divided the Church or Indian Christians on the basis of their caste background. Even the Lord's Table (Sacrament of Eucharist) was not spread, for they allowed the cup first to be taken by the so called upper caste Christians, and then the so called lower castes.[53] Again as referred earlier, influence of the medieval period European Church practice can be seen here clearly.

The missionaries' response to the problem of Christian Dalits included establishing 'mission compounds', 'Christian colonies', in the towns and cities, and for rural people 'Christians villages'. The main purpose of these establishments was to keep these new converts considered to be heathens.[54] But this approach of the missionaries only helped in creating a distinctive but narrow Christian culture at a low level.

4.3.3. Indian Church's/Christians' Response

Christian David's reference (see above), was atypical response of the Indian Christian, who declared the caste problem as a 'purely worldly idea'. In fact, today, the rank-and-file Indian Christians are evangelical in faith (followers of pietist traditions). Other worldly has become part of their blood and life, which was infused in them for the last two centuries by different missionary groups. The result is that they have become more deeply unconscious of their problem of dalitness.

Indian Churches/Christians have further strengthened some of the traditions followed by the missionaries. For example, the Christian educational institutions are continuing to nurture the values of the 'Upper Ten' representation of the oppressors.

'Sahibism' it seemed based upon the concept of 'Herr Pastor' of Medieval Europe has been fully inherited by Indian Church leaders. Today, every Christian leader is either 'Bishop Sahib' or 'Padri Sahib' or '… Sahib'.

The problem of the Dalits Christian has been deepened by a few Christians who come from the so-called upper caste background. For example, after India's Independence in 1947, at the time of drafting the Indian Constitution, all poor people belonging to the communities considered the low castes were to be given special economic privileges like getting free education for children, special privileges with regard to government jobs. But in the case of Christians, among whom a large majority had outcaste background and they were economically no better off than others of the same background belonging to other religion. But at the time, the Christian representatives were asked if they wished to have such privileges protected for their community, because a large majority of Christians were economically poor and originally belonged to the group of outcastes. But the Christian leaders refused to accept that offer. But who were these Christian leaders? These were H.C. Mookerjee, Rajkumari Amrit Kaur and Jerome D'Souza, the first one a so-called high-caste Bengali convert, second, a Panjabi convert from a royal background and the third, a Jesuit belonging to the upper classes. The leader of these three Christians, H.C. Mookerjee said, 'I am a member of the minority community myself and I feel proud that the community of which I am a member has decided to give up all special privileges….'[55] But this statement carries the ego and sentiments of a few upper caste/ class Christians, not of millions of Christians with Dalit background.

Because of the above stand of the so-called upper caste/ class Christians, as per the order of the president of India, 1950, the Dalit Christians not only have lost the benefits of the reservations but also their fundamental or civil rights as well as human rights have been taken away.[56]

In the recent decade, because of the awareness created by various organizations and action groups (both of Christians and others) of Dalits and non-Dalits, it seemed that a change in the attitude of Christian Community in India is taking place, but it is very slow.[57]

4.4. Conclusion

The historical discussion in this chapter, from the view of the Dalit Christians in India, makes the following main points:

First, on the basis of the historical data considered in this chapter, fundamental reason for the continuing unchanged conditions of Dalit Christians in India is more theological in nature than social. Theological, because of the particular understanding of their faith through early Christian missionaries. Due to this understanding (which was pietistic in nature), their main concern was to strengthen 'personal holiness' rather than deal with the problems of the whole community in an organized way. This understanding more or less continued to be followed by later missionary groups. It is an understanding of the Christian faith which made Christians in India, particularly from a Dalit background, passive in their approach to life issues. The Gospel interpretation inculcated in them, did not include the concerns of 'this world', it was related to the 'other world' and the individual salvation of the 'soul'. This understanding of Christian faith perhaps also continued to help the Christians from the so-called upper castes to continue in their old attitudes to-wards society, particularly towards Christians from the communities considered lower castes. So the theological understanding of the early missionaries, later on inherited by Indian Christians, became especially responsible for the continuing captivity of many Christians in their 'dalitness', instated of bringing them out of it.

Second, the discussion of the chapter makes it clear that perhaps the other major reason responsible for the unchanged conditions of Dalit Christians is the method of early Christian missionaries by which they not only accepted, but also encouraged the evil of caste distinctions within the Church. This helped in perpetuating old practices and attitudes among the Christians of India.

Third, the feelings of superiority of some deepened the problem. First, it was the gulf between missionaries and their converts and because of this, they failed to identify fully with the local people. This of course rendered the Christian principle of equality quite ineffective. All this encouraged the upper caste Christians as well as the other Indian Christian leaders to perpetuate the same complex within the Church.

Fourth, Indian Christians have accepted knowingly or unknowingly the language and expression used either by the dominant section of our Indian society or by the outsiders including missionaries, which only had helped in maintaining the status quo. Because through the use of such oppressive language and expressions, we have made the Indian Christians also the partners of the oppressive system, therefore, against the Dalits including Dalit Christians.

Finally, because Indian Christians have inherited the missionaries' theological understanding of the Christian faith together with methods and attitudes, their response to the Dalit Christians in India is mostly negative. Therefore there is a need to have a clear understanding of their real identity as well as to their own understanding of Christian faith in their given Indian context.

NOTES

1. Luke 22:24-27, Galatians 2:25-28, Ephesians 2:13-16, etc.
2. Minutes of the 8th Ordinary Meeting of the Synod of the Church of North India held at St. Stephen's College, Delhi, 6-10 October 1992, Minute no. S: 8:92-488 (e), p. 46.
3. Nirad C. Chaudhuri, *The Continent of Circe* (*An Essay on the Peoples of India*), Jaico Publishing House, Bombay, 1983 (rpt), p. 310.

4. Cf. C. Mathew and M.M. Thomas, *The Indian Churches of Saint Thomas*, ISPCK, Delhi, 1967, p. 7.
5. Joseph Thekkedath, *History of Christianity in India*, vol. II, Church History Association, Bangalore, 1967, pp. 22, 23. Also see John William Kaye, *Christianity in India*, Mission Publisher, London, 1859, pp. 17-23.
6. Kaye, ibid., p. 30.
7. Ibid., p. 32.
8. David Jenks, *Six Great Missionaries of the Sixteenth-Seventeenth Century*, A.R. Mowbray, London, 1930, p. 127.
9. William B. Anderson, and Charles R. Watson, *Far North in India*, Presbyterians Church of North America, Philadelphia, 1919, p. 146.
10. Kaye, op. cit., pp. 65-74.
11. Otto W. Heick, A *History of Christian Thought*, vol. II, Fortress Press, Philadelphia, 1966, pp. 23.
12. John Weborg, 'Pietisma: The Fire of God Which…Flames in the Heart of Germany', in *Protestant Spiritual Traditions*, ed. Frank C. Senn, Paulist Press, New York, 1886, pp. 199- 202.
13. Kaye, op. cit., p. 81.
14. Ibid., pp. 218, 230, 232.
15. Rev. C.F. Andrews, *North India*, A.R. Mowbray & Co., London, 1908, pp. 16, 17.
16. Ibid., pp. 14, 15.
17. Kaye, op. cit., pp. 252, 253.
18. Ibid., pp. 355- 6.
19. Weborg, op. cit., p. 202.
20. Ibid., pp. 192, 204.
21. Ibid., pp. 208, 209.
22. Ibid., p. 210 (top).
23. Ibid., p. 210 (bottom).
24. Otto W. Heick, op. cit., p. 441.
25. John C.B. Webster, *The Christian Community and Change in Nineteenth Century North India*, Macmillan, Delhi, 1976, p. 33.
26. James Massey, 'Ingredients for a Dalit Theology' in *Towards a Dalit Theology*, ed. M.E. Prabhakar, ISPCK, Delhi, 1988, p. 60.
27. Weborg, op. cit., p. 185.
28. Ibid., p. 186.
29. Ibid., p. 186.
30. Quoted in Stephen Charles Neill and Hans-Ruedi Weber, *The Layman in Christian History*, Westminister Press, Philadelphia, 1963, p. 162.
31. Kaye, op. cit., 1976, p. 253.

32. Mark Juergensmeyer, *Religion as Social Vision*, University of California Press, Berkeley, 1982, p. 188.
33. John Webster Grant, *God's People in India*, CLS, Madras, 1965, p. 15.
34. Andrew, op. cit., p. 24.
35. Mark Juergensmeyer, *Religion as Social Vision*, Berkeley, 1982, p. 184.
36. Rev. Andrew Gordon, *Our Indian Missions*, p. 446.
37. Rev. Frobert Clark, A *Brief Account of Thirty Years of Missionary Work of the Church Missionary Society in Panjab and Sindh*, 1852-1882 Mission Press, Lahore, 1883, p. 20.
38. Ibid., p. 42.
39. J. Aixala, *Jesuit Formation and Inculturation in India Today*, Gujarat Sahitya Prakash, Anand, Gujarat, 1978, p. 17.
40. Leslie Newbegin, *The Other Side of* 1984, World Council of Churches, Geneva, 1984, p. 1.
41. Andrew, op. cit., p. 160.
42. Ibid., p. 164.
43. Chaudhuri, op. cit., p. 332.
44. Duncan B. Forrester, *Caste and Christianity*, SCM, London, 1980, p. 70.
45. Cecil Tyndale-Briscoe of Kashmir, *An Autobiography*, Seeley Service, London, 1946, p. 70.
46. Ibid., p. 113.
47. Rev. C.D. Snell, 'Christianity in India', in *The Church Missionary Review*, vol. LXVI, no. 790, February 1915, p. 85. Also cf. Kaye John William, op. cit., p. 71.
48. I lived in Jullundher City (Panjab) from 1969 to 1974 and have seen such properties belonging to the converts from upper castes.
49. Again such an example can be seen today. If one visits Mission compounds in a city like Jullundher, Ludhiana in Panjab, one can meet such converts from lower castes living in small houses, who have worked for missionaries as servants.
50. Juergensmeyer, op. cit., 1982, p. 187.
51. Ibid., p. 186.
52. J.C.R. Ewing, letter to Dr. Gillespie, 19 March 1894, cited in John C.B. Webster, *The Christian Community and Change in the Nineteenth Century*, MacMillan, New Delhi, 1992, p. 60.
53. Cf. Juergensmeyer, op. cit., p. 188.
54. John Newton, *Historical Sketches of the Indian Missions of the Presbyterians Church in the United States of America*, Allahabad, The Allahabad Mission Press, 1886, p. 353.

55. Vide (for details) Jose Kananaikal, *Scheduled Caste in the Constituent Assembly*, Indian Social Institute, New Delhi, 1992, p. 14.
56. Vide (for the text of) the Constitution (Scheduled Caste) Order, 1950 with Amendment in the Constitutional Provisions for the Scheduled Castes by Jose Kananaikal, Indian Social Institute, New Delhi, 1984, p. 39.
57. See (a) Minutes of the 8th Ordinary Meeting of the Synod of the Church of North India, held at St. Stephen's College, Delhi from 6 to 10 October, 1992, S: 8:92-488 (e), pp. 45, 46.
(b) The resolutions passed during 1992 in the General Body Meeting of the Catholic Bishops Conference of India held at Pune in *Dalit Christian: A Socio-Economic Survey*, Archdiocese of Bangalore by Ambrose Pinto SJ, Bangalore, 1992.

CHAPTER 5

Dalit Roots of Indian Christianity

5.1. Case Histories

5.1.1. The Founder of Sialkot Region (Punjab) Christian Community: Ditt

The story of Ditt began when a Hindu of the Jat caste (a Panjabi forward class) by name Nattu was baptized on 17 November 1872 by the Rev. J.S. Barr. Nattu was not only from a high caste, he was also the son of a *Lambardar* (village head), and legal heir to his father's property and position. Missionaries were very happy, but later on they were unhappy, because Nattu forfeited his right to be his father's heir. For them he proved a failure, 'a weak brother'. But this was not true, because he became an instrument in bringing a person into the Christian fold, who later became one of the main founder leaders responsible for the present Church or Christian community of Panjab. This man's name was Ditt.

Ditt was from a small village named Shahabdike, which was about 3 miles south of a larger village named Mirali, and 30 miles from Sialkot (now in Pakistan). Ditt was born around 1843. The Rev. Andrew Gordon introduces him these words: '... a man of the low and much despised *chura* tribe, by the name Ditt, a dark man, lame of one leg, quiet and modest in his manners, with sincerity and earnestness, well expressed in his face, and at that time about thirty years of age'. By profession Ditt was a dealer of hides. He came in contact with Nattu, who taught him about Jesus Christ, and in June 1873 Nattu took him to Sialkot for baptism.

The Rev. Samuel Martin was hesitant to accept Ditt for baptism. After all his Christian teachings were based on the teachings of 'a weak brother' Nattu. But at the same time Ditt's knowledge of

Christianity was quite sound. He also appeared to Martin, an honest person. Still he wanted to delay his baptism, for which Ditt was not willing. In the words of Gordon: 'Mr. Martin finally decided to baptize Ditt, not because he saw his way decidedly clear to do so, but rather because he could see no scriptural ground for refusing.'

Martin faced another problem when immediately after the baptism, Ditt asked permission to go back to his village instead of staying in the protected mission compound. This was a new thing for Martin. The practice was that a new convert stayed with the missionary for more instructions and protection. Martin's worry was how this poor illiterate man would deal with opposition. Anyhow Ditt returned to his village and this action of his proved to be the starting point for a Christian movement among the ex-chuhras (Dalits) of Panjab.

On reaching home, Ditt did face bitter opposition from his own relatives. For example, one of his fellow villagers rebuked him by saying: 'Oh Ho. You have become a Sahib' (gentleman). Others said: 'You have become a "*be-i-man*" (one without religion). His own sister-in-law said: 'Alas, my brother, you have changed your religion without even asking our counsel; our relationship with you is over. Henceforth you shall neither eat, drink, not in any way associate with us. One of your legs is broken already, so may it be with the other.'[1]

But Ditt did not care about any opposition. Instead he witnessed his new faith in Christ openly and boldly, both to his family members and others. The result was amazing. Three months after his baptism in August 1873, he had the privilege of taking his wife, his daughter and two neighbours to Sialkot for baptism. He had to walk for 30 miles for the sole purpose of introducing his family and friends to the missionaries. Martin examined them and was fully satisfied and gave them baptism.

Ditt's work of buying hides from different places took him to many villages. Wherever he went on business, he preached about Christ also. In the eleven years (1884) after his baptism, he brought into the Christian faith more than five hundred persons from his community. By 1900 half the people of his community had accepted Christ and by 1915 almost all the Dalits known as *churas* of Sialkot district became Christians.[2]

5.1.2 *The Founder of Travancore (Kerala) Church: Vethamanikam*

'How Vethamanikam ... came to believe in one God is sure proof of the Spirit's work in the heart of a man who had never heard of Christ, and yet was led step by step until he found Him,' said Rebecca J. Parker.

Vethamanikam was a son of Dalit parents, who belonged to one of the Dalit communities of Travancore namely Sambavar. He hailed from a village Mailady which was a few miles from Cape Comorin, but part of the district of Travancore (at that time an independent state). He was brought up by a very pious mother, because his father died soon after his birth. She gave him basic education, which enabled him to read and write. She introduced in him the good moral values and also helped to love his family god. Even in the later years of his life, he built a temple for his family god. He used to read religious books including *Puranas*.

In search of truth, he went on a pilgrimage along with his nephew, to the temple of Chidambaram. But after reaching Chidambaram, he found that the life of the priests and others was not holy. While staying there for a night, he had a dream, which convinced him that Chidambaram will not be able to help him in his search for truth. So along with his nephew he returned, but on the way they stopped at Tanjore, where his married sister was living with her family. Both his sister and her husband were Christian. It is here Vethamanikam first heard about Christ. On Sunday while standing outside the church he heard the singing and message. At the end of the service, the missionary came to talk to him. He told him all about himself including the pilgrimage, which he undertook. He also told the missionary it looks like the Almighty God has sent them there. The missionary gave him a small booklet, which Vethamanikam read and while reading, he was filled with 'deep joy and satisfaction' about which he later remarked: 'My Lord and Saviour Jesus Christ! He touched my heart and it melted before God. A light from heaven shone upon my darkness and I did not want to leave the place.'

Then Vethamanikam stayed at Tanjore for sometime more and read more literature and asked more about Jesus. Finally he was fully convinced that his journey of search for truth had ended and he had found the true Saviour in Jesus Christ. Therefore he asked for baptism, which was given and he also spent some more time therefore further guidance after which, according to Parker 'he felt he was ready to return and take the good news to his own place, and staff in hand, he returned his face homewards.'

On return to Travancore, his relatives and friends asked Vethamanikam: 'Where is the holy gift of the Lord of Chidambaram and the sacred ashes?' Holding in his hand a copy of the Gospels, he answered, 'Lo, here is the Holy Gift of the Lord of all worlds!' Parker adds here:

> From that time forward Vethamanikam gathered round him day by day such as were willing to hear more of the good news he had brought, and to them he read and expounded the Scriptures. This patient teaching at last won its way to their hearts … and eventually they decided to join Vethamanikam.… A couple of hundred believers were thus gathered together… He gave Christian names to the members of his family.… Many listened and were won to join the growing band of believers.

But all this was not as easy as it looked, because at the same time a very strong opposition came from the Hindu community. They even excommunicated him from his caste and they persecuted him in many ways.

The news of his suffering and persecution even reached the royal family. His life as well as property became unsafe. But he decided to take his case to the highest Authority, therefore while reading the Word of God, the following prayer burst out from his inner being:

> O Thou dear Lord! When I worshipped idols which have no life Thou didst reveal Thyself to me, a great sinner, Thou didst pass by the rich, the learned, the honourable people, and didst choose me to be Thine. Now teach me, O Lord, What should I do. Put me in Thy right path, and let me know what I should do in this difficulty. Is it Thy will that the light which has begun to shine here should be quenched?

Vethamanikam received an answer to his prayer and refused to sell his property. Instead he took another pilgrimage to seek help from his friends at Tanjore. This was the time when services at Travancore were being held regularly under his leadership. The number of inquirers was increasing day by day. Therefore after making the arrangements, he undertook a journey to Tanjore. After reaching Tanjore, he was amazed to hear that in order to help him,

God had sent a missionary, who was already learning the local language in Madras. This missionary's name was Ringeltaube, who after completing his language course came to Travancore (in Vethamanikam's village Mailady) on 25 April 1806. Ringeltaube had the permission of the Maharaja (King) of Travancore. On his arrival Parker says: 'the heart of Vethamanikam was at rest. He had done his best. He know he had been led by the Spirit of God, and he gladly handed over to Ringeltaube the work that he had so well begun.'[3]

After taking charge, Ringeltaube found a group of believers, who were prepared by Vethamanikam for baptism. Therefore he baptized them and also appointed Vethamanikam as their catechist. For the next ten years till in 1816 when Ringeltaube left Travancore on health grounds, Vethamanikam worked with him always. Ringeltaube before leaving, made him in charge of the whole work, who held the church in Travancore together till in December 1817 when another missionary Rev. Chargles Mead arrived in Mailady. It is true in the early years only the Dalits from Sambavar community only responded to call of Spirit, but later on by 1819 a Spirit movement also began among the Nadar community of Travancore.[4]

5.1.3. *An Early Indian Christian Theologian: Krishna Mohun Banerjea*

Krishna Mohun Banerjea was the first Christian Convert, who made a serious attempt toward the formulation of an expression of theology known today as 'Indian Christian Theology'. He was also one of the earliest converts of the famous Scottish Presbyterian Missionary Alexander Duff. To begin with he was a member of the Free Church of Scotland, but later he joined the Anglican Church. Banerjea was ordained as Anglican priest and in 1852, he was appointed professor at Bishop College, Calcutta, where he worked till his retirement in 1867. It was after his retirement, he wrote two of his well known works namely *The Arian Witness or the Testimony of Arian Scriptures in Corroboration of Biblical History and the Rudiments of Christian Doctrine including Dissertations on the Original Home and Easy Adventure of Indo-Arians* (Calcutta, 1875) and *The Relation Between Christianity and Hinduism* (Madras, 1892). Two passages, one from each of these two works are given below, which will be referred as part of our later discussion.[5]

(a) We look to our Witness also for the disproof of an idea often broached against Hindoo Christians that they are rebels against the *sanatana dharma* of the country, and apostates from the faith that has animated the Hindoo mind, and the rule of life that has governed Hindoo practice from time immemorial. This essay aspires likewise to the patriotic honour of proving that while all Hindoo who have been instructed in Western literature, science, an history have departed from the faith derived from their immediate forefathers, Hindoo Christians can alone have the satisfaction of knowing that the fundamental principles of the Gospel were recognized, and acknowledged, both in theory and practice, by their primitive ancestors, the Brahminical Arians of India, and that if the authors of the Vedas could by any possibility now return to the world, they would at once recognize the Indian Christians, far more complacently as their own descendants, than any other body of educated natives.[6]

(b) The two propositions are:

1. That the fundamental principles of Christian doctrine in relation to the salvation of the world find a remarkable counterpart in the Vedic principles of primitive Hinduism in relation to the destruction of sin, and the redemption of the sinner by the efficacy of Sacrifice, itself a figure of *Prajapati*, the Lord and Saviour of the Creation, who had given himself up as an offering for that purpose.

2. That the meaning of *Prajapati*, an appellative, variously described as a *Purusha* begotten in the beginning, as *Viswakarma*, the creator of all, singularly coincides with the meaning of the name and offices of the historical reality *Jesus Christ*, and that no other person that *Jesus* of Nazareth has ever appeared in the world claiming the character and position of the self-sacrificing *Prajapati*, at the same time both mortal and immortal...[7]

5.2. Our Two Propositions

The three case histories are specially given here right in chapter section one in order to set a tone for our discussion on the two opposite sides of our subjects, 'Dalit Roots of Indian Christianity'. Number *one*, Indian Christianity basically owes its existence to the response, which various Dalit communities led directly by the Spirit of God offered to the Gospel of Jesus Christ. This truth becomes very clear from the two case histories, number one and two. Dalits' response to the call of the Spirit has contributed to the nature of the Indian Christianity both qualitatively as well as quantitatively, which helped in the formation of the body of Christ in India. Number two, the clue to the general European understanding of the Christian faith of the medieval period, we get in the case history of the first protestant Church of Germany as seen in chapter 4 section 4.3.1 which later on became not only responsible for the missionaries, passive response to the social and religious order of India, but also made the impact of Gospel ineffective in the life of Indian Christians. This had a negative result, deepening the 'dalitness' in the psyche of the Dalit Christians as well as non-Dalit Christians. The third case history of an earliest Indian Christian theologian helps in knowing the truth, how the current Indian Christian theological expression further made the Gospel irrelevant. So the two basic propositions, which are being discussed here in relation to the 'Dalit roots of Indian Christianity' are:

Firstly, Indian Christianity is the result of the works of the early Dalit Christian leaders and Dalit communities who responded to the Gospel of Christ under the direction of the Holy Spirit, are the basis of the Dalit roots of Indian Christianity.

Secondly, For the continuity of both individual as well as collective dalitness of Indian Christianity and Dalit Christians, the two expressions of theology namely the missionary theology of medieval period of Europe and the current Indian Christian theology are responsible, which is the basis of the roots of the perpetuity of the dalitness of the Dalits.

Here in our succeeding discussion, we will be dealing with these two propositions of ours specially the Dalit roots of Indian Christianity and the roots of the perpetuity of the dalitness of the Dalits. Our discussion will focus mainly on the four case histories stated in the beginning of this presentation, but we will refer to some more cases both from our Indian as well as European historical contexts.

5.2.1 *The Dalit Roots of Indian Christianity*

Much has been written during the past one decade about the attitude and work of early missionaries as well as Indian Christians, who have in general very little to contribute positively to the life of Dalit Christians. In fact the early missionaries like Roberto de Nobili, Ziegenbalg, Bishop Middleton, and Alexander Duff have reverse effects upon the future Church or the Dalit Christians in India. The same can be said about the upper caste Indian Christians, who have played such a role, which went against the Dalits. The best examples of such three Christians are H.C. Mookerjee, Amrit Kaur and Jerome D'souza, who represented the Indian Christian community at the drafting committee of the Indian Constitution after India's Independence in 1947. For detailed discussion on the early missionaries and the so-called upper caste Indian Christians one can refer to one of my earlier published works.[8] Here I want to only reconfirm the truth that for the basic task for which missionaries came was to proclaim the Gospel of Christ and to win human beings to faith and obedience in Him. This is exactly what Christian missionaries came to do in India. But interestingly, things in India did not turn out the same way as expected. To begin with the majority of the missionaries were interested only in preaching the Christian Gospel to the upper caste people. A pioneer missionary of the United Presbyterian Church of U.S.A. to Panjab admitted after his first thirty years experience of missionary work, when he said:

> In concluding these remarks, about my own evangelistic work in the last decade, I may say briefly, that I began with my eye upon the large towns and cities, but have been led from them to the country villages. I began with the educated classes and people of good social position, but ended among the poor and the lowly.[9]

The result of the above missionaries' approach in the case of Panjab (more or less true of other places also) was that from 1834 till 1885 – for 61 years they had only 477 communicant members and many of these were not Panjabi Christians. Even the first person to be baptised in Ludhiana on 30 April 1837 was a Bengali upper caste Hindu. But then after 1885 we see a quick change in numbers which grew and grew. The understanding of this change is important (which lies in the first case history of Ditt), because in the beginning this is what troubled not only the missionaries, but was also the factor which had almost shaken the whole Panjabi society. Through this we believe God's Spirit reveals its movement very clearly, and we see God's working and His option for the poor, lowly and downtrodden and turning this whole affair into a movement of the Spirit. But this 'Spirit Movement' in the beginning (which church historians have labelled 'Christian Mass Movement') was not a happy sign for Christian missionaries in Panjab. Because there have been very few so-called upper castes who accepted the Gospel.

In reality the Panjabi Christian community/church comes from the Dalit background and it is because of the 'Spirit Movement' among the Panjabi Dalits, in which an early Panjabi Dalit Christian, namely Ditt, played a major role.

The missionaries it seemed were not interested in the Dalits becoming Chrisitans. Some were really troubled about it, that is, about the way God's Spirit was working. This we see from a letter of J.C.R. Ewing who wrote to the Board of Foreign Missions on 19 March 1884 and in which he described this trend of poor, low castes becoming Christians as 'raking in rubbish into the church'.[10] Some other missionaries in their reports even hesitated to mention these converts' social background, and they were shown as 'common villagers' or 'illiterate menials'.[11]

But the above attitude of the missionaries concerning the conversion of the Dalits had twofold effect on Panjab Christianity; it left a negative cultural spot, which the Panjabi Christians even today would like to ignore, because they are afraid to talk about the past, that reveals their low social background.

When I say 'negative cultural spot', I mean that though the missionaries accepted the above trend as part of their mission work at a later stage, yet they were not fully convinced till the end. For the sake of a few from the so-called privileged castes, they were forced to maintain double standards in the church. The real problem occurred in the Holy Eucharist and Church services, which were after all the only occasions when the two groups of Christians could meet. According to Mark Juergensmeyer, in Panjab, they solved the problem in two ways:

> By establishing worship services for those who spoke English and those who spoke only Panjabi, which *de facto* eliminated the lower castes from English-speaking services; or failing this by ensuring that upper caste converts would sit at the front of the church so that they would use the communion implements first, before they become polluted by the Christians of lower castes.[12]

During my stay in Jalandhar city (Panjab) from 1969-74, I was told that the system of reserving benches for the privileged ones had been abolished only a few years back.

Besides the above administrative methods to deal with the problem, the missionaries used other methods also to solve the problem, for example, in the towns, 'mission compounds', in cities 'Christian colonies' and for the rural people 'Christian villages' were established. The main purpose of these settlements was to isolate these new Christians from other people, who were considered to be heathens.[13] Establishing separate places for these Panjabi Christians helped to create a very distinctive Christian culture and also projected an image which reflected the '*Churas culture*' or 'the Christian culture' in the negative sense.

But in spite of the above attitude of the missionaries the conversion process under the influence of the Spirit continued and today in Panjab we have about 3,00,000 Christians on the Indian side, of which 99 per cent come from the Dalit background. A large number of Christians are also in Panjab on the Pakistan side, who share the same background.

The second case history, of the founder of Travancore Church, Vethamanikan, makes the point still clearer about the work of Holy Spirit in the life of Dalit individual as well as communities. After reading carefully the case history of Vethamanikam, who was one of the most serious searchers of Truth, for which he went from place to place, before he reached Tanjore, where he had a direct encounter with the Gopel of Christ. Then he devoted years of dedicated work in his village Mailady before the first missionary Rev. William Tobias Ringeltaube arrived there in 1806. The kind of struggle Vethamanikam went through and the way God through his Spirit upheld him was a 'sure proof of the Spirit's work', not only in his life, but in the life of his Dalit Community Sambavar's. His biographer Parker is right when she said that Vethamanikam 'knew he had been led by the Spirit of God', therefore when Ringeltaube came he 'gladly handed over', 'the work that he had so well begun'.

But apart from Ditt of Sialkot and Vethamanikam of Travancore, there are similar other case histories also available. For example Venkayya (1811-91) of Kistna district of Andhra Pradesh. Venkayya became Christian in 1849.[14] He was baptised by Mr. Darling, a missionary of the Church Missionary Society. Darling during his first seven years of work could not get a single convert, because according to Bishop Picket: 'His eyes were upon the high caste Hindus, and he had preached to them and personally sought out individuals among them with constant diligence, but lack of interest discouraged him.'[15] But after Venkayya's conversion in 1849, God's spirit started working and in 1901 in Kistna district, the Christian number rose to 29,186 and by 1911, this number increased to 49,863 and in 1928, the Anglican alone had 122,500 members.[16]

These case histories are the sure proof of the work of the Spirit of God among the Dalit communities of India, which were led by Dalits such as Ditt, Vethamanikan and Venkayya, about whom Bishop Pickett has said: "The real founder of the Church in Travancore were not Ringeltaube, but Vedamanikam. In Kistna it was not Darling, but Venkayya. In Sialkot it was not Gordon, but Ditt.'[17] This testimony is indeed a living proof of dalit roots of the Indian Christianity.

5.2.2 *The Roots of the Perpetuity of the Dalitness of the Dalits*

Our second proposition is based on the thesis that the continuity of the dalitness of Indian Christians in general and Dalit Christians in particular is the missionary theology of medieval period of Europe. One aspect of the European understanding of Christian faith is well presented by the case history of the first Protestant Church of Idstein, of Germany.

Concerning the third case history of one of the earliest Indian Christian theologian, Krishna Mohan Banerjea's is one of the best examples of an Indian, so called upper caste convert and his laying the foundation of the Indian Christian Theology of today, as a successor to the missionary theology of Europe. Like his other fellow theologian A.S. Appasamy, who searched for evidence in the *Rigveda* for the Christian doctrines of *logos* and atonement, K.M. Banerjea went still further and made an effort to prove the common homeland of the Aryan and Abraham. The Dalit students of theology need to read K.M. Banerjea's work *The Arian Witness* (Calcutta, 1875),[18] in which he first made an effort to establish the historical relationship between the Biblical and Vedic, particularly Brahmanical Aryans and then attempted to formulate his theological expression, which today stands as a pioneering effort towards giving a direction to Indian Christian Theology, the roots of which lie in the Brahmanical orthodox Hindu traditions. And we also know that Brahmanical old Hindu traditions are historically responsible for the plight of the Dalits today or the 'Dalitness'.

In the case history of K.M. Banerjea two passages which have been quoted as examples, make our points very clear. In the first passage K.M. Banerjea is very sure that Indian Christians like him (who share like so-called upper caste background) are the 'descendants' of the 'primitive ancestors, the Brahmanical Arians of India', who according to him are 'the authors of the Vedas'.

Now on the other hand the history of the problem of the Dalits of today also began with the Vedas.[19] The defeated people (who were the indigenous people of India), whom the *Rigveda* addresses with different names including *dasa* (slave) are also shown in the same Veda, outside the purview of divine reality (*Purusa*). K.M. Banerjea in his 'Arian Witness' from which also the second passage is quoted in our fourth case history, has tried to see the fulfilment of both *Purusa* and *Prajapati* in Jesus Christ. According to this work *Purusa* was begotten in the beginning and in *Prajapati*, we see the Lord and Saviour of Creation. Here we see the so called upper caste Christian theologian's effort to convert Jesus Christ into their fold, where the Gospel reality is just the opposite. This dimension of Indian Christian Theology today makes it completely irrelevant to the Dalit reality, because logically it also joins hands with the missionary or traditional European Christian theology in perpetuating the dalitness of the Dalits.

5.3. Conclusion

We can conclude this chapter by stating that the response of Dalit individuals and communities all over the country during the nineteenth and twentieth centuries was a part of their response to the Gospel of Jesus Christ under the direct direction of the Spirit of God. Therefore one can find the roots of Indian Christianity in this response of the Dalits. This is the first key dimension, which Dalit theology has to capture in its contents, because it is indeed the content of the Dalit Theology.

The second key dimension which Dalit theology has to follow is that it being the exposure of the traditional Christian (European) theology as well as of today's Indian Christian theology (which are responsible for the dalitness of the Dalit) must come up with an alternative vision (through the formulation of the Dalit Theology) for Dalits as well as for others.

NOTES

1. The Rev. Andrew Gordon, *Our Indian Mission, 1855-1885*, Andrew Gordon, Philadelphia, 1888, pp. 421-32.
2. J. Waskon Pickett, *Christian Mass Movements in India*, The Abingdon Press, New York, 1933, pp. 46-9.
3. Rebecca J. Parker, *How They Found Christ: Stories of Indian Christians*, SPCK, London, 1940, pp. 122-32.
4. Pickett, op. cit., pp. 38-9.
5. Raj Baago, *Pioneers of Indigenous Christianity*, CLS, Madras, 1969, pp. 12-17.
6. Ibid., p. 95.
7. Ibid., p. 98.
8. James Massey, *Dalits in India: Religion as a Source of Bondage or Liberation with Special Reference to Christians*, Manohar, Delhi, 1995, pp. 86-103.
9. Gordon, op, cit., p. 446.
10. J.C.R. Ewing's letter to Dr. Gillespie, 4 March 1894, cited in John C.B. Webster, *The Christian Community and Change in the Nineteenth Century in North India*, Macmillan, Delhi, 1976, p. 60.
11. Mark Juergensmeyer, *Religion as Social Vision: The Movement against Untouchability in 20th Century Panjab*, University of California Press, Berkeley, 1982, p. 186.
12. Ibid., p. 188.
13. John Newton, *Historical Sketches of the Indian Mission of the Presbyterian Church in the United States of America*, Mission Press, Allahabad, 1886, p. 58.
14. Parker, op. cit., pp. 77-82.
15. Pickett, op. cit., p. 149.
16. Ibid., p. 50.
17. Ibid., p. 56.
18. Rev. K.M. Banerjea, *The Arian Witness or the Testimony of Arian Scripture in Corroboration of Biblical History and the Rudiments of Christian Doctrine Including Dissertation on the Original Home and Easy Adventure of Indo-Arians*, Asiatic Society of Bengal, Calcutta, 1875.
19. Massey, op. cit., pp. 38, 39.

PART 3

CONTEXT

CHAPTER 6

Present Context of the Dalits and Globalization

6.1. Dalit Oppression and a Multi-faceted Identity

Dalits as they stand today are divided into more than 750 sub-communities on the basis of the occupations assigned to them by their opponents).[1] But Dalits' opponents were not satisfied with these simple divisions, therefore they also told the Dalits among their occupations, some are higher and others are lower based on the degree of cleanliness or uncleanliness. For example cleaning the streets or toilets are considered to be the lowest and the work involved in making shoes or working with leather is higher than the other. In Hindi language the name given to Dalits involved in cleaning the streets is *bhangi* and one who works with leather is *chamar*. So a chamar will be higher than a bhangi and in this way the process of vertical division among the Dalits were introduced. Therefore today the Dalits are divided both horizontally as well as vertically. The Mandal Commission Report (1980) has made responsible for such division to the Caste system, which has even conditioned their minds in such a way that today they themselves have accepted these divisions as part of the natural order of the things.[2] This is the reason that most of the Dalits today have lost their self-respect to such an extent that they regard their work to which their community has been condemned not as a curse from which they should liberate themselves, but as a privilege which they must protect.[3]

Historically to their present captive state, Dalits have not reached in a single day or in a single month or a year, because, the ongoing oppression has forced them into this captivity since the time they have lost their first physical battle from the hand of their opponents (known as Aryan) 3,500 years ago.[4] But after that defeat, their oppression was not (even today) limited to physically suffering alone, because, they suffered much more socially, culturally and religiously. It is this multi-sided suffering and oppression based on a multi-faceted identity, that tells them that they are untouchable, they are subjects and they are slaves. It is to this state of their's, that they have named 'Dalit'. The 'Dalit' today for them is not mere a new name, it in reality has become a positive assertion of pride, because it is for them, first, the sign of their becoming consciousness of their historical captivity, second, it is a sign of the rejection of their oppression and third, it is a sign of their liberation.

6.2. Divide and Rule

Today Dalits are involved in ongoing struggle for regaining their lost human identity and for their full liberation. But then their opponents also have become fully aware of losing their hold on their historically slaves or slave communities. Therefore these opponents of the Dalits are continuing to use all possible means based upon the universal strategies,[5] which include conquest, manipulation, cultural invasion and specially 'divide and rule' in order to keep their hold over the Dalit communities.

To make our point clear, we can take the example of the reservation offered to both the Scheduled Castes and Scheduled Tribes after the Independence of India in 1947. At that time while recognizing the need to offer special care for the development of historically backward segments of our Indian society, which included 'Scheduled Castes' and Scheduled Tribes' in the Constitution of India, special provisions have been included to help them. But the Constitution does not tell who will be considered as Scheduled Caste or Tribe. The Constitution in Article 241(1) has only empowered the President of India to identify these segments of our society. The first President by exercising the power given to him in the Constitution, promulgated an Order in 1950 known as 'The Constitution (Scheduled Castes) Order, 1950'; in which he gave a list of Dalit communities, who will be considered as Scheduled Castes and will enjoy the developmental support of the Government. But at the end of that list, he added 'not withstanding anything contained in paragraph 2. no person who professes a religion different from Hindu, shall be deemed to be a member of a Scheduled Caste.[6] (*For more details see chapter 7 of this work.*)

Now the requirement of the Constitution was to identify the communities, who will be considered as Scheduled Caste, but not to fix a criterion. But then the above Presidential Order fixed the 'religion' as a criterion and by doing so, it had contradicted with two important Articles of our Constitution, which prohibits any form of discrimination on the basis of 'religion' (Article 15) and which gives a fundamental right to profess, practice and propagate religion according to one's choice (Article 25). Secondly, the Presidential Order of 1950 does not only takes away the two of the basic fundamental rights of the Dalits, it also has become a legal mean to divide the Dalit communities on the basis of religion. This is the reason; the issue like the restoration of Dalit Christians or Dalit Muslims' rights and the question of reservation has to be understood from this angle. These questions are part of the broader Dalit issue and are linked with the strategy based upon the principle of divide and rule of the oppressors or the opponents of the Dalits. This point became very clear, when during the mid 1990's a movement of the restoration of Dalit Christians' equal rights became first time visible, it was the Dalit Hindus specially the Dalit Hindu members of the Parliament, who opposed this move.

6.3. Dalits and Their Civil Rights

As mentioned earlier in the Constitution of India it has fully recognized the need for the development of Dalits in all areas of life: social, economical, political and educational. For example in social areas of life it has abolished the practice of Untouchability and declared it as an offence punishable in accordance with the law (Article 17). The Constitution also granted the special right to the Dalits to share the political powers by offering them the reservation of seats not only at the central or states' level, but in various local administrative bodies too (Articles 330-4). On the economic end, the Constitution not only prohibits any form of forced labour (Article 23), but makes a special provision for the Dalits to provide reserved posts in various government departments both at the central as well as states' level (Articles 16, 320, 335). These reservations have been offered according to their percentage of the total population of the country. The Article 46 of the Constitution offers a special provision to promote with special care the education and economic interests of the Dalits and it offers them a protection from social injustice and all forms of exploitation. Also educational and cultural safeguards are offered in Articles 15(4), 29(i) and 350A.

The Government of India even has passed Special Acts to protect the rights of the Dalits and to prevent atrocities on them at the hands of the so-called upper castes. These Acts include the Protection of Civil Rights Act, 1955 (specially to deal with the problem of Untouchability), Protection of Civil Rights Rules, 1977 and the Scheduled Castes and Scheduled Tribes Prevention of Atrocities Act, 1989. But here a point may be made that the protection and privileges under these Acts are applicable only to those Dalits who profess Hinduism, Sikhism or Buddhism. These do not apply to the Dalits professing either Christianity or Islam, because to the latter the Government of our country refused to give the status of Scheduled Caste. But this also does not mean that the other three Dalit religious groups are able to get their basic rights in different areas of life. There are number of works and studies, which prove this point of ours.

For example the 28th Report of the Commissioner for Scheduled Castes and Scheduled Tribes for the period 1986-7 reveals that there appears to have taken place many positive changes in the practice of Untouchability in the urban areas, but in rural areas this change is very slow. According to the report 'the denial of access to a common facility like drinking water is a normal feature. Separate settlements for members of the Scheduled Castes (Dalits) continue to be a rule in the village'.[7] The Report says in the urban 'slum areas, members of the Scheduled Castes (Dalits) will be found in the worst sectors.' The report makes a special reference to the rights of the Dalit. It says:

> The assertion of rights by members of the Scheduled Castes, particularly their refusal to accept humiliation, as a part of their being, is being retaliated in many areas by other communities through assertion of their rights inherent in the ownership of land and primacy in economic institutions which cannot be challenged formally under the law. Sometimes these formal postures can be grotesque and inhuman, e.g. when the right to live and even of easement are denied to those who can claim not an inch of land as their own in the village.[8]

Reports about various kinds of disabilities, insults and other atrocities suffered by the Dalit communities are reported daily in our newspapers. According to the Twenty-eighth Report of the Commissioner for Scheduled Castes and Scheduled Tribes the total number of atrocities committed on the Dalits during six years (1981-6) were 91,097,[9] but then the Fourth Report of the SC-ST Commission for three years alone (1995-97) gives 90,925.

6.4. Globalization and the Dalits

The most important point here needs to be remembered is that Indian society for the last 3500 years is controlled by (about) 18 per cent population of the country, which includes various caste groups and forward communities. Among these groups the most powerful, who were enjoying all the human rights were/are only 5.52 per cent Brahmins, because other had various reduced human rights according to their caste. For example Brahmins (priests) had the right to education as well as to teach others, *Kshatryia* (warriors) had the right to educate, but not teach. The same way third caste *Vaishyas* (traders) had a very limited need based right to education. The fourth caste *Shudra* (serving class) did not have any right to education, but they were still recognized as human beings. In the case of Dalits, who were considered as outcastes, they even did not have any human right as their own, because they were non-human for the caste people. Therefore it is 18 per cent minority (among these only 5 per cent Brahmins), who really enjoy the various human rights according to their grade.

So India as a country has been controlled by a minority, who also controlled all the economic and human resources. Related to the above point, we need also to remember that in today's context, the above caste based minority throughout history has supported politically the 'rightist' ideology, which has always opposed the existence of a secular state. On the other hand, the upholders of secular state or centrist ideology believed in the middle path, meaning partly state controlled planned economy, social justice for all, nationalism based on secular values and recognition of composite culture. But the believers of the rightist ideology, which is followed by the above minority, believe in one religion based culture or nationalism and a system of free enterprise and market economy.[10]

The next important point we need to note is that for Indian rightist political groups' both social and economic thinking runs almost parallel to the basic ideas of globalization particularly when we talk about it as privatization and liberalization of international trade and investment. Because if we look very carefully we find the meaning of this kind of globalization process matches well with the ideological meaning of both the cultural nationalism and a free enterprise cum market economy of Indian rightists' groups. The globalization mainly is understood today as the free movement of goods, services, people and information across national boundaries.[11]

6.4.1. *Defining the Globalization*

The above definition of globalization may look simple as well as harmless. But to understand the meaning and to fix a Dalit perspective, we need to look into the meaning and implication of globalization more critically. First, we all will agree with the view that: Globalization is now a fact, not an option. The communication revolution has turned the world into a global 'village' where everyone knows 'what is going on and what is available'.[12] The supporters of this process claim: 'The process of globalization is a central source of change in the world today. It can lead to widely shared inclusive prosperity or highly uneven development from which a significant number of countries and people are excluded. To benefit fully from it, to turn it into an opportunity, India has to adapt its policies.'[13] Now what are the policies behind the Globalization? *Human Development Report 1997* summarized the answer to this question by pointing out:

> A dominant economic theme of the 1990s globalization encapsulates both a description and a prescription. The description is the widening and deepening of international flows of trade, finance and information.... The prescription is to liberalize national and global markets in the belief that free flows of trade, finance and information will produce the best outcome for growth and human welfare.

This Report at the same place also adds: 'The principles of free global markets are nevertheless applied selectively. If this were not so, the global market for unskilled labour would be as free as the market for industrial country exports or capital.... Lacking power, poor countries and poor people too often their interests neglected and underminded.'[14] Also Globalization has its winners and losers.

The gainers include output, people with assets, profits, people with high skills, educated, professional, managerial and technical people, capital, creditors, those independent of public services, large firms, the strong, risk takers, global markets, sellers of technically sophisticated products, global culture, global elite and firms with market access and branding. The losers include: employment, people without assets, wages, people with low skills, uneducated workers, labour, debtors, those dependent on public services, small firms, the weak, human security, local communities, sellers of primary and standard manufactured products, local culture, global poor and firms without market access and no branding.[15] Now in the case of Dalits without any doubt we can say that as they stand today they are among the losers of globalization.

Here it is also interested to note that all the human development reports, which offered the analysis of the impacts of globalization agreed that it is not only the interests of the poor countries and the poor in general are neglected, but also the benefits of this process mainly have gone to the more dynamic and powerful countries of the North and South. These reports also agree with the fact that it is true liberalization, privatization and tighter intellectual property rights are shaping the path for the new technologies, determine how they are used, but then all this is controlled by the powerful Corporations and in the process: 'Poor people and poor countries risk being pushed to the margin in this proprietary regime controlling the world's knowledge.'[16] Besides this, the global gap between haves and have-nots, between knows and know-nots is widening, because of the following reasons: (a) as in private research agendas money talks louder than need, (b) tightened intellectual property rights keep developing countries out of the knowledge sector; (c) patent laws do not recognize traditional knowledge and systems of ownership and (d) the rush and push of commercial interests protect profits, not people, despite the risks in the new technologies.[17] All this actually means that the right to knowledge or education is limited to a small minority as part of the strategy. Here we must also add that when we talk about the education in relation to globalization, it means universal quality basic education both at the secondary as well as of higher level of education. Also there is a definite need of commitment to the social reforms on the government, without which globalization will not succeed either in transforming the local society or economy in any situation.

There are a number of other important aspects of globalization, which need our attention, but as we are restricting our discussion to the Dalit perspective mainly, therefore we can not deal here with all the aspects. But one last point here which need our attention is the history of globalization. Though the history of the present form of globalization goes back to the colonialist era of seventeenth, eighteenth and nineteenth centuries, yet its real history began after the Second World War. To begin the main purpose to establish this process was to formulate some global rules for trade to manage the global economy. For this purpose, to coordinate, three world institutions were founded: the International Monetary Fund (IMF), the World Bank (WB) and General Agreement on Tariffs and Trade (GATT)/World Trade Organisation (WTO). With these, within the given time by the last decade of twentieth century, the present form of the globalization came into existence, which went beyond the territories of nation states by the process of economic exchanges, political homogenization, technological advances and cultural influences. Presently globalization in the form of human power is, in truth without any control, because it does not recognize any boundaries such as political or national and even the boundaries of the natural world.

All what is said about the history of present globalization is true, but for Dalits, the history of their colonization cum globalization goes back to more than 3500 years. As pointed earlier in the case of India both the promoters as well as beneficiaries of globalization are the traditional groups belonging to the so called upper castes. The same way victims of this process are those, who were also the victims of caste based Indian social order. Dalits have been the most victimized among these groups. Globalization through the process of privatization and liberalization specially have added to the already faced woes by Dalits in the areas of economic, political, social and cultural. In these areas of their life already divisions have been imposed upon them both horizontally and vertically. Because caste is not only an instrument of division of labours, it was/is also an instrument through which Dalits as labourers have been divided or graded upon one another.

6.5. Impact on Dalits

Already some references have been made in our earlier discussion about the possible negative effects of globalization on Dalits. It has been also pointed out that the globalization process has already become an existent reality, therefore Dalits now cannot take it as an mere option, which can be either accepted or rejected. But what is important to take note of the fact is that Dalits are certainly more prone to the negative effects of globalization as compared to the other poor or weaker sections of our Indian society. It is because of their already existant historical context which is oppressive in nature. Therefore Dalits need to understand the nature of the threats or negative impact, which globalization is imposing upon them. The process towards this end has already begun. Therefore to face the challenge of globalization, they have to prepare themselves, both to save themselves from the negative effects of this process and also to avail the benefits of the same. For this Dalits need to be empowered by receiving a right kind of knowledge or education which can help them to become active participants of this process. It is here in this area Dalits need enabling support both locally as well as globally.

For example globalization can help Dalits in number of ways specially to deal with their old enemy, the Caste system, which has pushed them into a non-human state, socially, economically and politically. Because as long as they stay within the boundaries, in which Caste or Varna system operate, they cannot liberate themselves from the chains of slavery of this system. Therefore they have to get out of these boundaries and one way is, by becoming part of the global civil society, instead of sticking in the local existing society, which actually is founded on the principle of graded inequality. To go out from this slavery, now a possible opportunity is being provided to them by the process of globalization. Because this process possibly can provide them a chance to globalize or internationalize the 'Dalit Issue', which can help in breaking the control of Caste system. This means using a weapon of the enemy against the enemy. But this will be only possible if first, Dalits can come over the new threats, which are being imposed upon them by this process specially through the form in which this process is being introduced in our country. To understand this point further we need to probe into some areas of concern of the life of Dalits. We are proposing three such areas of concern to include in our further discussion: The State and Dalit Rights, Education and Dalits and Civil Society and Dalits.

6.5.1. *The State and Dalit Rights*

In India traditionally as well as historically the people's rights always have been restricted and controlled by the State, which include cultural, religious, economic, social and political rights. It is because the State always has been controlled by a minority group, in whose favour the major role has been played by the Indian caste based social order. This social order has literally followed the following three fundamental principles: the principle of the graded inequality, the principle of fixity of occupations and the principle of fixation of people within their respective classes.[18] These principles were to be followed as part of the *dharma* of a human being. If broken there will be a prescribed punishment. These principles were/are followed for the last 3500 years.

But thanks to the framers of the Indian Constitution which has recognized the follys of the Indian social order and has offered ways and means to deal with these follys. For example the Constitution itself, though has not attacked the Caste system, yet it offered the basic fundamental rights to all the citizens based upon the principle of equality (Article 14). It also has legally abolished the untouchability (Article 17). It offers everybody equal opportunity of employment in public sectors (Article 16). It also prohibits any form of discrimination on the basis of religion, race, caste, sex or place of birth (Article 15). The preamble of the Constitution also makes the intention of its framers very clear, concerning of the equal rights of all the citizens in the areas of social, economic and political. The principle of justice also fully has been applied to these areas of citizens life in the text of the Constitution. Besides upholding the principle of equality, the Constitution also has offered special safeguards for the rights of weaker segments of Indian society, which include religious and linguistic minorities, women, scheduled castes, scheduled tribes and other backward classes.

In the case of Dalits (constitutional expression used for them is scheduled caste), the Constitution has granted them special right to share the political powers by offering them the reservation of seats at all levels (Articles 330-4). On the economic end, the Constitution not only prohibits any form of forced labour (Article 23), but makes special provision for Dalits to provide the reserved jobs in various government departments and public undertakings (Article 16, 320, 353). These reservations have been offered to the Dalits according to their percentage of the total population of the country. The Article 46 of the Constitution offers a special provision to promote with special care the education and economic interests of Dalits and it also offers them a protection from social injustice and all forms of exploitation. But three points here need to be noted are: *one*, all these reservations and economic benefits offered to Dalits are limited to the government departments and public enterprises; *two*, presently these benefits are limited to Dalits professing Hindu, Sikh and Buddhist religions. These are not available to Dalits professing Islam and Christian religions; *three*, the benefits offered here have not reached fully to all those Dalits, who even are eligible to receive these.

So the first major threat of globalization faced by Dalits is with regards to their above constitutional rights. The Constitution of the country at least kept an open possibility for Dalits to share the economic rights through reservation in the government jobs as well as in the public sector. But now, as one of the essential element of the globalization of the market economy is privatization, which is one of the main recommendations of the Structural Adjustment Programme (SAP) and under the influence of SAP since early 1990s, India has opened its market and now the speed of this process has increased. Here the point need to be noted is that the privileges enjoyed by Dalits under the Constitution specially with regards to the jobs in the public sector are going to be affected directly. Because with the introduction of privatization policy in the public sector, Dalits going to lose even the possibility of having jobs there, which presently they are enjoying substantially, which very clearly can be seen from the table given below (which shows the percentage reservation of Dalits in Central Public Enterprises as on 1-1-96):

So the first major threat faced by Dalits is to their Constitutional rights, which are being taken away through the process of privatization of public sector. The most serious aspect of this problem is that the government by establishing a full time Disinvestment Ministry is ruthlessly busy in selling the various government owned enterprises.

Groups	Total	SC	%
'A'	1,98,625	16,710	8.41
'B'	1,64,402	15,921	9.68
'C'	11,32,860	2,16,801	19.14
'D' ('excluding Safai Karamcharies)	4,77,254	1,06,934	22.41
Total	19,73,141	3,56,366	18.06
'D' ('Safai Karamcharies)	24,623	21,506	87.34
Grand Total	19,97,764	3,77,872	18.91

Source: NC for SC&ST, Special Report January 1998[19]

On the other hand the State is supposed to be the guardian of the rights of the people, but then if State itself get involved in the process, which will take away the rights of the people, then in that situation who will protect the people's or Dalits' rights. Here a possible role of civil society comes, which we will discuss in our further discussion, but before that we will deal with other area of our concern namely Education and Dalits.

6.5.2. *Education and the Dalits*

UNDP's *Human Development Report* 1999 says: 'Education is a ticket to network high society. Globally 30 per cent of users had at least one university degree'.[20] About the same subject the report on *Human Development in South Asia 2001* says:

> Success in the global economy for individuals as well as for national economies, depends on their levels of education and training, that is, on their achievements Human Development then is more than crucial for further advance in economic growth, and for subsequently greater achievements in human development. Spreading education to everyone is an important means of spreading opportunities and incomes and countering the tendency for rising inequality and social exclusion.[21]

Here the first statement highlights the role of education in becoming the beneficiaries of opportunities offered by the process of globalization. The second statement which is based upon the contextual reality of South Asia (which includes India) and the human development has put education on the top as a means of not only getting opportunities and incomes, but also it will save the people from the rising inequality and social exclusion. This is possibly the reason why the report of *Human Development in South Asia 2001* laid a special stress on the need of the 'universal quality basic education as well as higher levels of education' including 'skill training', which can only enable a person 'to compete in the global market' and become beneficiaries of globalization in real sense.[22]

Here we must add also that 'education' as a basic means to develop a full human personality has been also recognized by the Universal Declaration of Human Rights of the United Nations (Article 26). The Constitution of India in Article 43 also has recognized the 'universal need of education'. It is true both globally as well as nationally that need for education for human development is fully recognized and in India after Independence many efforts have been made to educate the masses. According to the 2001 census the present general literacy rate of India is 65.38 per cent as compared to 1991 literacy rate of 52.21 per cent. In 1991 the literacy rate among the Dalits was 37.41 per cent, but unfortunately the 2001 census does not give the literacy rate of Dalits, which may be between 40 to 45 per cent.[19] This shows the gap between the national and Dalits' rate of education.

But even the growth in literacy as shown in various census reports, can prove to be very deceptive in nature. Because the truth is something else—when we talk about education in India specially if we are talking in terms of 'universal quality basic education as well as higher levels of education', which can enable a person to reap the fruits (opportunities) of globalization. Because in India such education is limited only to a very small percentage of the population. To make this point clear, we can refer to a study, conducted by Pushpa M. Bhargava, the gist of which was published in April 1993 in the *Indian Express*. In this study Ms. Bhargava in concluding added that it is largely hereditary in nature. She said: 'For about three to five per cent of population—about say, 40 million people—education would run in the family, with everyone, no matter how capable or incapable, going through high school to a college and finally ending up with a job,' she further added:

> For the remaining education-under-privileged 95 per cent even literacy is a struggle, leave aside education. ... It has been calculated that no more than 50,000 to 1,00,000 people from the hereditary non-educated move every year to the status of the educated ones. ... For all practical purposes,

therefore, a section of people has simply replaced the British within the hereditary educated class. Lack of education means lack of awareness and lack of ability to assimilate information even if one has access to it. Lack of education is also equivalent to economic trends to keep the majority equally backward.[23]

The roots of education as a hereditary affair goes back to the Vedic period and its caste based educational rights to few on the top. What Ms. Bhargava has said, that the real education is limited to 3 to 5 per cent of the population of India, was true 3500 years ago it was true in 1993, when Ms. Bhargava made the above statement and even possibly it is true today also. Historically education of different levels were reserved for those so-called upper caste people covering about to-day's 16 to 18 per cent population of the country and among them also only the real education was reserved for 5 per cent, which form the top rung namely Brahmins. 250 million Dalits were denied that special rights 3500 years ago and also today according to Ms. Pushpa M. Bhargava. If we take a positive side of Ms. Bhargava's statement that every year 50,000 to 1,00,000 people join the upper ladder of education, then we can imagine how many more centuries historically oppressed communities specially the Dalits will take to reach that level.

The truth about the reality of Indian education system and its beneficiaries, again makes our point further clear, which we have made in our earlier discussion that the benefits of globalization are limited to the traditional dominant caste groups of Indian population. Now is there any solution to this problem? Besides the role of Dalit theology and their whole liberation, which will be considered in detail in this last section of this work, here in the closing section of this chapter, the role of civil society is also discussed briefly.

6.6 Civil Society and Dalits

In our discussion of the earlier sections of this chapter, we have seen in the Indian context the possibility of the effective role of the State and getting enhanced the same through the quality education in favour of the historically the oppressed group like the Dalit is very little. It is because all the power structures historically are controlled by a small minority comprising of so called upper caste people. On the other hand it is also true, those who are concerned about the 'positive effects of globalization on economic growth as well as human development depend on how the globalization process is managed nationally and internationally.' But how a national government will save its people from the negative impacts of globalization? It mainly will depend 'on the commitment and capacity of government at all levels, from national to local, to manage their economic and social development policies and programmes in a socially-responsible way.'[24] In the case of South Asia (including India), the Report of 2001 rightly has made a point that 'to make an assessment of the impact of globalization on human development in South Asia, we must consider the initial conditions prior to globalization'. Here the expression 'initial conditions' is important because that points towards the reality of Dalits, which we have referred in our discussion of part one of this paper. The Report of 2001 adds the reason behind government's failures in protecting the rights of people mainly, because of the lack of commitment. Besides the lack of commitment to human development, this report also added two other reasons: inefficiency of administration of public sectors and poor governance.[25] It is in such a situation that Dalits have to find an 'alternative' to their problem in relation to globalization. Here comes in the picture a 'civil society' and its role, which possibly can offer enabling help to Dalits to face the challenge of globalization and changed the same into their benefits. Because we do agree unlike the Indian social order which is rooted in Caste system, 'inequality is not inherent in globalization'.[26] Also the globalization process provides the possibility of 'global connectedness and interdependence of societies' and also it can help in achieving other goals 'including those of world peace, environmental sustainability human rights, democracy and of course shared economic prosperity'.[27]

Human Development in South Asia 2001 specially has stressed on the roles of civil society in guarding the interests of poor groups like Dalits. But then what is civil society? It is a society, which recognizes the rights of an individual in every sphere of life. The twin principles of freedom and equality are the governing principles of such as a society. But this is only true at the conceptual level, because a civil society becomes only visible or it gets resurrected, whenever or wherever any oppressive structure including the power of the State is challenged and sought to be controlled. In such a context, a civil society becomes the instrument of defending human liberties and rights against such oppressive structure and it marked out an autonomous sphere of social practices, rights and dignity for the individual. Again the undergirded basic principle besides the twin principles on which a civil society is founded is the 'principle of justice'. 'Justice' here actually is the other name of fraternity, equality and liberty. These are the principles, which the Constitution of India through its preamble has endorsed as the basis of future Indian society according to which all its citizens will enjoy 'justice' in the spheres of 'social, economic and political; *Liberty* of thought, expression, belief, faith and worship; *Equality* of status and of opportunity and to promote among them all; *Fraternity* assuring the dignity of the individual and the unity and integrity of the Nation'.[28] But here we must remember that the Constitution has stated a vision of a civil society, which India still has to have. Therefore building a civil society is a continuous struggle, in which every citizen has to play a role and the role of Dalit and other weaker sections can prove crucial, because such a society is their need.

Here we must also add that actual civil society comprises media, social organizations, and in some cases non-governmental organizations. In fact when any group is willing to become a pressure group to bring a change in the existing oppressive structure of a society that becomes part of a civil society. Now because of the Caste system to have civil society organizations in a country like India is very difficult, particularly if we have to include the question of social justice as part of the process of human development. Therefore in India only such a group can take such a challenge, whose members historically have been considered as 'outcastes' meaning today's Dalits. Because Dalits theologically, ideologically and even historically do not form part of the Indian social order based upon the Caste system. Because of this reason and as human beings, they can get closer to their sister oppressed communities in the world. They need to enter into a process of global solidarity with all those who are carrying on their struggle based upon the principle of justice.

So the Dalits indeed have to strengthen first their own civil society movement in India and then it has to go across the borders to reach a global civil society, which will not only help them in restoring and protecting their rights, but also the rights of their follow oppressed human beings all over the world. So here comes the need of global solidarity of the oppressed and poor including Dalits of India. Besides global solidarity which include building of alliances, continuing stress on achieving the alternative approaches for getting the quality education and receiving direction towards collectively identifying their problems as well as formulating transformational solutions to them.[29]

NOTES

1. K.S. Singh, *The Scheduled Castes*, Anthropological Survey of India, Delhi, 1993, p. 1.
2. *Mandal Commission Report of the Backward Classes Commission*, 1980, Akalank Publications, Delhi, 1990, p. 19 (listed in further references as 'Mandal Commission'.
3. *Report of the Commission for Scheduled Castes and Scheduled Tribes for the Period Ending 31st December*, 1951, Government of India, New Delhi, 1961, p. 1.
4. James Massey, *Dalits in India: Religion as a Sources of Bondage or Liberation with Special Reference to Christians*, Manohar, New Delhi, 1995, pp. 38-9.
5. See for detail discussion: Paulo Freire, *Pedagogy of the Oppressed*, Penguin, London, 1990 (rpt.), pp. 108-35.
6. Quoted in: Massey, *Dalits in India*, op. cit., p. 134.
7. *Report of the Commissioner for Scheduled Castes and Scheduled Tribes, Twenty-eighth Report* 1986-87, Government of India, New Delhi, 1988, p. 6 (listed in further references as '28th Report of SC-ST Commission').
8. Ibid., p. 7.
9. Ibid., p. 238.
10. See for detail discussion: James Massey, *Emerging Political Scenario in India and Christian Response*, CCCC Study Document 3, Delhi, 1999, pp. 8-11.
11. *Human Development in South Asia* 2001: Oxford University Press, Oxford, 2002, p. 10.
12. *India Development Report* 1999-2000: Oxford University Press, New Delhi, 1999, p. 27.
13. Ibid., p. 28.
14. *Human Development Report* 1997, UNDP, New York, pp. 82, 97.
15. *Human Development in South Asia* 2001, op. cit., p. 15.
16. *Human Development Report* 1999, UNDP, Oxford, 1999, p. 6.

17. Ibid., p. 57.
18. See for detail discussion: Dr. Babasaheb Ambedkar, *Writings and Speeches*, vol. 3, Education Department, Government of Maharashtra, Bombay, 1987, pp. 106-15.
19. *National Commission for Scheduled Castes and Scheduled Tribes*, Special Report, January 1998, New Delhi, p. 23.
20. *Human Development Report* 1999, op. cit., p. 6.
21. *Human Development in South Asia* 2001, op. cit., p. 18.
22. Ibid., p. 2.
23. James Massey, *Alternative Approaches to Education for All*, CCCC Study Document 1, Delhi, pp. 10-15.
24. *Human Development in South Asia* 2001, op. cit., p. 135.
25. Ibid., p. 47.
26. *Human Development Report* 1999, op. cit., p. 82.
27. Jean Drèze and Amartya Sen, *India: Development and Participation*, Oxford University Press, New Delhi, 2002, p. 340.
28. *The Constitution of India*, Government of India, Ministry of Law Justice and Company Affairs, New Delhi, 1997, XXI.
29. Vernoika Bennholdt Thomsen et al. (eds.), *There is an Alternative: Subsistence and Worldwide Resistance to Corporate Globalization*, Zed Books, London, 2001, p. 69.

CHAPTER 7

Dalit Christians and their Civil Rights

7.1. Dalit Christian Issue

Historically, it is true, the problem which all Dalits including Dalit Christians face, is concerning their social, economic and political rights. Besides the Dalit Christians also suffered discrimination from the hands so called upper caste Christians within the Christian church. The worst level discrimination they face is with regards to the civil rights from the hands of their own government based upon the 1950 Presidential Order. These three levels of discrimination with regards to their civil rights are discussed in detail in this chapter.

7.1.1. *Discrimination Common with other Dalits*

First level discrimination, the Dalit Christians suffered along with the Dalits in general is concerning their social, economic and political rights.[1] The best example of this is the dwelling places of Dalits, which according to the Brahmanical scriptures particularly *Manusmriti* 10.51.82, has to be 'outside the village'[2] and this dictate even today is being followed through out the country. The author of this work comes from a largest village in Panjab named Zafferwal (dist. Gurdaspur), where even today both the Dalit Sikhs (known as *Majhabi Sikh*) and Dalit Christians (known as *Issai* or *Saa-i)* live side by side in *thathis* (means place of mockery).[3] The similar situation of Dalit Christians and Dalit belonging to other religions is found in south India also. For example study conducted in 1990 by Dr Jose Kananaikal in Tamil Nadu shows that in the vast majority of the villages (out of 142 in 257 villages), Dalit Christians live with the Dalits belonging to other religions.[4] Dr Kananaikal's study also have shown that the social, economic and educational conditions of the Dalit

Christians in most cases are similar to other Dalits, even majority of Dalit Christians are worst then the Dalits belonging to other religious.[5] The similar backwardness (social, economic political) prevails according to some studies among Panjabi Dalit Christians also.[6] So this is the first level oppression or discrimination, which the Dalits including Dalit Christians are subjected continuously for more than 3500 years along with Dalits in general.

7.1.2. *Discrimination within the Christian Community*

The second level discrimination, the Dalit Christians are facing is from their fellow Christians, who continue to claim their high caste status, even after becoming Christians. It is true, the Christian religion opposes any kind of discrimination on the basis of race or gender or social and political status or otherwise. It is supposed to be the most egalitarian faith. The *Magna Carta* of the Christian principle of equality is stated in the Christian Scripture in these words: 'There is no longer Jew or Greek, there is no longer slave or free, there is no longer male or female; for all of you are one in Christ Jesus.'[7] This egalitarian principle possibly is the one that Christians in India throughout their history have ignored. Here, a few examples of the views of from some of the highest authorities of the Christian world are given in support of this point.

First example, views expressed in the inaugural address of Archbishop George Zur, Apostolic Pro-Nuncia to India, which he gave to the Catholic Bishops Conference of India (CBCI), at their meeting held in Pune during December 1991, where he said:

> Though Catholics of the lower castes and tribes form 60 per cent of Church membership, yet they have no place in decision-making. Scheduled caste converts are treated as low caste not only by high caste Hindus but by high caste Christians too. In rural areas, they cannot own or rent houses, however, well-placed they may be. Separate places are marked out for them in the parish churches and burial grounds. Inter-caste marriages are frowned upon and caste tags are still appended to the Christian names of high caste people. Casteism is rampant among the clergy and the religious. Though Dalit Christians make 65 per cent of the 10 million Christians in the South, less than 4 per cent of the parishes are entrusted to Dalit priests.[8]

The situation of the Dalit Christians continues to be the same in society as well as the Church. This is clear from the CBCI's statement at the end of their meeting in March 1998, which says: 'The prevalence of the Caste system, not only in society but also in some parts of the Church in India even at the close of the 20th century, is a matter of shame and disgrace to all of us.'[9] As CBCI is the official representative body at the national level for the Roman Catholic Christians, the same way, the National Council of Churches in India, is the representative body of the Protestant and Orthodox Churches, which also has accepted the need to look to the issue of the Dalit Christians 'within the Church and outside.'[10] One of the major Protestant Church is the Church of North India (CNI), which has shown its serious concern about the Dalit Christians by recognizing it as a problem. For example, in its a few years back held 12th Ordinary Synod (supreme body) meeting from 16-21 October 2005 in Ranchi it once again has deliberated on this whole issue by recognizing it as a reality by saying:

> One of the most important issues continues to miss the attention of the CNI is the 'Dalit Issue'. We in the CNI have skirted around the issues related to the Dalits, particularly Dalit Christians, as if it did not mean anything to us. On the one hand, we claim that the Church in India, especially the Church of North India is predominantly the Church of the Dalits and the Tribals, and on the other hand, we seem to consciously ignore the sociological reality of the Indian Church.

By having said this the Synod once again adopted a resolution in which it in clear terms recognized the issue of the Dalit by saying: 'that we recognize the problem of Dalits particularly Dalit Christians both within the Church as well as outside'.[11]

These few examples of the major representative bodies of the Christians which include CBCI and NCCI and also examples given above of a major Protestant Church, CNI, makes our points very clear that the Dalit Christians even continue to face discrimination not only from the members of the society in general, but from the hands of the so called upper caste Christians also. Besides these two levels, the third level, the Dalit Christians are facing discrimination from the hand of their own government, which will be discussed in the next sub-section.

7.1.3 *Denial of Constitutional Rights*

The third level of discrimination, which the Dalit Christians are facing since 1950 about which the sad thing is that the source of this discrimination is the government of the country itself. Interestingly, this discrimination is related to the very first fundamental right granted to all persons in the Constitution of the country, the Right to Equality before the law in Article 14, which reads: 'The State shall not deny to any persons equality before the law or the equal protection of the laws within the territory of India'.[12] Here, important point to be noted is that this right in our Constitution is granted to all the 'persons'. But sadly, all the laws under which special protection is provided to Dalits belonging to Hindu, Sikh and Buddhist religions is denied to the Dalit Christians, because they are 'Christians'. The examples of these laws are: the Protection of Civil Rights Act 1955; Protection of Civil Rights Rules, 1977; and the Scheduled Castes and Scheduled Tribes (Prevention of Atrocities) Act, 1989.

The above laws, the Government of India has brought out in order to give protection to the Dalits. For example, the Protection of Civil Rights Act, 1955 deals with the question of religious and social disabilities met by the Dalits and how the offenders can be punished. Along with other matters, it also deals with the punishment for other offences arising out of 'Untouchabilty'. In short, it is 'an Act to prescribe punishment for the preaching and practice of 'Untouchabilty', for the enforcement of any disability arising there from and for matters connected therewith'.[13] The Protection of Civil Rights Rules, 1977, has given power to any State Government to appoint an officer not below the rank of a sub-divisional magistrate for the purpose of making an enquiry concerning the protection of any civil rights.[14] The 1989 Act for Prevention of Atrocities is

> an Act to prevent the commission of atrocities against members for the Scheduled Castes and the Scheduled Tribes, to provide for Special Courts for the trail of such offences and for relief and rehabilitation of the victims of such offences and for matters connected therewith or incidental thereto.[15]

It is clear from the contents of the above Acts that they have given some protection of rights to the Dalits, but it is also clear, both from the contents and their titles, that these are to provide protection only to those Dalits who are recognized as the 'Scheduled Castes'. So again, what about the Dalit Christians? Are they protected under these Acts? The answer is 'no'. What implication have these for the Dalit Christians/? Here, it may be worth referring to two actual incidents in one of the south Indian states, Andhra Pradesh, which will throw some light on the implications of these Protection Acts for the Dalit Christians.

The first incident took place on 17 July 1985 in a village named Karamchedu, Prakasam district. In this incident, the Dalit Christians were attacked by the upper castes Hindus and the persons killed were Tella Yehoshua (Joshua), Tella Moshe (Moses), Muttiah (Matthew), Duddu Ramesh, son of Yohan (John) and Duddu Abraham. The news was reported by a number of newspapers. All India Radio and television channels reported that some Harijans (Dalits) had been killed by the upper castes. No report stated the fact that all of them were Dalit Christians. These killings were discussed in the Andhra Legislative Assembly but again, only on the basis that all those killed were Harijans or members of the Scheduled Castes. A one-man Commission of Enquiry under Justice D.P. Desai was appointed by the Government of Andhra Pradesh to probe into the Karamchedu incident. The Commission enquired the case not on the basis of those killed being Dalit Christians but as only Madigas (a community belonging to a Scheduled Caste, which means by faith Hindu) and submitted its report on 28 March 1988.

The other incident of 1991 took place on 6 August when a mob comprising upper castes Reddis and other non-dalits raided a Dalit colony at Tsundura of Guntur district, where eight Dalits were killed. All those killed belonged to the Lutheran Christian Church. According to a report, 'the carnage was sparked off by the anger of the Reddis against a Dalit young man (a graduate) who had been accused of stretching his legs forward and kicking a Reddi young man sitting in the front row in a cinema show, a month before (July 4th)....' This news was discussed at an all India level including in the Parliament. But again, the basis of all discussions and enquiries was that some Dalits (not Dalit Christians) were killed.[17] The incident continued to appear in the national newspapers for many months.[18]

According to one analysis of Karamchedu incident of 17 July 1985, neither the Press including All India Radio nor even a High Court judge could differentiate between the Harijans (Dalits in general) and the Harijan (Dalit) Christians for the purpose of reporting or enquiry.[19] But the important point which needs to be noted is that the victims of both incidents were Dalit Christians, who, according to the Constitution (Scheduled Castes) Order, 1950 also known as The Presidential Order, 1950, are not considered to be Scheduled Castes and are therefore, not entitled to have any protection and care, neither under the special Articles provided in the Constitution (numbers 330, 332, 335, 338 and 46), nor under the Scheduled Castes and Scheduled Tribes (Prevention of Atrocities) Act, 1989 and Protection of Civil Rights Act, 1955. Here, a question may even be raised of the Dalit Christians have a right to live, about the Constitution of India says: 'No person shall be deprived of his life…'.[20]

Besides denying the equality before the law to the Dalit Christians, the Government is also discriminating with the Dalit Christians on the basis of religion. Such discrimination is prohibited in Article 15.1, which is also part of the Fundamental Rights and it reads as: 'The State shall not discriminate against any citizen on grounds only of religion, race, caste, place of birth or any of them.'[21] Again, sadly, our government on the basis of 'The Constitution has also denied to the Dalit Christians, rights granted in Articles 330, 332, 335 and 338 concerning jobs, education and share in the governance of the country. This also is part of the third level of discrimination which Dalit Christians are facing directly from the hand of their own government, because they are Christians. The third level of discrimination makes the case of Dalit Christian special as campared to the Dalits belonging to other religions. To understand this point more clearly, we have to look into the context of 'the Constitution' (Scheduled Caste) Order of 1950, which forms the main basis of today's problem of Dalit Christians and their civil rights.

7.2. The Constitution Order, 1950 and Civil Rights

Here, in this section, we will first deal with the background history of the expression 'Scheduled Castes' and the criteria used for deciding its denomination. The expression Scheduled Castes' was first coined by the Simon Commission (appointed by the British Government) between 1929 and 1932 and was later incorporated in the Government of India Act of 1935.[22] Prior to this, 'Depressed Classes' was used in Government (British) circles, and also by members of various reform movements.[23] This expression was used more or less for all kinds of depressed people including the 'Untouchables', without differentiating on the basis of religion. It was in 1932 that for the first time, the expression 'Depressed Classes' was used exclusively for the Untouchables. The British Government was then trying to help all other communities such as Muslims, Christians, Anglo-Christians and others (who, according to them, did not come under the Depressed Classes) and extending to them special benefits including giving them separate communal electorates.[24]

In 1931, a special committee was set up to draw a 'Schedule' of the castes covered under the Depressed Classes. The same year, the Round Table Conference in London was convened in which from the Indian side, Gandhi and Ambedkar were the key members. Here, Ambedkar demanded separate electorate for the Depressed Classes, whom he always referred to as Untouchables. But Gandhi objected. Ambedkar also suggested that Untouchables should be renamed 'Protestant Hindu' or 'Non-conformist Hindu'.[25] By that time, of course, Gandhi had also introduced another term for Untouchables, that is, 'Harijan' (meaning children of God), which he took from a Gujarati poem. But this was not accepted or liked by the Untouchables themselves.[26] As Gandhi and Ambedkar did not agree (at the Round Table Conference), no final decision was taken. Finally, the matter of communal electorates was left to the chairman of the Conference, Prime Minister Ramsay MacDonald, who in 1932, issued the Communal Award in which he also replaced the expression 'the Depressed Classes' with the 'Scheduled Castes'.[27] From then onwards, the Untouchables of India were known as the Scheduled Castes. Later, the expression Scheduled Castes were included in the Government of India Act, 1935, which was followed by the Government of India (Scheduled Castes) Order, 1936, according to which 'no Indian Christian…should be deemed a member of a Scheduled Caste'.[28] This was the first time that 'religion' was used as a criterion to define Scheduled Caste. (At this stage, the effect of this decision was not felt by Indian Christians as they were still enjoying the status of a minority community with full rights.)

The definition of the expression the 'Scheduled Castes' was given in the Government of India Act, 1935, which said: 'The Scheduled Castes means such castes, races or tribes or parts or groups within castes, races, tribes, parts or groups which appear to the Governor-General to correspond to the classes of persons, formerly known as the

Depressed Classes as the Governor-General may by order specify'.[29] This definition of the Scheduled Castes, more or less literally, was adopted by the authors of the Indian Constitution and later by the Government of India in 1950. The Indian Constitution's exact words are given in Article 366, clause 24: 'Scheduled Castes means such castes, races or tribes or parts of or groups within such castes, races or tribes are deemed under Article 341 to be Scheduled Castes for the purpose of this Constitution.'[30] The Indian Constitution, on the basis of the Article 341(1) empowers the President of India, '...by public notification, to specify the castes, races or tribes or parts of or groups within castes, races or tribes which shall, for all purpose of this Constitution be deemed to be Scheduled Castes....'[31] Again, the Constitution without defining who is of a Scheduled Caste in Article 366 (2) only refers to the power given to the President of India in Article 341.[32] But once the President has issued such an order saying who can be included in the list or Schedule, this list of Scheduled Castes, on the basis of Article 342 (2) can be changed only through an Act of Parliament.

While exercising the powers conferred to him in Article 341 (1), the President of India promulgated in 1950 an order known as The Constitution (Scheduled Castes) Order, 1950. This Order of 1950 almost re-enacted the list of the Government of India (Scheduled Castes) Order, 1936.[33] As stated earlier, concerning the Scheduled Castes, the Indian Constitution has followed all the bases that the British Government had laid down in 1936. Reference has already been made to the list, but the fundamental criterion of the Government of India (Scheduled Castes) Order, 1936 has been used by the Order of 1950 also. On that basis, the third paragraph of this Order reads: 'Notwithstanding anything contained in paragraph 2, no person who professes a religion different from Hindu shall be deemed to be a member of a Scheduled Castes.' This paragraph was amended in 1956 by Parliament to read 'the Hindu or the Sikh' and again in May 1990 to 'the Hindu or the Sikh or the Buddhist'.

The British Government did include various other tests to decide the Scheduled Castes list. Stephen Fuchs says: 'The test applied for inclusion in the list was the social, educational and economic backwardness arising out of historical customs of untouchability.[34]

But it is also true that originally, it was the British Government which in 1935-6, introduced 'religion' as a criterion and debarred the

Christians of Scheduled Caste origin from getting the concessions and facilities available to members of other religions of Scheduled Caste origin. The same basis was used to debar Dalit Christians from these concessions and facilities in 1950 when the Presidential Order was promulgated. Until 1947, Christians in general enjoyed minority rights. But then three Christians belonging to dominant background, who happened to be members of the Constituent Assembly, became satisfied with the fundamental rights and because of that action, Christians in India forever lost their basic minority rights for which the Dalit Christians had to pay later the price of their decision. Because now the Dalit Christians neither have full fundamental rights nor other civil rights (as seen in section 7.1.3), as a result of which, they had to continue to suffer all the discriminations, in spite of the fact that a number of arguments have been put forward by different individuals and commissions in their favour, which we will see in the next section.

7.3. Struggle for their Civil Rights

The nature and size of the Dalit Christian issue or problem have become very clear from the discussion, which we had in this chapter. The Dalit Christians' issue as stands today and is seen in section 7.1, is much more serious and three times bigger as compared to their fellow Dalits belonging to Hinduism, Sikhism and Buddhism. They share the general disabilities along with other Dalits in the areas of social, economic and political. These disabilities are recognized in the Constitution in Article 46 and to deal with them, provisions are also provided in Articles 330, 332 and 338. But these provisions will be applicable only to those Dalits who will enjoy the status of 'Scheduled Castes' under the Presidential Order, 1950. In the beginning, these rights were given only to the Dalit Hindus but later, the Parliament through amendments in 1956 and 1990, extended the same to the Dalit Sikhs and Dalit Buddhists. To understand this point more clearly and the kind of responses we had from different official sources, we will refer here to one of the well-known legal cases of a Dalit Christian and some of the arguments offered and their affects, which took place in the Parliament at the time of the second amendment of the Presidential Order, 1950.

7.3.1. *Supreme Court on Soosai Case*

A Dalit Christian, by profession a cobbler, Soosai, challenged the validity of the discriminatory Presidential Order, 1950 on the basis of religion. His case went to the highest court of the country. While dismissing his writ petition on 30 September 1986, the Division Bench of the Supreme Court of India consisting of the Chief Justice P.N. Bhagwati, Justice P.S. Pathak and Justice A.N. Sen made the following remarks:

> It is not sufficient to show that the same caste continues after conversion. It is necessary to establish further that the disabilities and handicaps suffered from membership of such caste membership in the social order of its origin-Hinduism continue in their oppressive severity in the new environment of a different religious community.[35] [*The discussions of section 7.1.1, 7.1.2 and 7.1.3) proves very clearly that the Dalit Christians suffer the same 'disabilities and handicaps' which their fellow Dalits belonging to other religions are having.*]

7.3.2. *Parliament Debate on the Dalit Christian Issue*

The case of the Dalit Christians was also debated during the summer session of Parliament (May 1990), when the last amendment was made to the Presidential Order, 1950. A number of members, both Christians and those belonging to other faiths, argued in favour of the Dalit Christians. During the discussion, two main points were raised against the Christian Dalits. *First*, as to why the Dalit Christians should not be given equal rights. In this regard, Uma Bharati argued: 'Point of Order. Dividing the Christians into Harijan Christians and high-caste Christians, I think the hon. member has to ask the permission of John Pope Paul. He does not divide Christians into Harijan Christians and Savarna Christians, all are equal. What the hon. member is saying is against the Christian religions (interruptions).'[36] *Second*, as to why a Buddhist Dalit should be granted equal rights, Kalka Das said: 'Had he not understood the importance of Buddhism, its Indian identity and its inseparable links with Hinduism, he (Ambedkar) could have embraced Islam or Christianity, but he did not turn to any foreign religion.'[37]

Finally, at the end of May 1990 debate, Parliament once again could not extend equal rights to the Dalit Christians. What is the implication of this act of Parliament? First, it means that Dalit Christians continue to lose one of their most important fundamental rights which prohibit any kind of discrimination on the basis of religion which has been stated in Article 15 of the Constitution (*see for details, discussion in section* 7.1.3).

7.3.3. *Change of Religion does not Change Social and Economic Status*

Already reference has been made to debate, which took place in the Parliament, but in that debate, the views expressed was only of one political group (rightist). There were other views, which were also expressed at the time of the second amendment in 1990. For example, regarding the criterion, used to decide the status of Dalits as 'scheduled caste' the point made by Shri Ram Vilas Paswan in 1990 needs to be noted. Shri Paswan, who was then the Union Minister for Labour and Welfare, made the remark while stating the object and reasons for proposing to include Buddhist of Scheduled Caste origin in 'the list of Scheduled Castes'. He said:

> 'Neo-Buddhists are a religious group which has come into existence in 1956 as a result of a wave of conversions of the Scheduled Castes under the leadership of Dr. Babasaheb Ambedkar. Upon conversion to Buddhism, they become ineligible for Statutory concessions....Various demands have been made, for extending all the concessions and facilities available to Scheduled Castes to them also on the ground that *change of religion has not altered their social and economic conditions*. As they objectively and deserve to be treated as the Scheduled Castes for the purpose of various reservations, it is supposed to amend the Presidential Order to include them therein.[38]

The important point here is Shri Paswan's statement need to be noted is that the amendment of 1990 to the Presidential Order, 1950 has now changed the criterion about religion, which very clearly has stated 'that the change of religion' does not alter 'social and economic conditions'.

7.3.4. *Other Views on Rights of Dalit Christians*

The fact that change of religion has not changed the socio-economic and educational status of the Dalit Christians has been proved by the number of Commissions appointed by the Government and by the Judiciary. Some of the extracts from some of the documents which give the views of some Commissions and Judiciary on this issue are given here for ready reference. These also very clearly prove that the Christians of Scheduled Caste origin continue to suffer the socio-economic and other discrimination, even after their conversion to Christian religion. These views are:

Prof. Madhu Dandavate, while expressing his views before the Mandal Commission (1980) stated that conversion from one faith to another did not change the socio-economic status of a person. It was, therefore, desirable that converts from Scheduled Castes to Buddhism, etc., should be treated as Scheduled Castes. Similar is the situation among Indian Christians 'Christians in Kerala are divided into various denominations on the basis of beliefs and rituals and into various ethnic groups on the basis of their caste backgrounds… even after conversion, the lower caste converts were continued to be treated as Harijans by all sections of the society including the Syrian Christians.'[39]

In 1980, the Minorities Commission on its report also stated, 'The Commission has *prima facie* felt that since the Christians, Muslims and Buddhist of Scheduled Caste origin continue to suffer from social and economic disabilities even after conversion, there should be no objection to their availing of the concessions admissible to them before conversion'.[40]

Supreme Court through the 9 Bench Judge Majority Judgement in the Mandal case with regard to Christians, categorically established the fact that change of religion doesn't change caste disabilities of the Scheduled Caste and it continues after conversion. This view is supported by 8 of the 9 judges. A relevant passage from the judgement reads as:

> Though Christianity also does not recognize caste system, there are upper and lower castes among Christians. In Goa, for example, there are upper castes Catholic Brahmins who do not marry Christians of lower castes. In many Churches, the low caste Christians have to sit apart from the high caste Christians. In Andhra Pradesh, there are Christian Harijans, Christian Malas, Christian Reddys, Christian Kammas, etc. In Tamil Nadu, converts to Christianity from Scheduled Castes-Latin Catholics, Christian Shanars and Christian Gramani are in the list of Scheduled Castes. Such instances are many and vary from region to region.[41]

A recent response to the Dalit Christian issue is referred here, which represents in real sense the response of a civil society. This response came in the form of a public interest litigation filed in the Supreme Court of India by 'Centre for Public Interest Litigation' through its General Secretary and Mr T. Franklin Caesar on 22 March 2004. Here below the section are related to the grounds on which this petition was made and what it has asked from the Hon'ble Court are quoted, which in fact, represent the summary of the discussion of this article:

Ground

(A) The Constitution (Scheduled Castes) Order 1950, as amended is discriminatory and volatile of Articles 14 and 15 of the Constitution in as much as it discriminates against Scheduled Caste converts to religion other than the Hindu, Sikh and Buddhist religions. It is submitted that the social and economic disabilities of Scheduled Caste converts to Christianity continue to persist in most cases even after their conversion. In this conversion, there cannot be any distinction between Scheduled Castes converts to Sikh and Buddhist religions and Scheduled Caste converts to the Christian religion. It is submitted that the theory that Christianity does not recognize castes cannot be a valid justification for excluding Christians from this, since in theory, even Sikhism and Buddhism do not recognize castes. The Discrimination is also clear from the fact that Scheduled Tribe convert to Christianity continue to remain within the preview of the Scheduled Caste Order 1950, while Scheduled Caste converts to Christianity are denied this benefit.

(B) The denial of benefits to Scheduled Caste converts to Christianity in the matter of reservation of jobs, political reservation and other benefits extended to the Scheduled Caste in general caste, is discriminatory and violates their Fundamental Rights guaranteed by Articles 14 and 15 of the Constitution. It is submitted that since the social and economic disabilities suffered by Scheduled Castes person in most cases do not cease even after their conversion to Christianity, such conversion cannot be a legal and constitutional basis for denying them the benefits available to other Scheduled Caste persons. It is submitted that the petitioners have not filed any other similar petition before this Hon'ble Court of the country.

Prayer

It is therefore, respectfully prayed that this Court may be please to:

(A) Allow this petition and declare unconstitutional and void, clause 3 of the Constitution (Scheduled Castes) order 1950, and
(B) Declare as unconstitutional and void, the denial of the reservation of the benefits to Scheduled Castes converts to Christianity in respect of reservation of jobs, political reservation and other benefits given to Scheduled Castes persons under the various laws and notification in the country and,
(C) Pass any other orders, as this Court may deem fit and proper in the facts and circumstances of this case.[42]

The case in the Court is still going on. The verdict of the Court either once again may go against the Dalit Christians or it may go in favour of them. This only time will tell.

7.4. Conclusion

As the discussion and analysis of Dalit Christians issue as well as the implication of the Presidential Order, 1950 are very clear in this Article, but still in the concluding remarks in order to sum our discussion by making few important observations will not be out of place. These observations are:

First observation is about the general discrimination and disabilities as discussed in section 3, which are faced by all Dalits in India. In the case of Dalit Christians, the evidences based on empirical studies and surveys given in section 7.1.1, two incidents referred in section 7.1.3 and the various views given in section 7.3.4 very clearly state that they also suffer all the disabilities and discriminations which their fellow Dalits belonging to other religions are having.

Second observation is related to the constitutional Fundamental Rights, which are granted to all the citizens in Articles 14, 15, 21 and 25, but in the case of Dalit Christians, these rights are directly violated on the basis of the Presidential Order, 1950. These rights include, right of equality before the law, discrimination on the basis of religion, right to life and right to freedom. The discussion of section 7.1.3 has fully spelt out the reasons behind these violations and even it has revealed that besides the four Fundamental Rights, the Dalit Christians are also denied those rights, which are granted to their fellow Dalits belonging to other religions in Articles 330, 332, 335 and 338 concerning jobs, education and share in the governance of the country.

Third observation is concerning the expression 'Scheduled Caste', which as seen in section 7.2, first time was used by the Simon Commission between 1929 and 1932. The Simon Commission used this expression for all the 'Depressed Classes' without differentiating on the basis of religion. But later, it was used exclusively for the Hindu untouchables, but then their counterparts belonging to Christian and Muslim religions were given all the special benefits including separate electoral rights as part of their minority rights. The same position was stated in the Government of India Act 1935, which after the independence in 1947, the Indian Government also copied, but it did not give the special benefits to Dalit Christians. To make this correction, the Government of India for the use of 'Scheduled Castes' expression will either have to go back to its original position of 1929 to 1932 by removing the third paragraph of the Presidential Order, 1950, in which religion has been used as criterion to define 'Scheduled Castes' or it has to give all the special benefits to Dalit Christians, which have been given to their fellow Dalits belonging to the Hindu, Sikh and Buddhist religions as were given in the Government of India Act 1935.

Fourth and final point about the Dalit Christian, we need to note is, the way they are treated within their own Christian Community, proves that they are gone into a deeper captivity. They still far away from their whole liberation or salvation. It is to this the Dalit theology has to lead to them finally.

NOTES

1. See for detailed discussion: James Massey, *Dalits in India, Religion as a Source of Bondage or Liberation with Special Reference to Christians*, Manohar, New Delhi, 1995, pp. 21-39.
2. See for further information: Arthur Coke Burnell (tr.): 'The Ordinance of Many', Motilal Banarsidass, New Delhi, 1971, p. 312.
3. Vidya Sagar, 'The Christian Community in Panjab: An Analogy',

in *Religion and Society*, vol. XXXVIII, no. 2, June 1991, Bangalore, pp. 30-35.

4. Jose Kannanaikil, *Scheduled Caste Converts and Social Disabilities*, Indian Social Institute, New Delhi, 1990, p. 8.
5. Ibid., p. 33.
6. Sagar, op. cit., pp. 14, 15. Also see: C.O. MacMullen et al., The Amritsar Diocese: A Preliminary Survey, Baring Union Christian College, Batala, 1973, pp. 40, 41.
7. Letter of Paul to the Galatians (NRSV), 3: 28.
8. Quoted in Editorial: The Examiner (*The Catholic News Review*), 143/3. 18 January.
9. S. Lourduswamy, *Towards Empowerment of Dalit Christians, Equal Rights to all Dalits*, CDS, New Delhi, 2005, p. 30.
10. Ibid., p. 63.
11. Minutes of the 12th Ordinary Synod Meeting of the Church of North India held from 16- 21 October, 2005, Ranchi, p. 361.
12. *The Constitution of India* (as on the 1st January, 2000), Government of India, New Delhi, p. 6.
13. The Scheduled Caste and Scheduled Tribes (Prevention of Atrocities Act, 1989 (no. 33 of 1989) and The Protection of Civil Rights Act 1955 (72 of 1955) with short notes, Lucknow, 1990, p. 11.
14. Ibid., p. 23.
15. Ibid., p. 3.
16. Kande Prasada Rao, *Freedom of Religion for Harijan in India*, Vijaya Printers, Ongole, 1990, pp. 17- 19.
17. See for details XVIII Biennial Council Meeting, Hyderabad, 22- 24 January 1992, Christian Institute for the Study of Religion and Society and Joint Programmes, pp. 40-3.
18. *Indian Express*, 2 December 1992, Madras, p. 9.
19. Kande Prasada Rao, op. cit., p. 18.
20. *The Constitution of India*, op. cit., p. 9.
21. Ibid., p. 6.
22. Louise Ouwerkerk, *The Untouchables of India*, Oxford University Press, London, 1945, pp. 40-1.
23. See for details: *Karnataka Backward Classes Commission, Government of Karnataka Report*, vol. 1, pt. 1, 1975, pp. 55-8.
24. Harold R. Isaacs, India's Ex-Untouchables, Asian Publishing House, Bombay, 1965, p. 36.
25. Ibid.
26. Ibid., pp. 39-41.

27. Ouwerkerk, op. cit., p. 41.
28. Marc Galanter, 'Competing Equalities: Law and the Backward Classes in India', Oxford University Press, Bombay, 1984, p. 143.
29. Cited in *Karnataka Backward Classes Commission Report*, op. cit., p. 60.
30. *The Constitution of India*, op. cit., p. 160.
31. Ibid., p. 143.
32. Ibid., p. 160.
33. See Galanter, op. cit., p. 132.
34. Stephen Fuchs, *At the Bottom of Indian Scoiety*, Munshiram Manoharlal, New Delhi, 1981, p. 2.
35. Text of Judgement: Soosai Case given in S. Lourduswamy: op. cit., p. 147.
36. Jose Kananaikil, 'Scheduled Castes Converts in Search of Justice, Constitution (Schedules Castes), Orders (Amendment) Bill', 1990, p. 5.
37. Ibid., p. 17.
38. Taken from the proposed text of The Constitutional (Scheduled Castes) Order (Amendment) Bill, 1990.
39. *Report of the Backward Classes Commission*, Government of India, vols. I & II, pt. 1, 1980, p. 46.
40. *Third Annual Report of the Minorities Commission*, New Delhi, 1980, p. 31.
41. Article 477, Mandal Case Judgement, vol. 6, no. 9, Nov. 1992, Judgement Today.
42. From the text of Writ Petition no. 180 of 2004 in the Supreme Court of India, quoted in Lourduswamy, op. cit., pp. 172, 173.

PART 4

MULTI-RELIGIOUS APPROACH

CHAPTER 8

Historico-Religious Traditions

8.1. Inclusive Approach

First, the 'Dalit Issue' taken in this section is inclusive, because it embraces the experience of all the Dalits numbering about 250 million belonging to all the major living faiths, which include Hinduism, Islam, Sikhism, Buddhism and Christianity.

Second, because it is inclusive in nature, therefore for its search of Dalit heritage it does not depend on one particular source or text, instead it goes even beyond the origin of the so called 'great traditions' and search for these in all the possible texts. For example, in this chapter reference will be made to the contributions of a Dalit Hindu saint Ravidas, a Dalit Muslim saint Kabir and a Hindu Sudra saint Jotirao Phule. In sub-section four on 'Faith Traditions' reflection includes my personnel Christian experience.

Third, the discussion of this chapter is based upon a broad based theme 'Historico-Religious Traditions'. The subsequent discussion of this chapter will be carried under the following four sub-heads: Historical Traditions, Religious Traditions, Spiritual Traditions and Faith Traditions.

8.2. Historical Traditions

In this chapter the discussion is limited to the 'Dalit traditions'. But we will not use the standard dictionary meaning ('the handling down of statements, beliefs, legends, customs, etc., from generation to generation esp. by mouth or practice'[1]), because very little in that sense is left behind either written or oral by the forebears of the Dalits. What is available in writing is what is left mostly by their rivals in some odd forms, which now is being researched, reconstructed and re-interpreted by the Dalits as well as non-Dalit activists. In this process a number of Dalit traditions are uncovered, which not only throw light on the lost human identity of the Dalits, but also reveals that once upon a time, they owned a most developed civilization, to which the twentieth century historians and archaeologists have referred to as 'Indus Valley Civilization'.[2] (*See for detail discussion chapter 2 of this work.*)

Today a large number of Dalit and non-Dalit scholars have also accepted that well-civilized people were living in the cities of Harappa and Mohenjodaro before 1500 BC, who were part of the Indus Valley civilization. These cities had spacious streets, market places and godowns.[3]

It is true the unearthed and re-discovered story of the Indus Valley Civilization tells us that it had indigenous origin and the people who inhabited it belonged to a pre-Aryan race. But a question may be asked if these pre-Aryan people were today's Dalits. Based upon the existing traditions, historical data and archaeological sources, a good number of scholars have looked into this question of 'Dalits' as being indigenous people and have an affirmative answer.[4] (*See for detail answer in section 3.4 of this work.*)

So the earliest historical traditions revealed that Dalits once had a glorious past and were living with full human dignity and also they represent one of the sections of the indigenous settlers of India. But although their opponents made all efforts to destroy their humanity, still they could not succeed fully. To make this point clear, we will refer to the two stories, which are narrated in the two great Hindu epics, *Ramayana* (fifth century BC) and *Mahabharata* (600 BC-AD 500).[5]

The first story is told by Valmiki, the author of *Ramayana* who reveals, how far Sudras (the fourth caste), had became degraded (not to speak of the Dalit or outcaste). According to this story, in Lord Rama's time only the three upper castes were allowed to do *tapasya* (penance and meditation). Yet a Sudra undertook penance in order to attain divinity, as a result of which, a Brahman boy of 15 years died. The bereaved father complained to Lord Rama, who after learning the cause of the death, went in search of the Sudra. On meeting him, Lord Rama said to him:

> You are indeed blessed. Tell me in which caste you have been born. I am Rama, son of Dasaratha. Out of curiosity I have asked you this question. Tell

me the truth. Are you a Brahman, Ksatriya or a Sudra? The ascetic replied, 'O King! I am born of Sudra caste. I want to attain divinity by such penance. When I want to attain divinity I won't tell lies. I am a Sudra by caste, and my name is Samvuka.' As soon as the ascetic uttered those words, Rama drew forth his sword and severed Samvuka's head.[6]

In the continuing narrative it is said that Lord Rama asked the gods to restore the Brahman boy to life and he was told that he had already been revived the moment the Sudra ascetic was killed. But it was Sudra's yearning for divinity and his being truthful that led him to be murdered.

In the *Mahabharata* also there is a reference to the degraded state of the Dalits. The story of Eklavya, an indigenous boy, tells us how he had to lose his 'right hand thumb' because he had learned archery and was in no way inferior to Arjuna in his skill.[7] Again the main point of the story is how at the time of *Mahabharata* low castes or the Dalits did not have even the basic right to education or attain any skill, but still Eklavya represents a Dalit's power of humanity by the use of which he could supersede, the so called Ksatriya warrior Arjuna.

8.3. Religious Traditions

About the existence of Dalit religious traditions, even the oldest Hindu religious literary source *Rigveda*, bears testimony to the fact that the Dalits had their own laws to govern their religious life, which as expected, the Aryans regarded as 'alien laws'.[8] However, we do find remnants of Dalit religious traditions of which some forms have been preserved by the Dalits in different parts of India. The traditional scholars of religion have labelled the religious traditions of the Dalits as 'little traditions' and those of their opponents, the Aryans as 'great traditions'.[9]

The roots of Dalit religious traditions lie in the veneration of nature, earth, water, trees and animals, etc. In contrast to the so called great religious traditions who worship in a temple or in a building, the Dalits practise corporate worship in an open space. For instance, in my village Zafferwal (Panjab), the Dalits worship a human-made dome shaped mound of earth, called *Bala Shah*. This mound faces east and is placed under a tree or on an open spot with an earthen lamp (*diya*) burning over it and also a red flag on top of it. On an auspicious day, the devotees worship here with their offering. Burning lamp and the red flag are for security from all kinds of evil forces.[10]

The other example which I want to refer to is of a song sung by a Dalit community of Pulayas in North Malabar (Kerala), which they use from ancient times to worship a god named Pottan Teyyam. This song is known as 'Toṭṭom (song) of Pottan Teyyam'. This song contains a very powerful message against the practice of untouchability and caste discrimination. It also affirms the basic human equality. Presently this song has two versions: a Dalit (Pulaya) version and non-Dalit *(Brahminized)* version. The later version came into existence during eleventh century as part of the assimilating process of the so-called upper caste. Today both the versions are available in a long poems' form. Both the poems follow dialogue between a Dalit character and a non-Dalit character. In the Dalit version these characters are Chinna Pulayan (a little Dalit) and Chovar, a Sudra. From the Dalit version, here a passage is given, which not only offers a criticism against religious beliefs and practices, but also brings the message how all the human beings belonging to different groups (even so called castes) are same and equal. This passage reads thus:

Why you Chovar quarrel over caste?
Suppose Chovar and we break a coconut
Shan't we find inside the same kernel?
The knives of the Chovar are sharp
And also are our knives
When you are wounded blood comes out
When we are wounded blood comes out
Why you Chovar quarrel over caste?.[11]

Besides the remnants of ancient Dalit religious traditions, a great number of Dalit liberative traditions are available from the fifteenth century onwards from which a large majority can be listed under religious traditions. Some of these are in literary form and some represent the spirituality of the Dalits. We have labelled them as 'spiritual traditions' in the sense of 'Dalit spirituality', which actually is the 'spirituality of liberation'. Some of these I will briefly reflect upon.

8.4. Spiritual Traditions

8.4.1. *Dalit Bhakti Saints*

(a) God in the beginning created Light all human beings belong to Him.
Since from one Light is the whole world created, Here who is noble or who is inferior?[12]

(b) You considered upper caste! well-known is my cobbler's caste.
But still in my heart, I continue to praise my Lord.
You should know even the wine made with sacred Ganga water, the real devotees will not drink.
Even after impure liquids, if gets mixed up with the sacred Ganga water, is not different from it.
The Tar tree is considered impure.
So also the paper (made from it) is considered such.
But when words of the Lord's devotion over it are printed, it is worshipped and bowed to.
People of my caste are hide-beaters and binders, carrying dead animals around Banaras.
Yet upper caste Brahmins to me make obeisance.
As Ravidas, Thy servant with Thy Name has taken shelter.[13]

In Panjabi language there is a saying, *'Jis tan lage, soi jane'* (the real pain is known by the victim). The two examples given above reflect the harsh truths of Dalit spirituality and the anguish felt by saints and poets as Dalits.

The two passages are quoted from Sikh scripture *Guru Granth Sahib*. The first passage is written by a Dalit Muslim saint, Kabir, who has boldly declared that all human beings are equal as they share one source or origin (Light). Therefore he asked, 'who is noble or who is inferior?'

The second passage represents a testimony of a Dalit conscience in the middle ages, that of a Dalit Hindu saint Ravidas, whose spirituality even the Brahmins respected. His poetry clearly shows that the Brahmins respected him and therefore attempted to elevate his status in the hierarchy though on their own terms. This is reflected in the line: 'Yet upper caste Brahmins to me make obeisance.' The reason for this was because Ravidas' relationship with God had been set right.

8.4.2. *Mahatma Jotirao Phule*

Phule's major contribution to Dalit theological thoughts we find in his interpretation of the personhood of Jesus Christ by linking his coming into this world as part of the fulfilment of the oldest Dalit legend based prophecy, which reached us through a folk song sung by the women of Maharashtra, which has the following opening sentence in Martathi: *'Ida pida jao anni Balliche rajya yeo'* which means 'let all troubles and misery go, and the kingdom of Bali come'. Phule saw in Jesus Christ, the second coming of Baliraja, who according the legend was the most righteous non-Aryan King. He ruled a large part of ancient India at the time of Aryan's coming to India.[14] Phule's own words about this read as follow:

Thus the prophecy of our venerable old ladies

> May Bali's Kingdom Come'! seems to have materialized (partially). When Baliraja (Jesus Christ) was crucified by a few wicked desperadoes a great moment of liberation was set in motion in Europe, and crores of people became his followers (embraced his teachings) and he strove ceaselessly to establish His Kingdom on earth in consonance with the dictates of our creator.[15]

But before moving to any discussion, we may have to briefly narrate the Baliraja's story (legend), which will also introduce to us his personhood and characteristics, because of which Phule saw Baliraja's second coming in Jesus Christ.

If one reads Phule's work, one will see that Baliraja and his second coming in Jesus Christ is one of the main themes of his works. After introducing in part one to five, who are the Aryans and their origin, he gave details of their coming to India and their battle with Baliraja, in parts five to nine. In part six he tells about the extent of Baliraja's Kingdom. According to Phule, beside his rule in the whole of western India and part of today's north India up to Ayodhya and Kashi (Banaras), it was also 'spread over wide areas of other parts of India'. He also adds: 'It may be conjectured that he controlled some islands round about Ceylon (i.e. in South-East Asia) one of the islands was "Bali" (in Malaysia)'.[16]

About the Baliraja's righteousness and truthfulness, according to Phule, he never attacked his enemy from the back, 'he always hit them on their fronts or faces. Hence, he came to be known as "hitter on the front (mouth)"...He was a friend of the downtrodden. He was fond of music also.'[17]

How Baliraja's end came? Phule narrates a legend in this regard, according to which it was Adi-narayan (Aryan supreme God) who got incarnated and took the form of a poor and short Brahmin (priest). Waman in order to banish Baliraja into the nether world, appeared before Baliraja as a poor beggar and asked him the gift of three steps (of the earth). He knew Baliraja was very kind and compassionate in heart, who will never say 'no' to the needy and the poor. So according to his nature, Baliraja told Waman to take three steps from anywhere in his kingdom. At that moment the size of the wicked Waman increased and reached to the skies, so much so by his first step, he could cover the whole earth and by his second step the whole sea, then he asked Baliraja, where he should put his third step. He made Baliraja helpless, but then Baliraja offered his own head for Waman's third step. At that moment the treacherous Waman after putting his step on Baliraja's head, pressed him down to the nether word. This is how the end came of a righteous king Baliraja, about whom the Marathi Dalit women pray 'May Bali's Kingdom come'![18]

About the second coming of Baliraja in Jesus Christ and about the fulfilment of the prophecy of old ladies and its purpose, Phule says:

> The universal Creator of us all and our universal Father the Almighty God – so ordained that the sacred knowledge of the Truth and human rights that he generously bestowed on us all should be enjoyed by us all in amity and harmony. To translate this desire of the Almighty into reality, Baliraja, the champion of the oppressed, the holy, the repository of the wisdom, and always spoke the truth—manifested himself on this earth after a few years. He undertook the great mission of emancipating his depressed, oppressed and weak brethrens from the trammels of the treacherous, wicked and cunning ensnarers—the Bhats (Brahmins)—and strove to establish the 'Kingdom of God' in this land of ours.[19]

First part of this passage is already quoted earlier. Phule says here that it is in Jesus Christ that Baliraja has come again to establish God's Kingdom on this earth and here he added 'in this land of ours' means India. Phule also has seen the Christian missionaries' work in India as actualization of the mandate to preach 'the true teaching of their Messiah'.[20]

8.5. Faith Traditions

The Faith traditions to which I am going to refer now are common to all of us. In my case, I am a third generation Christian to receive these, because my grandfather, the late Mr. Bhagh Singh became a Christian at the beginning of twentieth century. I still remember my father, the late Rev. Jalal Masih (22 March 1907-18 September 1980) used to gather all our family members to read the Bible everyday followed by singing Psalms in Panjabi and followed by prayer by my father or mother (the late Mrs. Fazl Bibi, died 26 March 1983) and to end with Lord's prayer said by all the members of the family. I continued to take part in the family gathering till the age of twenty-one, then I went for higher studies to university, where I lived in different hostels. But the practice of reading the Bible and saying prayer every morning continues till today. The practice of my Bible reading today has taken other forms, like reading the Bible from the perspective of the Dalits.

Secondly, the 'faith traditions' instill in us the 'faith commitment', which in truth is not only the proof of an authentic believer, but it is the first requirement or step to enter into the process of doing theology from any of subaltern perspectives including the 'Dalit'. In the case of a Dalit theologian, he or she has to bring into the process a personal commitment, on one side with God and on other side with (fellow) Dalits and the world around (which needs transformation). Now this personal commitment is not possible without getting grounded in one's 'faith traditions' and in the various 'Dalit traditions'. But then these faith traditions we inherit from our parents (the family) and the communities called the Church and the society in which we move, live, think, worship and act.

One main source of our faith traditions is the Scripture, in my case the Bible, which also needs the same personal commitment. When we read it, it actually gives us a perspective to read the Text. Once this happens even our way of reading the Text also changes and we will not only start perceiving new meaning of the Text and its relevance to our specific context, but also start perceiving the Word getting incarnated in that context and finally becoming a liberative force for bringing about a change in the given context. (*See detailed discussion on 'Biblical Models of Liberation'*, in chapters 9-11 of this work.)

Now how this happens? I will answer this question by giving an example of my personal experience of reading the Text while working on the commentary of the Gospel according to Luke.

While reading the text of Luke, I found myself dialoguing with him. Sometimes instead of dialoging with Luke, I suddenly found myself in dialogue with some of the characters of his Gospel. These characters sometimes help me to perceive the meaning of phrases and words. But in these dialogues, I always tried not to lose myself and the situation of my people, the Dalits. These dialogues sometimes take the form of hopping flights and I find myself journeying between two worlds that of Luke and the biblical world, and of Dalit. The purpose of these hopping flights is to search for the meeting points or relevance between the two worlds. In the process many times I was directed by one text to another to perceive the intended meaning of the text and to see its relevance to the world of the Dalits. Here an example of such a dialogue which I experienced while reading Luke 22:8-30, to this experience the title given is 'Self Gift as Foundation of a New Community':

By the time Jesus reached Jerusalem, he was about 33 years old. In Jerusalem before his arrest, Jesus did two key things: *one*, he introduced a new way of resistance (19:28-22:1-6; 22:31-71; 23:1-56) and *two*, he laid down the foundation of a new community (21:1-4; 22:7-30). The process of a new community was begun through education and mobilization. The selection of the twelve apostles was a very concrete step towards the foundation of a new community (6:12-16). But his real intention behind this action becomes clear with his creation of the institution of the Lord's Supper (22:4-23). Historical background of this institution was the festival of Passover, which was related to the liberation of Israelites from the house of slavery in Egypt. This festival was the day of remembrance and also of passing on of information to their children, of their slavery and of their liberation (Ex 12:1-28; 13:3-10).

With full care all preparations for the Passover meal, which was to take place over the sacrificial Passover lamb, were made (vv 7-13). The Passover meal was usually eaten with the immediate kin (Ex 12:3-4). But Jesus was going to eat the Passover with his disciples (v 11), an event from which a new faith based community was going to take form.

Jesus reinterpreted the Passover meal in terms of his impending death and the coming of God's kingdom. In verse 14, the 'hour' refers to the beginning of the Passover, but it also anticipates the appointed hour of Jesus' arrest (22:53). Similarly in verse 15 'suffering' refers to Jesus' death (24:46).

Jesus also declares this Passover meal to be the last till the coming of the kingdom of God (22:16-18). Two elements 'a loaf' and 'cup' represent the 'body and 'blood' of Jesus, which were 'given' and 'poured' respectively on behalf of those who will partake of these elements. The expression 'remembrance' points towards the continuity of this practice in future (v 19) and the expression 'new covenant' refers to the fact that it is going to replace the old covenant, which was sealed with the blood of an animal (Ex 24: 3-8); but this new covenant was going to be sealed with the blood of Jesus. Sharing a piece of a broken bread indicates the fact that those who were going to share that one bread, representing Jesus' own body, were to become part of one body. In the same way those who were going to drink from the one cup, representing Jesus' blood, were going to become blood relations from that moment onwards. Here all kinds of social divisions based upon any racial, ethnic or caste system was going to come to an end; in fact every person who eats the broken bread and drinks from *one* cup, becomes part of the new covenant, meaning that person enters into a new relationship with God and with the fellow human beings without taking into account any kind of social, cultural, economic and ethnic differences. This is what the expression 'new covenant' means....[21]

This is one example of reading the Text from the Dalit perspective. But a similar experience I have every morning at the time of my brief personal devotion and reading of the Text.

8.6. Conclusion

I want to close this chapter, with two concluding remarks:

My First remark is about the Dalit traditions. In brief the historical and religious traditions reveal to us that the Dalits once were also full human beings—enjoying all the benefits of a normal human being. They had their own religious and social rules to govern their life. This is what we learn from the Dalit religious traditions. But the main point which these traditions reveal is how the opponents of the Dalits made efforts to separate the Dalits from other human beings on one side and on other side to sever their relations with God. But then our reflection on 'spiritual traditions', we also saw, how the early Dalit saints like Ravidas sought to re-establish the relationship of their community with God. All the movements of conversion to Christianity and other religions grew out of this quest.

Phule's seeing the righteous king Bali's second coming in

Jesus Christ according to the plan of Father the Almighty God to emancipate (liberate) the depressed and oppressed from the yoke of the caste system, and his seeing Jesus Christ and his coming as the second coming of King Bali as a 'refuge' and emancipating source for the Dalits, are part of the laying down of the foundation of doing theology from the Dalit perspective.

The last and final remark is based on the Dalit traditions particularly the 'faith traditions', which directly lead to the process of doing theology from the Dalit perspective. Because as held by the theologians of various liberation theologies that the 'theology' is a critical reflection on the relationship of God and human beings in different historical circumstances—we can trace the roots of Dalit theology back to the very dawn of the history of the Dalits. By looking into the contents of the Dalit traditions, we not only come to know the lost human identity, but also the truth that, it is the Dalits of Indian society, who represents the undivided humanity of the created world. Dalit theology's role includes enabling them to recover this original state of theirs, which their opponents tried intentionally to destroy.

NOTES

1. Webster's *Encyclopedic Unabridged Dictionary of the English*, Gramercy Books, New York/Avenel, 1994, p. 1502.
2. James Massey, *Roots: Concise History of Dalits*, CIS, New Delhi, 2004 (5th edn.), pp. 5-19.
3. M.C. Raj, *Dalitology: The Book of the Dalit People*, REDS, Shantinagar, Tumkur, 2001, p. 98.
4. Suresh Narain Srivastava, *Harijans in Indian Society*, The Upper India Publishing House, Lucknow, 1930, pp. 3, 9-10.
5. Fr. Zacharias, *An Outline of Hinduism*, Ap. Seminary, Alwaye, 1956, pp. 375-6.
6. Makhan Lal Sen (tr), *Ramayana*, Rupa & Co., Calcutta, 1989, pp. 699-702.
7. Jaydal Goyandaka, (ed.), *Srukhipat Mahabharat* (Hindi), Gita Press, Gorakhpur, N.D., pp. 69-72
8. *Rigveda* 10.22.8.
9. Henry H. Presler, *Primitive Religion in India*, CLS, Madras, 1971, pp. 245-6.

10. James Massey, 'Popular Religious Beliefs among Rural and Urban People', in *Popular Religioun in the Punjab Today*, ed. John C.B. Webster, ISPCK, Delhi, 1974, pp. 81-2.
11. Abraham M. Ayrookuzhiel, 'Chinna Pulayan: The Dalit Teacher of Sankaracharya, in *Religions of the Marginalized*, ed. Gnana Robinson, UTC, Bangalore and ISPCK, Delhi, 1998, pp. 24-5.
12. Kabir, *Sri Guru Granth Sahib* (in Panjabi), Sri Damadami Bir, p. 1430, Parkash Bhai Jawahar Singh Kirpal Singh and Kampani, Amritsar, p. 1389.
13. Ravidas, *Sri Guru Granth Sahib*, ibid., p. 1293.
14. Jotirao Govindrao Phule, *Slavery* (in the Civilized British Government under the Cloak of Brahmanism), translated by Prof. P.G. Patil, Education Department, Government of Maharashtra, Bombay, 1991, p. xxx (first introductory essay).
15. Ibid., p. 36.
16. Ibid., pp. 13-15.
17. Ibid., pp. 13-14.
18. Ibid., pp. 20-1.
19. Ibid., p. 36.
20. Ibid., p. 38.
21. James Massey, 'The Gospel according to Luke, New Testament', *Dalit Bible Commentary*, vol. 3, CDS, New Delhi, 2007, pp. 205-6.

CHAPTER 9

Peace, Reconciliation and Justice

9.1. Case Histories

9.1.1. *Andhra couple stoned to death for 'honour'* (The Times of India, *Friday, 28 May 2010)*

NIZAMABAD: Honour killing isn't restricted to north India: a young Reddy girl and her Dalit husband were stoned to death on Wednesday night. Six people, including the parents of Baddam Swapna Reddy (22), were arrested and charged with murder on Thursday. Swapna, belonging to the high-caste Reddy community, married Sunkari Srinivas (28) about three months ago. The couple was found stoned to death on the outskirts of Krishnajiwadi village in Nizamabad. Swapna's father B. Lal Reddy, mother Radha, uncle N. Ram Reddy and three aunts—Yadava, Padma and Shoba—were all booked for murder and under SC/ST Prevention of Atrocities Act. Cops were deployed in the village after locals staged a dharna outside the girl's parents' house on Thursday. According to villagers, Srinivas—who was first married to Savithri and has two daughters Nandini and Harini—met Swapna, fell in love and the two got married at Vemalavada temple in Karimnagar district about three months ago. Srinivas hadn't divorced his first wife but she apparently had no objections to his second marriage. Fearing that their families would not accept their union, the couple began living in Hyderabad after their wedding. Srinivas, a trained computer mechanic, worked with a private firm. Locals said the couple returned to the village on Wednesday and tried to convince the elders in Swapna's family to accept their marriage. The girl's family members were still in a rage. Later in the day, they allegedly descended on Srinivas's house in the village and attacked the couple.

Kamareddy DSP D. Udaykumar Reddy said all the guilty in the double murder would be brought to book. Locals apprehend that those who carried out the crime belonged to the upper caste and hence would get away. 'About 20 members of Swapna's family came barging into our house late last night, dragged them out and lynched them in front of me,' said Savithri, Srinivas's first wife, who is now a witness to the death of her husband and his second wife.

9.1.2. *Dalit Sarpanch ostracized for contesting poll* (The Times of India, 9 *June 2010)*

ROHTAK: Bhoop Singh, a brick kiln worker in Army chief V.K. Singh's village in Bhiwani district, could be walking proud. Afterall, a Scheduled Caste sarpanch is a rarity in this socially conservative, caste-conscious jat belt. But Bhoop Singh now moves sleathily with armed escorts provided by the state administration to protect him from the upper caste community leaders of Bapora village who insist that all major panchayat and zila parishad posts were wrongly reserved for SCs. The upper caste leaders had forced most villagers to boycott Monday's local election and say they won't recognize the lower caste man as the village panchayat head. Soon after Bhoop Singh was elected unopposed on Monday, villager elders held a meeting and issued a fiat ordering residents to ostracize Singh and his family. Villagers said they were told not to talk or have any relations with the family of the new sarpanch. 'We have decided not to keep any relations with his family and we have decided not to acknowledge him as sarpanch of the village,' said Mitersein, a villager. Bhoop Singh could not be reached for comment. A villager said he had not been seen in the village since May 27 after the village elders held a meeting and resolved to boycott the local election.

9.1.3. *Dalit cooks in UP schools spark outrage* (Hindustan Times, *Kanpur*, 16 *July 2010)*

The Uttar Pradesh government directive to state-run schools on employing Dalit cooks has brought into focus the caste tension that prevails even among primary students. In the districts of Kanpur Dehat, Kannauj and Auraiya (all in central UP), an atmosphere of confrontation has been created in 22 primary schools between upper orders and Dalits, with the former refusing to eat what scheduled caste (SC) cooks prepare. The April 24 order says all primary schools having 26-100 students will have to employ two cooks, one of whom must be SC. A school with 101-200 students must have three cooks—one from the general category, one SC, and one from the Other Backward Classes.

A school with 201-300 students has to hire two SC cooks, one from the Other Backward Classes, and one from the general category. Each cook is being paid Rs 1,000 a month. In Kannauj there have been protests on this issue. The parents of upper-caste students assaulted district officials when Sub-Divisional Magistrate Manoj Singhal forced students to have food prepared by an SC woman. Government vehicles were set afire. Looking to arrest trouble, Kannauj District Magistrate Govind Raju NS has cancelled all the appointments of cooks made by village heads. Kanpur Dehat District Magistrate S.K. Tewari has a different take on the issue on the problem in his district. He said, 'People were angry with the local village headman. They prevented their children from going to school as a protest against non-development.' 'The issue was twisted and politicised,' he said.

9.1.4. *Dalit man lynched in Ghaziabad* (Hindustan Times, *Ghaziabad, 3 August 2010)*

A 48 year old Dalit man was lynched by eight men after they suspected he was to taking an animal for slaughtering late Sunday night. The incident took place near Chitora locality of Masoori area near NH 24, police officials said on Monday. Surender Jatav, a resident of Noorpur, was returning home by the side of the Upper Ganga Canal area with his wife and daughter. They were taking along a cow along with them police said. 'Near Chitora area, the victim was obstructed by eight youths at around 6.30 pm. These men questioned him about the ownership and purpose of taking along the animal. The victim did not reply. Thereafter, the accused thrashed the victim and lynched him,' Superintendent of Police (SP) Capt. M.M. Baig said.

Police officials said that the victim had earlier been to jail for suspected cow slaughtering which led the accused to believe that he was taking another cow for slaughtering. The accused later threatened victim's wife and daughter with dire consequences if they tried to inform the police.The accused were reported to be in the age group of 22 to 25 years. The victim's wife later lodged a police complaint stating that her husband was forced by the accused to work as a daily wager in their fields and was killed after he denied their offer. Eight people were named in the FIR while six of them were arrested till late Monday evening, Baig said. A case for murder and other provisions of SC/ST Act was registered at Masoori police station, police said.

9.2. Dalit Perspective

This chapter intends to understand the subject of 'peace, reconciliation and justice' from the perspective of these ex-outcastes or ex-untouchables or those who addressed themselves as 'Dalits'. To clear further this perspective, three more general observations are being offered.

The first observation is with regard to the present state of the Dalits in India. Even to-day different forms of atrocities are on the increase against the Dalits, deliberately perpetuated by the so called upper caste, which include—murder, hurt, rape, kidnapping, abduction, dacoity, robbery, arson, etc. For example, according to a Government Report for the period 1981-6 (six years), atrocities committed against the Dalits were 91,097[1], and the next report covering only three years (1995-97) was 90,925.[2] These atrocities are caste based community violence, which in this sense are structural in nature. Such atrocities are recurring phenomena in rural India owing to the increasing awareness of their rights among the Dalits. Four case histories, which contain incidents of violence against the Dalits during the months of May, June, July and August 2010 are listed in the beginning of this chapter in order to show the kind of structural violence going on against the Dalits even in recent times.

Second observation is related to the nature of peace. The absence of organized violence between major groups or nations is the most common understanding of peace.[3] But at the same there is another meaning, which is more related to the question of justice as against structural violence, because this aspect of peace is not covered by 'negative peace' from which we mean absence of peace. Structural violence is the key to understanding this peace. Because many people today are facing life at extreme poverty, particularly in a country like India.[4] In such situation, there may not be a war, but still life is by no means peaceful. This chapter is concerned with this peace.

The third observation is about the nature of reconciliation, it should be noted that it does not merely apply to good relations in general, but to the doing away of enmity. Reconciliation actually means that the parties being reconciled were formerly were hostile to one another. The prerequisites for such reconciliation are repentance and justice, because without these there can be neither genuine reconciliation nor peace. Then reconciliation actually means the complete removal of the root cause of the enmity. It is in the wider sense in our chaotic world this will happen only, if the rights of those who are living a life of disadvantages, will first be restored and this restoration will be possible only when renewal takes place in life or both individuals as well as the communities. It is because the individual's renewal always becomes the basis of the renewal of a nation to which they belonged. Because once the individuals as well as a nation get renewed, then automatically those who have lost their rights and dignity regain these and it is at this point when the real reconciliation takes place. It is about such peace and reconciliation based upon 'repentance and justice' the focus of discussion is carried out in this chapter.

Four case histories given in section one and the three observations made in this section, very clearly reveal to us that the issue of 'peace and reconciliation', and 'the violence' is as old as human history. But in the case of India this takes the form of structural violence because of the caste based divisions in Indian society. At the same time almost all the religious or faith communities have tried to offer some form of solution to this issue, and the efforts made by them to this end has a long history, when the processes of structural violence begin itself. Here in the remaining discussion of this chapter, we will be looking to some of the approaches, which have come into existence by the efforts made by the various faith communities and their leaders and in section four, we will discuss an alternative approach namely 'holistic approach' to the whole issue of peace, reconciliation and justice. The chapter will conclude with a call for 'united action' all the Faith communities and other for the establishment of a 'just society, based on the principles of 'peace, reconciliation and justice.'

9.3. Already Available Approaches

In this section we will discuss two sets of already available approaches to the issue of 'structural violence and peace' under the sub-headings, 'Early Approaches' and 'More Recent Approaches'.

9.3.1. *Early Approaches*

By looking into the nature of the 'structural violence' against the Dalits in India as revealed in the four case histories in section one, one will find that the roots of this problem are in the *Varna* system or Caste system. This caste system besides creating divisions also gave birth to the principles *of* graded inequalities, fixity of place for each caste or class, and the fixity of occupation for each class or caste.

These principles to be followed strictly and each group has to live according to rules of life prescribed in the holy texts prepared by the Brahmans. If any person (specially belonging to Shudra (serving four caste) and Dalits will break these rules, he was to be punished severely. These penalties included the cutting of body organs, going into exile and even the penalty of death.[5]

It in response to this situation created by the *Varna* system, the earliest alternatives in the form of revolts were initiated by two Kshatriya (second warrior caste) princes, Lord Mahavira (540-468 BC) and Gautam Buddha (563-483 BC), the founders of Jainism and Buddhism respectfully. The main point of Jainism approach was based upon the notion of complete non-violence as against the most violent methods used by the Brahmans (first priestly caste) to control the people in general, and Shudra and Dalits in particular. The Brahmans used all kind of methods to extract wealth from all the people of society .They laid extreme stress on the pleasure of the other world, which was based upon the deeds done in the present life. Even to fulfil the *dharma* (code of conduct), they encouraged peoples to go for wars and kills animals. They had no respect for life. The Jain approach was basically a response to this situation, which they tried to introduce through an extreme form of non-violence, which according to them was the main way to protect every life. But as the Jain approach was not conducive to human existence at that time, so it did not work out well....[6] Also at a later stage, Jains were forced under the influence of Hindu *Varna* system to create their own caste system, which also become a serious hindrance in the implementation of their approach.[7]

The next most important approach to deal with the conflictual situation created by divisive forces of *Varna* system was introduced by Gautama Buddha, who rejected birth-based divisions in society.[8] He ignored the soul theory (transmigration) as prescribed by the Brahmans. He laid stress on the perfect life and conduct in this present world. He also preached the principle of equality by organizing *Sanghas* (Fellowships), in which he welcomed the Shudra, Dalits (Chandalas) and Tribals.[9]

Buddhists' approach to counter the Brahmanic approach of life prescribed both non-violent and violent means. About the violent means, Lord Budhha's teaching was that it can be used as energy, but not as in instrument of oppression. In place of four-fold *Varna* system, the Buddhism preached the *Varna-less* or casteless society, in which the stress was laid upon '*Dhamma* (justice), which essentially focused on the right to life and liberty and its ideal objective was socio-economic equality.'[10] As the Buddhist way of life was becoming more and more acceptable by the people in general especially to Shudras and Dalit therefore the Brahmanical forces opposed and blocked its growth. In fact the time of *Manusmriti* the followers of lord Buddhist were also considered untouchable by the caste people.[11]

After the efforts of Lord Buddha, for the next approach, we have to wait for the saints of Bhakti (Devotion) movements, which begin during the eleventh century AD. According to the *Varna* system thereare three ways for the human salvation, which include *Gyan* (knowledge), *Karma* (goods deeds) and *Dhyan* (reflection). But these ways were the monopoly of the caste *(first* three) Hindus, particularly the Brahmans. But the saints of Bhakti movement questioned the authority of the caste people and introduced *bhakti* (devotion) to God by everyone. Some of the well-known Bhakti saints of this period were Ramanujacharya, Madhvachrya, Ramanand, Vallabhacharya, Tukaram, Meerabai, Guru Nanak Dev, Chaitanya, Namdev, Eknath and Tulsidas. Among the Dalit saints prominent in south India were Chokhamela and Kanaka, who tried to assert their right of spiritual equality. In the north among the well-known Dalit saints were: Kabir and Ravidas. The main emphasis of Bhakti saints was to direct the people to the religious reform particularly of spiritual equality and an equal status before God, but they never question the *Varna* system .Because of which approach also did not become effective in the case of the subaltern fully.[12]

9.3.2. *Some Later Approaches*

There are a number of movements-based approaches, which came into existence during the nineteenth and twentieth centuries as Anti-Brahman movements. For example Mahatma Jotirao Phule (born in 1827), who was from a Shudra caste, believed Shudras and ati-Shudras (Dalits) have common historical roots and the divisions among them have been introduced by their opponents (Aryan Brahmans). In 1873, he started a society named Satyashodhak Samaj with twenty-eight rules to follow. The ninth rule of it, gives the summary of his approach to deal with the problems of Shudras and Anti-Shudras. This rule in the forms of vows read as:

- I will not worship anything except our Creator.
- I will not bring into discredit the pure rights that have been given by our Creator by countenancing either those who through the arrogant assumption in their books, behave as though others were inferior, or those who accept such inferiority.
- I will stop being party to the killing of animals, and will give up alcohol, as far as I can.
- I will hold firmly to my pride in the truth, will help the old, the lame, and the very young in our society , and will strive to give enough education to all our children that they may understand their rights.[13]

Like Mahatma Phule in south India it was Periyar Ramaswami Naicker, who started in 1925 the 'Self-Respect movement' as an anti Brahman movement. He openly opposed the doctrine of God, caste and Brahmanism. His main objective to start the Self-Respect movement was to remove crookedness, jealousy and cruelty and build a society that was natural. According to him, it was natural for a human being to discuss origin of everything and know the cause. A human being is a slave, who refuses to know things.[14]

Space does not allow us to give more examples of the movements, which gave birth to various other similar approaches in different regions of India, but still before moving to the final section on 'Holistic Approach' we will briefly discuss two of the well-known approaches, one, of Mahatma Gandhi and the second, of Dr. B.R. Ambedkar.

9.3.2.1. Mahatma Gandhi's Approach

Mahatma Gandhi's full name was Mohandas Karamchand Gandhi (1869-1948). He belonged to Vaisya *Varna* (third caste in hierarchy). From 1894 to 1915 Gandhi lived in South Africa, where he had a successful career as a political organizer against the whites. There he could unite all Indians; because almost all of them were from his own *Vaisya Varna* (caste). But he could not repeat that experience in India, because of the caste division, for which he himself was the upholder. Anyhow, on his return to India he entered Indian politics as member of the Indian National Congress, which was dominated by caste Hindus. It was only when in 1920 he became the President of the Congress, the issue of untouchability was brought on the agenda of the Congress. In 1922 a sub-committee was appointed to deal with this issue. But it never worked effectively, either because of the lack of funds provided or the leadership involved in it and also there continued to be all along a big gap between precepts and practice.[15]

According to Mahatma Gandhi himself, for Dalits there were three options open: *one*, they can join hands with the British, who will help them, but in this way they will commit a sin against their fellow country people; *two*, they can reject Hinduism, but it was not advisable to reject religion for worldly betterment, nor was it correct that untouchability was a part of Hinduism, and the *third*, alternative was self-help and be self-dependable, for which they should oppose and refuse to deal with those who observed social ostracism, but this needed an organized intelligent effort and a good leader, which Dalits at times did not have.[16]

Gandhi certainly had a firm belief in the *Varna* system, about which he even in a *Gujarati Journal* gave a long statement, which began as follows: '1. I believed that Hindu society has been able to stand, it is because it is founded on the caste system. 2. The seeds of Swaraj (self rule) are to be found in the caste system.... 3. A community which can create the caste system must be said to possess unique power of ogranisation...'.[17] In another place even said: 'I believe that the divisions into *Varna* is based on birth.'[18]

Now if we look carefully to Gandhi's approach, which was basically concerned with the problem of untouchability and its removal, it will become clear to us that his main emphasis was centred around the idea of social reform leading to a religious partial equality. He never touched the area of economic upliftment of the Dalits and he also bitterly opposed the empowerment of the Dalits politically. Also he himself as an orthodox Hindu upheld the *Varna* system, which were the reasons why Dalits never accepted his approach.

9.3.2.2. Dr. B.R. Ambedkar's Approach

Dr. B.R. Ambedkar began his discussion with the definition of the nature of a society, with which he wanted to replace the existing one. For example in one of his observations, he pointed out that in the caste based society, an individual person has no place, where in his proposed society individual is the final end. Also in caste based society a person's relationship with the member of his or her class or with the members of other classes were already fixed, but in his ideal society these relations have to be based on liberty, equality and fraternity. Here the onus on the society was to protect the individual's human rights.[19]

According to Dr. Ambedkar 'the norm or the criterion for judging right and wrong in the modern society is justice'[20] and again 'justice' according to Dr. Ambedkar 'is simply another name for liberty, equality and fraternity'.[21] He has also given the meanings of these expressions, which we need to note to understand the nature of his approach. He divided liberty into two categories namely, 'civil liberty' and 'political liberty'. But he also added that it must be accompanied by following three social conditions: social equality, economic equality and knowledge (education) made available to all. Because in the *Varna* based society all these three social conditions were restricted to a particular *Varnas*.[22] While talking about 'equality', emphasis must be placed on the moral aspect of equality. Because 'moral equality' asserts in ethical value, a belief to be sustained, and recognition of rights to be respected.[23] Concerning the meaning of 'fraternity' Dr. Ambedkar said, 'Fraternity is the name for the disposition of an individual to treat men as the object of reverence and love and the desire to be in unity with the fellow beings.'[24]

So in the above sense 'justice' (based on liberty, equality and fraternity) was the basis of Dr. Ambedkar's approach to an alternative society or 'just society'. Again at the end how to establish a 'just society', he was very clear. *Varna* system was the basis of the existing Indian social order and it was this system, which was responsible for all the evils in the existing Indian society. Therefore according to him this system must be destroyed. But he was also very clear that 'it is not possible to break caste without annihilating the religious notions on what it, the caste system, is founded.'[25]

The main point of Dr. Ambedkar's approach was without a real structural change in the existing *Varna* based social order, the new 'just society' will not come into existence. His method to bring this change included his special emphasis on education, organization and agitation, which according to him will provide the Dalit community with a general sense of security and self-confidence.[26]

9.4. Alternative Approach

As pointed out in the three observations made in the beginning of this chapter, we made ourselves very clear that we will be dealing here with the whole issue of 'conflict and peace', which is related directly with the question of justice. Because the subaltern people particularly the Dalits in India have been victims of this 'structural violence' and thereby they have been denied all kinds of justice in their whole life. Therefore any approach which we have to follow from their point of view has to be holistic in nature. 'Holistic' here means affirmation of the view that an organic or integrated whole has a reality independent of and greater than the sum of its parts.[27] It means entire society is involved in the process of peace and is willing and geared to be concerned about all human beings in his or her totality. As seen in the earlier discussion in this chapter, the purpose of the Order created through the Varna system was to control and to dominate the lives of all Indian people. Therefore, the role of all the members of our society to struggle against such structures and systems, which oppress human beings resulting into a conflictual and unpeaceful situation.

The idea of holistic approach to the issue of 'violence and peace' is also dealt in biblical literature. For an example the Hebrew word *Shalom*, which is used in the Old Testament basically means 'completeness' or 'wholeness'.[28] This is of course the general meaning of 'peace' in the Bible. But it certainly get broadened in nature in the later Biblical tradition. For example, Prophet Isaiah in his book (9:6-7) talks about a future Coming King and about the qualities of his reign. Prophet also used the number of titles for this king, who includes: 'Prince of Peace'. According to the Prophet Isaiah, reign of this Prince of Peach will 'grow continually' and 'there shall be endless peace' (Isaiah 9:7). This actually means, the 'justice and with righteousness' (right relationship) will be the foundation of the reign of the Coming King and the basis of 'endless peace' in his reign. Peace according to Isaiah is the fruit of justice (32:17). Most religious traditions accept Prophet Isaiah's position including Dr. B.R. Ambedkar (as seen in the discussion on his approach).

For example according to Rabbi Muna 'if justice is done, truth has been effected and peace brought about....'[29] Pope John Paul II in his address to the world religious leaders in Assisi during January

2002, pointed out that peace rests on two pillars: commitment to justice and readiness to forgive. He added a comment on these two pillars by saying:

> Justice, first of all, because there can be no true peace without respect for the dignity of persons and peoples, respect for the rights and duties of each person and respect for an equal distribution of benefits and burdens between individuals and in society as a whole. It can never be forgotten that situations of oppression and exclusion are often at the source of violence and terrorism. But forgiveness too, because human justice is subject to frailty and to the pressures of individual and group egoism. Forgiveness alone heals the wounds of the heart and fully restores damaged human relations.[30]

The Pope John Paul II's words are the summary of a holistic approach to the question of violence (conflict) and peace, because the test of 'authentic peace' is the freedom from threat to the powerless of society, which includes the Dalits in India. Such peace is the outcome of the process of reconciliation and with 'justice' both will not be operative in a real sense.

9.5. Conclusion

The undergirded challenge from the discussion of this chapter to all of us is: in whose side we are? Are we going to stand (in solidarity) with the oppressed communities or with the traditional dominant groups, who are going to fight in future more aggressively in the name of 'cultural nationalism' at the local level and 'globalization' at the world level leading to their proposed 'One World Order' (*See for detailed discussion chapter* 6.) Both these phenomenon are dangerous in nature. Because the historically oppressed communities are going to be further marginalized.

Already painful cries are heard in India from the *Adivasi* (indigenous) habitats, because their rights over the natural resources including 'land' are being taken away in the name of development. The Dalits as they are becoming more and more aware about their basic human rights are facing increased atrocities from the hands of their traditional oppressors. Religious minorities are now directly under many forms of violent attacks, many countries including India, because the plurality of religions and cultures are facing a direct threats from the hands of the propagators of 'cultural nationalism' or 'One World Order', the small farmers are faced with a new economic crisis, because of the 'structural adjustment programme', the subsidies given to them are being withdrawn, and job opportunities even for the educated youths belonging to these communities are already on the decrease.

The phenomenon of globalization is also going to add a large portion of India's population to the number of those people, who are living 'below poverty line' and the number of ordinary poor is going to increase at the same time. In the case of India, the worst prediction has come from the World Bank, according to which India will have soon the largest concentration of illiterate population in the world. India will have 54.8 per cent of the world's illiterate population in the age group of 15 to 19. Needless to say, a larger percentage of these illiterates will belong to Dalit, tribal and other weaker sections of Indian society. These are only some of the realities, which are going to increase all over the world.

In the context of said challenge we have to reflect on the spirituality, on which we till now have been fed. This spirituality basically has been something otherworldly, purely private and individualistic in nature. On the other hand socio-cultural including political matters have been taken as affairs of this world, which have nothing to do with the spiritual concerns of the Church or her members. Therefore the demand upon us is the review of our this attitude urgently.

There is a dire need for a prophetic spirituality, a spirituality, which always call for repentance, conversion and change (in real sense for a real reconciliation). It is confrontational in nature and it enables a person to confront the evil and injustice. It is always ready to take a stand. It always is rooted in social, economic and religious conditions of a particular time. It always brings hope for the victims or oppressed by denouncing the oppression and announcing the good news of salvation.

The most serious challenge, which in future we are going to face from the oppressed communities, is: how much we are going to be committed to the change or empowerment of these communities. Because some of those, who belong to these communities have experienced, during 1980s and 1990s, many of the senior workers of the various Faith Communities and the senior most social activists belonging to the voluntary organizations, willingly, with a lot of concern joined the struggle of Dalits and Adivasis, but they went to an extent, which gave them the right of control over the struggle or movement of these communities. It has been seen even such social and religious activists never trusted the abilities of the empowered Dalits and Adivasis. Their attitudes even have put a big question mark about their integrity and commitment of empowering the Dalits and Adivasis. Therefore the challenge to various faith communities as well as to their leaders is going to increase in the time to come.

Ultimately the religious communities and the social activists have to accept the truth that people (in the case of India, Dalits, Adivasi, etc.) are subjects of their own destiny and history and therefore one day they have to become their own voices. It is at that point of history, the role of the all the faith communities will change specially in the area of advocacy. Also a call of the present time for all of us is to be in solidarity, which is a step further than mere advocacy, a move from 'ambulance ministry' to a 'ministry of involvement and participation' in the struggle of the oppressed communities for their redemption. So that a 'just society' or kingdom of God on this Earth may get established, in which peace will reign with justice, and all will live with fuller redeemed dignity and recovered humanity. This will be possible through our unified action and Dalit theology has to play this enabling role.

NOTES

1. *Report of the Commissioner for Scheduled Castes and Scheduled Tribes, Twenty-Eight Report* 1986-87, Government of India, New Delhi, 1988, p. 238.
2. *National Commission for Scheduled Castes and Scheduled Tribes, Fourth Report* 1996-97-1997-98, vol. 1, Government of India, New Delhi 1998, p. 240.
3. Colleen Roach, 'Information and Culture in War and Peace-Overview', in *Communities and Culture in War and Peace*, ed. Colleen Roach, Sage, Newbury Park, 1993.2.3.
4. Naohiro Kiyoshige, 'Old Testament Lessons on Peace', in *Called to be Peacemakers*, ed. Saguru Matsuki and David L. Swain, Ecumenical Books, Tokyo, 1989, p. 81.
5. R.B. Mishra, *Caste and Caste Conflicts in Rural Society*, Commonwealth Publishers, Delhi, 1989, p. 53.

6. Kancha Ilaiah, 'Dalitism Vs Brahmanism: The Epistemological Conflict in History', in *Dalit Identity and Politics*, ed. Ghan Shyam Shah, Sage, New Delhi, 2001, pp. 16-17.
7. Marcus Banks, *Organizing Jainism in India and England*, Clarendon Press, Oxford, 1992, p. 27.
8. G.S. Ghurye, *Caste and Race in India*, Popular Prakashan, Bombay, 1979 rpt. 5th edn.).
9. Ilaiah, op. cit., pp. 117, 118.
10. Ibid., p. 119.
11. B.R. Ambedkar, 'The Untouchables: Who are They and Why They Become Untouchables', in *Dr. Babasaheb Ambedkar: Writings and Speeches*, vol. 7, Education Department, Government of Maharashtra, Bombay, 1990, p. 315.
12. See for detail discussion; James Massey, *Dalits: Issues and Concerns, India 50 Years of Independence: 1947-97, Status, Growth & Development*, vol. 20, Delhi, 1998, pp. 122-3.
13. Rosalind O'hanlon, *Caste, Conflict and Ideology: Mahatma Jotirao Phule and Low Caste Protest in Nineteenth-Century Western India*, Cambridge University Press, Cambridge, 1985, p. 231.
14. Katti Padma Rao, *Caste and Alternative Culture*, Gurukul Lutheran Theological College, Madras, 1995, p. 124.
15. S.K. Gupta, *The Scheduled Castes in Modern Indian Politics: Their Emergence as a Political Power*, Munshiram Manoharlal, New Delhi, 1985, 212-17.
16. Ibid., pp. 208-9.
17. B.R. Ambedkar, 'What Congress and Gandhi Have Done to the Untouchable and Mr. Gandhi and the Emancipation of the Untouchables', in *Dr. Babasaheb Ambedkar: Writings and Speeches*, vol. 9, Education Department, Government of Maharastra, Bombay, 1991, p. 275.
18. Ibid., p. 277.
19. B.R. Ambedkar, 'The Hindu Social Order: Its Essential Principles', in *Dr. Babasaheb Ambedkar: Writings and Speeches*, vol. 3 compiled by Vasant Moon, Education Department, Government of Maharashtra, Bombay, 1987, p. 55.
20. B.R. Ambedkar, 'Philosophy of Hinduism', in *Dr. Babasaheb Ambedkar: Writing and Speeches*, vol. 3, compiled by Vasant Moon, Education Department, Government of Maharashtra, Bombay 1987, p. 25.
21. Ibid., p. 25.
22. Ibid., pp. 38, 39.

23. Ambedkar, 'The Hindu Social Order: It's Essential Principles', op. cit., pp. 96, 97.
24. Ibid., p. 55.
25. Ibid., pp. 97, 98.
26. D.R. Nagaraj, *The Flaming Feet: A Study of the Dalil Movement in India*, South Forum, Bangalore, 1993, p. 40.
27. See for general discussion:
CNI Synodical Programme: Towards a Holistic Understanding of Mission, A Report, CNI, Delhi, 1993, pp. x, xi (Intro).
28. Rabbi Rami M. Shapiro, 'Great is Peace: An Introduction to Shalom', in *Voices from World Religions—Peace in Our Time*, ed. Henry O. Thompson, ISPCK, Delhi, 1993, p. 10.
29. Ibid., p 10.
30. 'Address of His Holiness Pope John Paul II to the Representatives of World Religions, Assisi—24 January 2002', in *FELLOWSHIP—A Quarterly Newsletter of CBCI Commission for Ecumenism and Dialogue*, vol. 7, April 2002, no. 2, CBCI Centre, New Delhi, p. 3.

PART 5

BIBLICAL MODELS OF LIBERATION

CHAPTER 10

Role of Community Leaders

10.1. Two Divine Interventions in Human History

A careful reading of the Bible will reveal that, though it contains many books written by authors both known and unknown, at different times of human history, yet it is centred around the two basic divine interventions in human history. Both the interventions began with those people, who were considered to be the lowest according to the human standards. The details of these interventions run through the pages of the Bible, in the First Testament (Old Testament) and the Second Testament (New Testament). The central message of the first divine intervention is that 'God is on the side of the oppressed' and of the second divine intervention, is that 'God liberates the oppressed'. Both these interventions bring good news for the oppressed communities of this world (including the Dalits in India) for their liberation and also stands as a test for any authentic expressions of theology including 'Dalit theology'.

This chapter on the alternative role of community leaders amidst oppression is centred on three biblical models: the model of Moses; the model of Gideon; and the model of Jesus. The Moses model focuses on the issue of an enslaved community—its brokenness and its restoration. The Gideon model presents to us a young person who was faced once with a 'Divine challenge' and who, with a convincing pastoral persuasion, accepted that challenge. These two models are excellent archetypes for community leaders and the religious group leaders who are offering or intend to offer services to the members of the weaker sections of our Indian society such as Dalits, Adivasis and Tribals. The Jesus model embraces the whole question of the community, the methodology and the ongoing process of empowerment of God's people, which would finally lead them to a full liberation or full salvation. Let us now consider each model in detail.

10.2. Moses Model

The Book of Exodus (the second book of the Bible) that recounts the story of the enslaved broken community of Israelites reveals in detail the Moses model of community formation. The model is very relevant to various historically oppressed groups of people in our country, like the Dalits. The situation and circumstances of the Dalits bear a very close resemblance to that of the Israelites, as described in the Book of Exodus. Both had to face structural oppression and violence from the hands of the ruling and dominant community (Exodus 1: 13-22). In the case of Israelites however, it was the Divine-human partnership (God-Moses) which made possible their liberation. But first and foremost, their liberative process could begin only when they became conscious of their oppressed state (Exodus 2:23-25). It was after this that Moses could begin his role of a liberator under the Divine guidance. The process of liberation began by changing the location of the enslaved people which was assigned to them by their oppressors as part of their 'status' in that society as lesser human beings (Genesis 43:32, 34). With this proposed change in location began the community formation process of the Israelites. This gives a clue to the first step in the alternative role that the community leaders are trying to understand while working amidst the oppressed community of our country.

The next important step in the process of community formation was the issue of leadership, which indeed is most important for any group of people. Here we see God intervening to choose Moses (Exodus 3:1-12). In the process came the assurance to Moses that God was on the side of the oppressed. This assurance went a long way to help Moses in putting his people on the way to liberation (Exodus 12:1-14; 31) even though he had to face the most powerful political authority of his time in Pharaoh the King (Exodus 6:28-11; 10).

With the process of liberation we also witness the foundation of community formation being laid out for the Israelites. The future community of the Israelites was to be rooted in 'memory'. The beginning of the liberative history of Israelites took place with God passing through their community on the eve of liberation. From then on they were going to have their own history of which they would be the 'subject'. This move certainly was one of the most significant steps taken towards the formation of a community. God's passing through the land of slavery symbolized that the divine power was on the side of the oppressed. Every Israelite was asked to slaughter a lamb and mark the doorpost and lintel of his house with some of the blood of that lamb (Exodus 12:7). They were told that by doing this the Lord's presence would be felt by them, for He was going to 'pass through' the land of Egypt and shall cause every firstborn of the Egyptians to die (Exodus 12:12). But on seeing the 'sign' of blood on the houses of the Israelites He would Passover those houses 'and nothing would happen to them' (Exodus 12:13). In future this event was celebrated by the Israelites as the festival of 'Passover', and it became their central festival.

Before celebrating the festival of Passover, certain rules were laid down for the community of the Israelites that were to be observed for seven days prior to the festival. Among these rules, the first was with regard to their daily food which they were to eat with 'unleavened bread' throughout the week for all seven days. Anybody who broke this rule was to be excommunicated from the community. To avoid such mishap, the Israelites were told to remove leaven from their houses (Exodus 12.15). According to the second rule, they had to have the whole congregation/community gatherings (assembly) on the first day and the seventh day; no one will do any work on these two days apart from preparing food that they were to eat (Exodus 12:16). The third rule was that the 'festival of unleavened bread' that marked the day of their deliverance from Egypt, was to be observed as a perpetual ordinance by all—even by the future generations of the Israelites (Exodus 12:17).

Apart from the community festivals which Moses introduced as part of the formation process, the next important thing on his mind was the need of a common 'ideology' or a 'theology', that would usher in a standard norm for keeping together a body or a community. This shows how important it is for the Church that they should have a 'faith and order' which can be in the form of a statement. Now, faith has two parts: *one*—the 'rules', which a community or a Church is supposed to follow collectively; and *two*—the 'rules' which every individual member has to follow. These two parts can be clearly seen in the faith statement which Moses had prepared for the Israelites (Exodus 20: 1-26).

The part one contains four commandments which the community collectively had to observe. The Israelites were told to always keep in mind the foundational truth of their history: that although they were a liberated community then, they were once slaves in Egypt and 'the Lord their God' brought them out from that slavery. Their conscious awareness of their historical liberative experience would impart to them an undivided loyalty to the Lord God. No other god or gods should ever be a part of their faith. According to the second commandment, they were forbidden to make any kind of idol for worship. Again linked up with the second commandment was the third, according to which the people were not to 'make wrongful use' or 'misuse' the name of the Lord God. The fourth commandment was to observe 'the Sabbath day and keep it holy' by not doing any work on that day. All their work should be carried out during other six days of the week. The 'seventh day' or 'the Sabbath day' belonged to the Lord God, because He created for six days and 'the seventh day He rested' and set apart this day for Himself. The spirit behind this fourth commandment was that by observing the Sabbath day, one does what God does, and this becomes a visible 'sign' of His followers. Because all the four commandments were to be followed as the collective action of a community, it would give an 'identity' to them as 'His people' or 'His body'. This would also represent the kind of relationship and solidarity that the community of the Israelites was required to have with the Lord God. In fact this part forms the 'faith' statement of the Israelites.

The next six commandments laid emphasis upon the personal relationship among the community members. The fifth commandment enjoined the right relationship with one's parents which would be a source of blessing for one's long life. The next five commandments define the basis of right relationship with the community members, which included 'shall not murder' 'shall not commit adultery', 'shall not steal', 'not bear false witness against your neighbour' and finally not to covet one's neighbour's houses, wife, slave, animal or anything that belonged to the other. Apart from these commandments, Moses also introduced a 'central place of worship' for the community, which was to play an important part in the process of community formation (Exodus 25:1-31). The Church leaders should understand the importance of this factor because it would significantly help in the sustenance of community solidarity.

10.3. Gideon's Model

Gideon's model is in chapters 6, 7 and 8 of the Book of Judges. Before explaining its implications for the Community or Church leaders of today with regard to the oppressed communities of our country, I shall like to quote some verses from these chapters.

10.3.1. *A Divine Challenge and a Young Person's Response*

The Israelites did what was evil in the sight of the Lord, and the Lord gave them into the hand of Midian for seven years….

'When the Israelites cried to the Lord on account of the Midianites, the Lord sent a prophet to the Israelites; and he said to them, 'Thus says the Lord, the God of Israel, I led you up from Egypt, and brought you out of the house of slavery…' and 'I said to you I am the Lord your God; you shall not pay reverence to the gods of the Amorites…' But you have not given heed to my voice.

'Now the Angel of the Lord came and sat under the oak at Ophrah, which belonged to Joseph the Abiezrite, as his son Gideon was beating out wheat in the wine press, to hide it from the Midianites. The angel of the Lord appeared to him and said to him, 'The Lord is with you, you mighty warrior'. Gideon answered him, 'But sir, if the Lord is with us, why then has all this happened to us? And where are all his wonderful deeds that our ancestors recounted to us, saying, 'Did not the Lord bring us up from Egypt?' But now the Lord has cast us off, and given us into the hand of Midian.' Then the Lord turned to him and said, 'Go in this might of yours and deliver Israel from the hand of Midian; I hereby commission you.' He responded, 'But sir, how can I deliver Israel? My clan is *ha-dal* (the weakest) in Manasseh, and I am the least in my family.' The Lord said to him, 'but I will be with you…' Then he said to him, 'If now I have found favour with you, then show me a sign that it is you who speak with me. Do not depart from here until I come to you, and bring out my present and set it before you.' And he said, 'I will stay until you return'….

'Then all the Midianites and the Amalekites and the people of the East came together and crossing the Jordan they encamped in the Valley of Jezreel. But the spirit of the Lord took possession of Gideon; and he sounded the trumpet, and the Abiezrites were called out to follow him…Then the Lord said to Gideon, 'with three hundred that lapped, I will deliver you…'.

'The Midianites and the Amalekites and all the people of East lay along the valley as thick as locusts, and their camels were without number, countless as the sand on the seashore. When Gideon arrived, there was a man telling a dream to his comrades.... And this comrade answered, 'This is no other than the sword of Gideon, son of Joash, a man of Israel; into his hand God has given Midian and all the army.'

'Then the Israelites said to Gideon, 'Rule over us, you and your son and your grandson also; for you have delivered us out of the hand of Midian.' Gideon said to them, 'I will not rule over, the Lord will rule over you.'... So Midian was subdued before the Israelites, and they lifted up their heads no more. So the land had rest forty years in the days of Gideon.' (Judges 6:1, 7-18, 33-34; 7:7, 12-14; and 8: 22, 23, 28)

10.3.2. *Gideon became an Instrument of Liberation of his People*

These verses from the three chapters of the book of Judges, briefly tell us the story of Gideon. One most important point in these lines is that the story of Gideon began with the description of a very oppressive situation in which once again the Israelites were forced to live in. But with the appearance of a divine messenger (an angel), the scene changed, because this divine messenger began his message on a very positive note while addressing Gideon. He said 'The Lord is with you, you mighty warrior.' Interpreting this message for a Dalit in our Indian context would appear something like this: 'The Lord is with you, you mighty (*no less than the so-called Kshatriya*) warrior!' It is different, however, when one human being addresses another with such expression, because such expression sometime can contain sarcasm. But coming from the mouth of a divine messenger, the psychological impact was quite different and that impact could be seen through a sudden change which took place in Gideon.

In verse eleven of chapter six (Judges), it is clear that like any average Israelite of his days, Gideon was also afraid of the Midianites and because of their fear he toiled secretly to earn his living. But the positive address of the divine messenger immediately reminded him of the history of his people and the role played by the Divine in it. His answer to the divine messenger therefore, reflected the pain of abandonment by the Lord of His children. 'If the Lord is with us, why then has all this happened to us? ... Did not the Lord bring us up from Egypt?' By connecting to the history of the past slavery and oppression of the community in Egypt, and recollecting how

God the Lord liberated his ancestors from that slavery, Gideon at once enhanced the canvas of his suffering and saw his situation in a new light. At that time the divine action became the foundation of a nation, transforming the slaves or 'no people' into '*a people*' or 'a nation'. It is this feeling that inspired Gideon to dare to seek the Divine help once again for his community. Not only Gideon received the divine assurance—'I will be with you, and you shall strike down the Midianites'—but he was commissioned by the Lord in no uncertain words: 'Go in this might of yours and deliver Israel from the hand of Midian; I hereby commission you' (Judges 6:14).

Initially Gideon's response to the divine commission reflected his lack of confidence in himself, which is typical of an oppressed person. His response was 'But sir, how can I deliver Israel? My clan is the weakest (*ha-dal*) in Manasseh (a tribe) and I am the least in my family' (Judges 6:25). The Hebrew expression '*ha-dal*' means 'dalit' by the use of which Gideon confesses his own and his community's downtrodden state. A Dalit would also respond similarly to such a situation, and would say, 'I am a Dalit, how can I undertake such a great responsibility?' But we know how Gideon finally took up the Divine challenge and became an instrument of liberation of his people. How could this happen? The answer to this question will spell out the role for a Church leader working amidst the community in an oppressed state.

10.3.3. *Pastoring, Empowerment and Liberation*

The most important aspect of the story of Gideon for the Church and the Christian community in India is its relevance to the current context. The negativity reflected in Gideon's use of the word 'weakest' and the 'least' is in fact described in Hebrew Bible by the word 'dal' which has been translated as 'low' (*in Revised Standard Version*) or 'impoverished' (*in New Revised Standard Version*). This word is also the root of '*dalit*' or '*dalot*' in Hebrew. Therefore the author definitely is laying stress on the 'dalit state' or 'dalitness' of the Israelites into which they have been forced to live by the Midians. The text emphasizes that in this Dalit state the Israelites not only lost their 'economic rights', but their cultural (religious) and political rights as well.

To sustain one's integrity and honesty in the midst of such oppressive state of living is indeed amazing. Gideon's initial words to the divine angel telling him that his clan is the 'weakest' and 'he is the least in the family', reveals that rare inner strength in a person. Gideon did not feel shy or hesitate to accept the truth about himself. Majority of those who belong to the oppressed communities of our country, especially those who are Dalits and tribals, find it very difficult to admit this truth about them. They even offer many reasons to wriggle out of the situation. For example, 'Now that I have become a Christian, why should I say I am a Dalit or a Tribal?'. Such people must be guided to boldly accept their identity. That shall be their first step towards empowerment in life. They must be bold enough to declare 'who I am', instead of looking for scapegoats. The pastors and the religious leaders can play an important role in this regard.

It is interesting indeed to see the divine messenger as a successful model for a religious leader. It tells us how the 'process of a genuine pastoring' can empower even the weakest person among the Dalits / oppressed, whose psyche has been irreparably impaired through caste and other oppressions. The most important point in the pastoral words of the divine messenger was that he never used a negative expression, which could have affected Gideon adversely. In most of the cases in the Christian Church (including other religious groups) and outside the situation generally is completely opposite. Instead of encouraging the oppressed people positively, we use expressions and language negatively; and this we do to such an extent that instead of helping those people, we push them deeper into the oppressive state. Therefore any pastor who intends to work among the weaker and oppressive communities needs to take note of the approach and pastoral methodology that the divine messenger had adopted in the case of Gideon. And in my opinion this is the key to successful role of a pastor and other Church leaders who are working amidst the oppressed.

It is because of the approach of the divine messenger that Gideon's whole self could transform. After this, the first step that Gideon took was to bring a change in the life of his people by steering their faith back to the Divine power, which had been responsible for their liberation in the past and would also liberate them in future. For this he dismantled the existing religious structures, which his people had erected, such as 'the altar of Baal', that represented the false gods and religion. Once the challenge was taken up by Gideon, he earnestly devoted himself to the task, as if once for all he had entered into a partnership with the Divine in achieving the liberation for his people. The expression used in the text 'A sword for the Lord and for Gideon' remarkably represents this 'Divine-human partnership'. Human empowerment means getting empowered with the Spirit of God. Once that happens, then nothing can stop a person becoming an instrument of change or liberation for his or God's people. This is how Gideon became an instrument of liberation for his people. But then the liberation of the Israelites could stay with them only for 40 years more—that is, till the death of Gideon—because his future generations could not sustain their faith commitment. Throughout the Old Testament, we find years of struggle between Divine and human, through which God continued to send His prophets to remind His people about their faith commitment. But finally He took an extreme step, when He saw that human beings are failing continually in their responsibility to carry out the Divine challenges. It was then that He Himself offered to appear as a model human being and lay down the foundation for the full salvation (liberation) of His whole creation.

10.4. Jesus' Model

The Bible is the story of the numerous encounters of the Divine and the human. Each encounter is supposed to carry a challenge from the Divine and a response from the human being. According to the book of Genesis (chapters 1-3) the story of these encounters began with the first human beings, Adam and Eve. After making the entire world God placed the responsibility of its care on the human beings. However, while doing so He also directed the humans to adhere to certain discipline. But both Adam and Eve failed to keep themselves within that discipline, as a consequence of which they were thrown out of the garden. How to restore their original status in His creation, God continued to work with the human beings. The authors of the Bible selected one case history of a nation, namely Israel, to show how God worked in human history. Old Testament is the account of the stories from that case history. We have already referred to two such stories, of Moses and Gideon. In both these stories the people of Israel were inspired by these leaders and struggled to get liberated; but they were unable to sustain their freedom after the death of the leaders. There is similar end in most of the Old Testament stories of the prophets and other biblical leaders. Finally God had to take an extreme step: He opted to become a human being Himself so that He could show how an ideal human should live on this earth. In the four Gospels of the New Testament we come across the story of God who came to us in the human form. Jesus Christ, in whom God became human (John 1:1-3, 14-18), represented for us a model of a perfect 'Divine-human' partnership', and also a most authentic and sustainable model for community formation.

How does Jesus' perfect model of 'Divine-human partnership' relate to our reflection? The unknown author of the book of Hebrews helps in understanding this relationship. This he does by introducing Jesus Christ as a priest, whom he compares with the Levite priest, Aaron. We are aware of the role played by Aaron along with Moses in the liberation of Israel from their slavery in Egypt. Also it was he who later on became the first priest of his community and founded the highest order of the priestly class known as 'Aaronite' (Leviticus 3:2, Hebrew 7:11). But to reach that level, Aaron had to go through the gruelling experience of becoming a 'spokesperson' (Exodus 4:16) not only of his brother Moses, but also of his enslaved community during their trials and tribulations in Egypt and in the period immediately following it. All the Aaronites—who in fact were Aaron's offsprings and other members of the clan of Levi—had to go through a most comprehensive and intensive training by becoming a part of the liberation struggle of their people. The training of these priests was organic in nature, and was not based upon any pre-planned theological education as most of us have today.

Beside the Aaronite order of priesthood, the other order which the Bible refers to is the non-priestly or non-Aaronite order, the head of which, according to Hebrews chapter 7 is Jesus Christ. The writer of Hebrews also sees Jesus in the model of Melchizedek, the king-cum-priest, who also did not belong to any priestly class. It becomes clear from the four Gospels that Jesus also had to encounter a number of power-structures and authorities on behalf of the poor, prisoners, blind and broken victims of his time (Luke 4:14-19). But the difference between Aaronite order and Jesus' order, according to the author of Hebrews, is that in spite of his belonging to the non-priestly order, the priesthood of Jesus is perennial in nature. The reason for this is that Jesus had victory over death (through resurrection), and he lives forever, and so does his priesthood.

What I am pointing to is that unlike other deliverers and liberators in the Old Testament—like Moses and Gideon—whose influence came to an end with their death, the ministry of Jesus Christ continued non-stop. It did not end with his death. But then how this 'Divine-human partnership' model will help us today in our ministry particularly when we have to minister a community or Church whose 80 per cent membership is composed of either Dalits or Tribals? The answer to this question can be seen in the principles, on which this model was based.

10.4.1. *Identifying with the People in their Actual Situation*

The first of these principles is related to God becoming a human being. In different stages of human history the response of human beings to the Divine challenges were more or less ad hoc in nature. In order to rectify this, God Himself chose to become a human through His 'incarnation' act. We can find the summary of this act of God in John 1:14. Through this act, God not only identified himself with the human beings, he also fully became a part of the human history. Another concrete picture of the same Divine act can be seen in Luke 2:1-7. Here we find a human child 'wrapped…in swaddling clothes, laid…in a manger' (Luke 2:7). With this were also fulfilled two prophecies of the Old Testament that were predicted several hundred years earlier. Both these prophecies were made by prophet Isaiah which had predicted God's direct participation in human history. In Isaiah 7:14, it was prophesied that 'a young woman… will give birth to a son', who will be called 'Emmanuel' (meaning 'God with us'); and in Isaiah 53:4 it was made clear further that God as a human being will have 'no form or comeliness'. We see these prophecies fulfilled in word and spirit in Jesus Christ. In him we meet God as a full human being, and that too as one who came to us as the poorest of the poor (in real sense a Dalit). In other words, he chose to abandon his other-world-identity for the sake of the liberation/salvation of His whole creation.

Why did God identify himself in Jesus Christ with the lowest human being *(ha-dal)*? It was only to make his act inclusive, so that the 'Divine-human partnership' that comes forth from this act, and the services offered through it, are also inclusive. And this leads us to the core of the alternative role for community or Church leaders who intend to work amidst the oppressed. Today the first challenge before all of us, particularly before those who are going to the field to begin their ministry, is to identify with those among whom we plan to work, if we want that our ministry should be acceptable, creative and fruitful. We should begin from the lowest, and with the least one. This is the first secret of any sustainable ministry. But how such ministry becomes operational? Our answer to this question is in the second principle of Jesus' model.

10.4.2. *Carrying Service to the People where they are*

Jesus began his public ministry when he was about thirty years old. But right on the first day of his ministry, in his own local village of Nazareth, he made his manifesto public, by describing very clearly, the purpose, focus, goal and scope of his ministry. The text of his manifesto was:

The Spirit of the Lord is upon me,
because he has anointed me
to bring good news to the poor.
He has sent me to proclaim release to the captives
and recovery of sight to the blind,
to let the oppressed go free,
to proclaim the year of the Lord's favour. (Luke 4:18-19)

We know Jesus was rejected by his own village people. My dear friends and colleagues, people should be ready for such rejection also. One example for this is the author of this work himself. For everyone who intends to serve such an experience is very hard to bear. One needs a real empowerment of the Spirit to do so. But once you overcome that state, then nothing can stop you to fulfil your ministry. St. Luke in his Gospel tells about this aspect of the ministry of Jesus. 'Soon afterwards he went on through cities and villages, proclaiming and bringing the good news of the Kingdom of God' (Luke 8:1). The result was amazing. When the disciples of John the Baptist came to find out from Jesus, if he is the one who was to come? Jesus in his answer told them: 'Go and tell John what you have seen and heard: the blind receive their sight, the lame walk, the lepers are cleansed, the deaf hear, the dead are raised, the poor have good news brought to them' (Luke 7:22).

According to his Nazareth manifesto, Jesus began his work with the various excluded and oppressed groups of people. Among these people were the tax collectors, the outcasts (Luke 15:1), and the women (who were regarded lowest in the social structure—John 4:7-9). He inspired the change in the poor (Mark 12:41-44), in the rich like Zacchaeus (Luke 19:1-9), in non-Jew Canaanite women (Matthew 15:21-28) and in sinful persons (Luke 7:36-50). According to the Gospel writers, Jesus continued 'visiting all the towns and villages' with his message of Good News of the Kingdom of God, bringing together the poor, the blind, the captive and the oppressed. But then he had to pay the price for that. He was rejected and abused with all kind of titles and names. About this, once he himself had said: 'For John came neither eating nor drinking and they say, 'He has a demon', the son of Man came eating and drinking, and they say, 'Look, a glutton and a drunkard, a friend of tax collectors and sinners!' (Matthew 11:18-19).

This second challenge is for all. This challenge demands from us that we identify the people we intend to serve. This is the second part of the alternative role of a community or church leader. Which are our target groups? Are we clear with the terms of manifesto of our ministry? For effective and long-lasting results of our ministry, we should follow Jesus' model by being clear both of our target groups and our goals; and also, we have to be ready to face all kind of reactions for the same. But then what about the sustainability and continuity of our ministries? This question brings us to the third principle of Jesus' model.

10.4.3. *Continuing of a Service by Organizing and Empowering the People*

Continuing the ministry, especially which deals with the people is the most difficult task. In the Old Testament we have come across the accounts of the wonderful work of liberation that was carried out by Moses and Gideon in their times; and we have also seen how their influence petered off after their death. The efforts of all other prophets and leaders mentioned in the Book met similar fate. Even today we are faced with the same problem: most of the good work carried out by most of the peoples' movements and organizations begins with very clear vision and sincere efforts of some persons, but in most cases everything dwindles out and vanishes from the scene in due course, once the founder or key persons die. Today the Christian community as a whole and the institutions and organizations related to it, also face the same problem. But then how did Jesus plan for the continuity of his ministry?

According to Gospels and other books of the New Testament (second part of the Bible), Jesus was aware of this problem and therefore he took care of it by planning in advance. According to the Gospel writers, Jesus started organizing his close circle of disciples from the very beginning (Matthew 4:18-22, Mark 1:16-20 and Luke 5:1-11). Soon he selected twelve disciples, whom he gave the status of 'apostles' (Matthew 10:1-4, Mark 3:13-19, Luke 6:12-16). This he did after spending many hours in prayer to God. Then according to St. Luke, he expanded his work by picking seventy two of his disciples and training them so that they get empowered to carry on his work in the right spirit. In order to create faith commitment in his followers he instituted a sacrament known as 'the Lord's Supper' or 'Holy Communion' (Luke 22:14-23, 1 Corinthians 11:23-25). Every time his believers take part in it, they are reminded what the Lord has done for them. It also helped the believers to be in solidarity with one another like in a relationship of flesh and blood. Because Jesus' own flesh and blood is the foundation of this sacrament (Ephesians 2:13-16), it helped the believers to be in solidarity with one another like in a relationship of flesh and bread. Besides working on his mission, he completed this task of empowering his disciples and entrusting them into the safety of the Lord, before leaving this temporal life. He prayed for them to God the Father: 'Sanctify them in the truth.... As you have sent me into the world, so I have sent them into the world'. This prayer of sanctification he also offered 'on behalf of those who will believe' in him 'through their word' (John 17:9-18).

After his resurrection when Jesus met his disciples, he told them about their future task as his witnesses. To empower them with the 'power' from above, he promised them a 'Helper', who would replace him as the enabler (Luke 24:44-49; and Acts 1:8). It is this Helper, which actually is the Holy Spirit, and which was meant to guide every believer into all the truth (John 16:5-15). This process of empowerment began when the first set of disciples received the Holy Spirit (Acts 2:1-12). The change in their life was amazing. Now they were ready to face any challenge or power of this world. The story of the early Christian community is most powerful testimony to this truth as narrated by St. Luke in the Book of Acts.

10.5. Conclusion

In conclusion, I want to stress that there is a great need of right kind (an alternative) of service today. One of the most important goals of such service is to empower God's people, so that they themselves may become instruments of their liberation as well as if their oppressors and finally transfer the whole society into a 'Just Society'.

CHAPTER 11

Prophet Jeremiah of the Captives and Oppressed

11.1. A Risk Taking Community Leader

Jeremiah of the Old Testament (second part of the Bible) can be addressed as 'a prophet of the captives and oppressed' (Dalits) about whom he himself said, 'They are only poor (*dalem* or Dalits) for they do not know the way of the Lord, law of their God' (Jeremiah 5:4).

Some aspects of his life are briefly discussed here in this chapter in order to offer another case to the Dalit leaders, what kind of role is expected from them even at the risk of their life. Five aspects, which includes, as a 'liberationist' theologian, a contextual prophet, his work for the Dalits of Jerusalem, his views about the people considered 'outsiders' (out caste) and his final prophecy of new life for his community people.

11.2. Jeremiah as a 'Liberationist Theologian'

There are two parallel theological streams running in the time of Jeremiah, namely, the 'Exodus theology' and the 'Zion theology'. Jeremiah upholds the 'Exodus theology', which had its roots in the liberation history of the Israelites, from the slavery of Egypt. He made his stand on this 'expression', while indicated the people of Israel for breaking their faith covenant (Jeremiah 2:1-13). It is against this understanding of Israel's faith, their priests, rulers and prophets have led their people (Jeremiah 2:8). Again and again, Prophet Jeremiah referred to the historical basis of this expression of theology (Jeremiah 7:21-26; 23:7; 31:31-34; 32:20-23). The Exodus theology's basis was God's liberation of Israel from Egyptian slavery, divine guidance through the wilderness wandering towards the gift of the land of Canaan and finally the covenant at Sinai between God and

His people of Israel. It is this understanding of the faith of Jeremiah as a prophet, which puts him in the traditions of the 'liberationist theology', which also brings him closer to the 'Dalit theology', which is also rooted in the oppressive and captive historical experience of the Dalits in India.

The second expression or stream of theology, which in a way is an opposite expression to Jeremiah's expression of 'theology of Exodus' is the 'Zion theology', which stood upon two pillars: religio-cultural symbolizing with Jerusalem's 'temple' and political power symbolizing with the royal 'place' in Jerusalem. But both these pillars did not have any important place in Jeremiah's theological understanding of the relationship between God, Israel and Judah, and 'other nations' (Jeremiah 10:19-21; 21:11-23:8). On the other hand, Jews who followed the 'Zion theology' believed that God will defend their city against its enemies (see Psalms 44, 48, 76, 90, 31:4-3).

Finally, the basis of 'Exodus theology' or Jeremiah's theology was to: 'Act with justice and righteousness, and deliver from the hand of the oppressor anyone who has been robbed. And do no wrong or violence to the alien, and the orphan, and the widow, or shed innocent blood in this place' (Jeremiah 22:3; see also 7:5-7 and 33:15).

In the case of Dalits in India, they also when they first encountered Christian preaching, they received it in the form of missionary theology rooted in the European context of the rich and poor, namely pietistic theology, which was addressed to rich, but the missionaries used the same for poor specially Dalits in India. This missionary Christian theology instead of helping them made them more poor or increased their 'Dalitness'. Therefore there came a need of Dalit theology which to be rooted in the Dalit context. The project Dalit Bible Commentary is part of the same process and Jeremiah's theology is model of the same.

11.3. Jeremiah's Context of Prophecy

Here we must remember that if Jeremiah's theology of liberation was rooted in the experience of the exodus of his community from the slavery of Egypt, then his immediate prophecy was rooted in the context of his community situation of his days. The details of their situation we find in Jeremiah 2:1-13:27. The political summary of the context is put in the question form, which says, 'Is Israel a slave? Is he a home born servant? Why then has he become a plunderer?'

(Jeremiah 2:14). Their religio-culture is summed as: 'But where are your gods that you made for yourself? Let them come, if they can save you, in your time of trouble, for you have as many gods as you have towns, of Judah' (Jeremiah 2:28). About the social conditions, it says, 'Also on your skirts is found the lifeblood of the innocent poor, though you did not catch them breaking in' (Jeremiah 2:34).

As a prophet, Jeremiah not made full analysis of the context of his people but he also encountered it with his full strength as well (Jeremiah 14:1-33:36). He fully identified with his community's suffering (Jeremiah 12:3-4), but still his own people wanted to take his life, because of his prophetic messages (Jeremiah 11:18-23). Through his bold sermons in the temple, he tried his best to expose the conditions of his people (Jeremiah 7:1-15; 11:1-17; 16:1-13; 22:1-5; 23:1-8; 25:1-14 and 26:1-24). In our own time, among Indian Christians, most of the leaders, including Bishops and priests will say, we preach what people want us to preach and what they want. Most of them do not dare to touch the issues like Dalit or caste issues. But it was not the case with prophet Jeremiah. Here, few of the extracts of his sermon as examples are given:

In one of his sermon to those who came to worship in the temple, Jeremiah said in his sermon the word of the God:

> Amend your ways and your doings, and let me dwell with you in this place. Do not trust in these deceptive words. This is the temple of the God.... For if you truly amend your ways and doings, if you truly act justly one with another, if you do not oppress the alien, the orphan, the widow, or shed innocent blood in this place, and if you do not go after other gods to your own hearts then I will dwell with you in this place, in the land that I gave of old to your ancestors forever and ever (Jeremiah 7:3-7).

Another example of sermon, in which we found the rejection of 'temple based theology' or 'Zion theology' and upholding the 'Exodus theology' in which stress is laid on the liberation of the oppressed, we found in Jeremiah 11:1-17. The example of a 'judgement' based sermon is found in Jeremiah 16:1-13. The direct reference to the rejection of 'Zion theology' in Jeremiah's sermon is found in Jeremiah 21:11-23:8. His sermon on the theme of 'repentance' is in Jeremiah 25:1-14.The complete demolition of 'Zion theology', which is more or less equal to the 'Pietistic theology' and which came into existence during the medieval period in Europe, which was meant to be preached to the rich, but the same was brought by missionaries to India, which they preached to the poor Dalits and made them captive to the structure of the church/temple.This theology made them further poor in their life. including spiritual life. The complete rejection of such 'theology' is found in Jeremiah's sermon in Jeremiah 1-26. He was put under divine compulsion to preach his sermon and was asked 'not hold back a word'. For this sermon he was directly threatened for his life by the so-called 'believers' of the 'Zion theology', who asked him 'why you prophesied in the name of the Lord', saying, 'This house (church/temple) shall be like Shiloh and this city (holy city Jerusalem) shall be dissolute...' (Jeremiah 26:3, 9).

Prophet Jeremiah was not only a preacher; he also fully identified and had direct experience of the suffering of his people (Jeremiah 12:3-4). His laments are the direct proof of his personal sufferings along with his community (Jeremiah 11:18-23;12:1-6;15:10-21;17:4-8; 18:18-23;20:7-13 and 20:14-18).Here is a model of Jeremiah for the Dalit leaders which includes, the Christian pastors, priests and bishops, if they intend to play any role in the liberation of the Dalits in India.

11.4. Jeremiah and the Dalits of Jerusalem

Prophet Jeremiah was indeed a prophet of the oppressed and captives as seen in the discussion earlier section of this essay. Based on some of the references he can equally be addressed as the 'prophet of the Dalits'. He at least used in his work five times the Hebrew expression '*dal*' in its different grammatical forms. In Jeremiah 5:4, he used for the dalits '*dalim*', which refers to the process and deeper sense of its meaning in Hebrew. With a special meanings Jeremiah has used this Hebrew expression in Jeremiah 39:10; 40:7 and 52:15, 16, where it has been translated as 'the poor people' or 'the poorest of land' or 'the poorest people of the land'. But who are these poorest people of the land? One possible answer is that these poor people were the original dwellers of the land of Jerusalem, who were defeated by the Israelites (Judges 1:21, 28, 32, 33).

Jebusite Community was the best example of an indigenous group on whose land the temple of Jerusalem was built (2 Samuel 24:18-25). So it is possible these people or community like the Dalits of India, 'who owned nothing' (Jeremiah 39:10) were left behind to take care the land. These are the people rightly addressed 'the poorest of the land' (Jeremiah 52:16).

11.5. Jeremiah and the non-Jews Religious Sect and Ebedmelech the Ethiopian

The two notable case histories are: first of a community name Rechabites (Jeremiah 35:1-19) and second of an individual called Ebedmelech the Ethopian (Jeremiah 38:7-13; 39:15-18). The detailed discussion on these two case histories is given in his book, which show how the Rechabites as a community of nomad people like the de-notified tribes (a community, which shared the historically similar roots whom Britishers named as 'criminal tribe') of India become model of 'faith' for the Israelites, who considered themselves special people of God like the so-called the upper caste people of India. Can Dalits in India ever become a model faith as well?

The case of Ebed-melech, the Ethiopian, who was 'alien', but most faithful to the Lord, who in return offered full liberation to him and his family. Here again is a case, which can be a model for the oppressed communities of the world including Dalits in India.

11.6. Jeremiah's Prophecy and 'New Covenant'

Jeremiah's life goal and theology can be summed up in terms of, what he prophesied about the future 'new covenant' (Jeremiah 31:31-34).Here in this covenant a promise of full salvation/liberation is made, which will be a new covenant, not a law (either of Moses or of Manu), according to which the old covenant had been broken, but the new covenant will continue, because it bring an inward transformation of the human heart that will allow all people equally to know God intimately and to be obedient to the commandments or Divine will. And God will forgive and forget all people's sins, which will lay the foundation of a new community based on a new theology rooted in the new-covenant.

What Jeremiah as a prophet tried to offer by giving a call in order to build a new community rooted in the new covenant or a new theology, same is true with the Dalits, when Dr. B.R. Ambedkar gave them call to get converted to any of the religious truth, which upheld the egalitarian principle, which included Buddhism, Islam, Sikhism and Christianity.

CHAPTER 12

Prototype Leadership for Community Liberation

12.1. About Three Works

Three works with which we are concerned in this chapter are found in the Old Testament of the Bible. All these are historical works, namely Ezra, Nehemiah and Tobit. The first two works, of Ezra and Nehemiah, give important historical information about the early post exilic period or captivity of Israelites, from 539 to ca. 430 BCE. Both the works bear the names of two best-known leaders of the Jewish community of that time, who themselves were part of the Babylonian captivity. Ezra was a scribe and priest (in the present sense Professor Theologian and Reverend) and Nehemiah was a Governor (a bureaucrat cum politician).

The third work 'Tobit' is historical fiction, which most probably has been put in written form in the fourth or third century BCE. The point here which needs to be remembered that like most of the classic historical works, though it be a fiction, it opens a window into a social world view of its author by narrating about real-life characters, which includes Tobit, his son Tobias and daughter-in-law Sarah.

The common point of all three works is the captivity of the community, which is a central point of subject of these works. Ezra and Nehemiah directly had the experience of captivity as part of their community and Tobit, represents a prototype real character of Jewish community living in Nineveh. The common factor of 'captivity', on one side brings them closer to the Dalits in India and on other side their world of captivity and struggle for liberation brings their world closer to the world of the Dalits. Besides the three biblical prototype leaders, discussion here in this chapter (section 3) includes also

Dr. B.R. Ambedkar, who in a real sense falls very close to these biblical characters as a prototype Dalit leader, historian and theologian.

12.2. Common Context and Common Agenda

Among the three historical works, two of the works deal with post-captivity or exilic context of the Jewish community of Ezra and Nehemiah and the third work of Tobit narrates the condition of the same community, when it was still in captivity. In a way Dalits of India share both of these aspects of captivity even though today they are living in the post-independence era of India. But their captivity is not having one or two layers of captivity, their captivity has multiple layers and now they are under internal captivity, which is actually continuing for more than 3500 years. But at present they are enjoying a number of constitutional freedoms and rights, which brings them closer to Ezra and Nehemiah's time, who were freed at that time and they were engaged to re-built their broken community, but Dalits presently are like Tobit, who at individual level had regained his liberation, but his community was still in captivity and was living in the region of Nineveh. It is the book of Tobit which gave the glimpses of social context of the life of Tobit's community, which included customs related to family life, marriage, burial, the eating of meat, relationship between parents and children, inequalities between the sexes and conditions of the rich and the poor. This work further presents the nature of persecution and how members of a captive community were dealt by the authorities including brutally killing them and denying them the right of burial (Tobit 1:16-21).

The context of all the works of Ezra, Nehemiah and Tobit included the key symbols of their communityhood, their central place of worship in Jerusalem and both the political capital city and its walls were broken and ruined, which their means their political and cultural identity was no more left behind. The story of Ezra is centred around the re-building of the central of place of worship (Ezra 3:1-6:22) and the story of Nehemiah was to re-build the defence walls of their city (Neh. 3:1-7:73). The story of Tobit adds another dimension to the whole concern of community, 'Human and Divine partnership', which paves the way to liberation (Tobit 3:16-11:16). So the context of all the three historical works was the broken conditions of the Jewish community, because of the captivity; and common agenda of all these were to re-claim or re-build that broken community, which is also supposed to be the context and agenda before the Dalit community in India.

Because in the case of the Dalits, the very term or name 'Dalit', which they have chosen to gave themselves, describes the 'state' which is oppressive in nature and into which they have been forced to live for centuries by their opponents or oppressors by using the instrument of caste. Secondly it is this common name of 'Dalit', which has created a urge in them, to overthrow the captivity of dalitness and reach the final goal of liberation. One difference between the captivity of the community of Ezra, Nehemiah, and Tobit was that they were captive in the foreign land, but in the case of Dalits, they were/are in their own land, because their land has been taken away from them by force by others. The present Dalit context includes their inferior social status, their being politically powerless and their economic poverty (slavery or captivity). The worst thing of all this is that it has become part of their inner being and they have accepted this as a part of their natural life. This has given them a multi-faceted identity, which tells them they are untouchables, they are outcaste and they are slaves. How such context can be dealt with, it is here the examples of Ezra, Nehemiah and Tobit can become handy and specially the Dalit leader Dr. B.R. Ambedkar can possibly help the Dalits to achieve their final goal of liberation, if they are willing to follow his model.

12.3. Prototype Dalit Leader

World's oppressed communities besides having 'commoness' in their context and agenda for their future, also having number of leaders, who have 'commoness' in their approaches to deal with the oppressive contexts of their times. Some of these leaders and their approaches fall in the categories of 'prototype' means have in these a preliminary form of methodology to deal with the issues or have basic seeds of a theology or an ideology, which later if developed can become a binding force for the broken or enslaved communities for their liberation or transformation. Here are a few such prototype Dalit leaders are referred, who have tried to respond to their community context either for the whole community or part of it. One is the prominent Dalit leader Dr. B.R. Ambedkar from our own time, an Indian and other three are Dr. Ezra, Governor Nehemiah and a spiritual man of action called Tobit. Among the last three leaders, two are historical persons, who led their freed community members to build their broken Jewish community, in Babylon. The third character of 'Tobit', who actually is a fictional one, but who had a real resemblance with leaders still living in the captivity in Nineveh.

Dr. B.R. Ambedkar upto some extent stands very close to Ezra and Nehemiah, but who as a Dalit was born a Hindu and later he got converted to Buddhism, but he in real sense fulfils all the parameters of a Dalit Christian theologian, whose approach and method in a way lay down the foundation of today's 'Dalit theology'. He also had deep concerns to deal with the whole issue of 'Dalits' numbering today more than 250 million, the root of their oppressive dalit state (dalitness) is the 'caste or varna system', whose creator was the Hindu priestly caste of Brahmins. Here before referring to the work of Rev. Dr. Ezra and Governor Nehemiah and Spiritualist Tobit, we will state briefly the views of Dr. B.R. Ambedkar on the issue of 'caste' and on the issue of 'Dalit Christians'. His proposal with regard to these two issues, can be considered as a 'prototype' in nature which is being summarized here.

12.3.1. *On 'caste'*

After reading Dr Ambedkar's main writings, it becomes very clear that he was not just a critic or a person having some new ideas, he was also at the same time a person, who had concrete suggestions for the implementation of the same. For example in his analysis of the existing social order based on the caste, he was very clear what evils it carried particularly enable to keep the Dalits in captivity for centuries now. Based on his analysis, he talked about the annihilation of caste, concerning which he was also very clear that it 'is not possible to break caste without annihilating the religious notions on what it, the caste system, is founded'. This according to him was only possible through a *kranti* (revolution), not through a simple reformation. In order to do it, he suggested the following three main steps:

First, *New Doctrinal Basis*—Dr. Ambedkar suggested the first step to formulate the new doctrinal basis of the Hindu religion, which according to him, has to 'be in consonance with Liberty, Equality and Fraternity'. Here it means to reinterpret part of the scriptures such as Upanishads, which carries the philosophical basis of Hinduism. Dr Ambedkar's stress here was on the radical reinterpretation which involves 'a considerable scraping and chipping off the ore they contain', which presently go against the principle of fraternity or fellow-feeling and does not allow the practice of 'the associated mode of life', which is one of the important ways to deal with or coming over a broken (dalit) community.

Second, A *Complete Change in the Fundamental Notions of Life*—The above stated first step, automatically leads to the second by entering into 'the associated mode of life', asking for 'a complete change in the fundamental notions of life'. It means adopting a new set of 'values of life', which in the strict sense 'conversion' is leading to a 'new life'. In this regard again he offered the following three practical possibilities:

The first action he suggested was to abolish the caste and the various *sub-castes*, because these came into existence only through imitation and excommunication. But he was not fully convinced with this, because he thought the process may stop with the abolition of sub-castes, therefore,

He suggested another action, according to which *inter-caste dining* may be the solution. But again he himself argued against this suggestion. Because there were many castes which allow inter-dining, but it has not succeeded in killing the spirit of caste and the consciousness of caste, therefore,

Lastly he suggested an action, which involved *inter-caste marriage*. About this, he said: Fusion of blood can alone create the feeling of being kith and kin and unless this feeling of kinship, of being kindred, becomes paramount, the separatist feeling, the feeling of being aliens, created by caste will not vanish.

Third, *The Old Body Must Die to Receive a New Body*—means to conversion through a 'u-turn' leading to a new life actually means going through a death experience, rejecting completely the old life before entering into a new one. This according to Dr Ambedkar was possible if one was willing to 'discard the authority of the Shastras and destroy the religion of the Shastras'. He strongly suggested: 'You must take the stand that Buddha took. You must take the stand which Guru Nanak took. You must not only discard the Shastras, you must deny their authority, as did Buddha and Nanak.' Here the point which needs to be remembered is that though Lord Buddha and Guru Nanak belonged to a Kshatriya caste and the Shastras only allow their caste to study not to teach; yet they both became founder teachers of the two great religions, which means they took the role of Brahmins and through this action they rejected the authority of the Shastras.[1]

12.3.2. *On 'Dalit Christians'*

According to Dr. B.R Ambedkar the Indian Christians are living in sheltered waters. They are, at any rate, a large majority of them are living in the laps of the missionaries. For their education, for their medical care, for religious ministration and for most of their petty needs they do not look to Government. They look to the Missions. If they were dependent upon Government they would be required to mobilize, *to agitate, educate and organize* their masses for effective political action. For without such organization no Government would care to attend to their needs and their requirements.

Secondly according to him that the Indian Christians are 'disjointed', it is a better word than the word disunited-community. All that it has in common is a common source of inspiration. Barring this one thing which they have in common everything else tends to keep them apart Indian Christians like all other Indians are divided by race, by language and by caste. Their religion has not been as to make difference of language, race and caste as though they were mere distinctions. On the contrary their religion which is their only cement is infected with denominational differences. The result is that the Indian Christians are too disjointed to have a common aim, to have common mind and to put a common endeavour. In short, the term 'Indian Christian' is just a statistical phrase. There is no community feeling behind this phrase. Indian Christians are not bound together by what is consciousness of kind, which is the test of the existence of a community.[2]

Besides the above state of affairs of Christians in general in India, Dr. B.R. Ambedkar adds also three basic reasons for the failure of Dalit Christians to raise for them a movement for their liberation, who almost form 70 per cent membership of Christianity in India.

The *first* reason is the complete absence of desire among the educated Christians (both non-Dalits and Dalits) to take up the cause of the community and fight it. Because there is no community feeling among the educated classes and the masses. They are divided into high class and low class without having any concern for one another. The result is that Dalit Christians are leaderless and therefore unable to mobilize for the redress of their wrongs.

The *second* reason is to be found in the mental snake-up of the Dalit Christians, which is 'characterized by a complete absence of any urge to break his bonds' with the past or with their old faith. A Dalit might become a Christian, 'But the case is very rare of an untouchable becoming a Christian because of a positive discontent or dislike of the Hindu religious teachings. The result is that Christianity becomes only an addendum to his old faith.'

The *third* reason for the absence of any urge is due to the teachings of the Christian Church. The teaching that the fall of humanity' is due to his/her sin and the reason why one must become Christian is because in Christianity there is promise of forgiveness of sins.[3]

What Dr. B.R. Ambedkar said about the Christians in general and Dalit Christians in particular, about that we do see by careful going through the works of Ezra, Nehemiah and Tobit, how close they were in their approaches and theological thinking with Dr. B.R. Ambedkar. Here a brief discussion is offered on the works of these three in the light of views of Dr. B.R. Ambedkar in order to see where these four prototype Dalit leaders have meeting points and where they have departing points in their approach to the liberation of their oppressive communities in their various contexts.

With regards to the Indian Christians in general Dr. B.R. Ambedkar as a prototype Dalit Christian historians observed that they mostly depended for their needs on foreign missions and he further adds: 'If they were depended upon Government they would be required to mobilize, *to agitate, educate and organize* their masses for effective political action. For without such organization no Government would care to attend their needs and their requirements....' The opposite to Indian Christians and their leaders, on the other hands, we see Ezra and Nehemiah, though were part of the captives community, yet when time came, they both did not hesitate to take help of even foreign rulers of their time, even though these rulers were non-Jews (see Ezra 1:1-11; Neh. 2:1-10). Even for enforcing the religious teaching of Law, Ezra could use the legal assistance of King Artaxerses (Ezra 7).

According to Dr. B.R Ambedkar Indian Christians were a

'disjointed' body in other words of 'Christ', not simply 'disunited, which some Christians think particularly in the ecumenical circles, because which they lay stress on an 'organic unity'. But Ambedkar as a prototype Christian theologian is laying stress on much deeper truth by using the expression of 'disjointed', which points to the deep down factor of 'dalitness' or 'brokenness' of Christian community. Here again two biblical prototype Dalit leaders, Rev. Dr. Ezra and Governor Nehemiah exactly recognized the truth behind the destruction of their community's nationhood or communityhood which their enemies did by destroying the two pillars of their nationhood namely the 'central place and worship', the temple of Jerusalem, the source of religious faith and the palace of their king in Jerusalem at the destruction of their capital city (see Lam. 2:6). Therefore, challenge before them was first to-build their temple or central place of worship (Ezra 6) and to re-fortified the city of Jerusalem (Neh. 2) and leads their community back to original faith in the Mosaic Law (Ezra 7 and Neh. 13). Here the focus was both on their re-claiming their 'national identity', by enclosing the walls of Jerusalem with a wall, which was done under the leadership of Nehemiah and purge the community from all things of foreign origin. It is at this point Dr. B.R. Ambedkar as a prototype of Dalit leaders takes different stand, because of difference in the Jewish captive community and Dalit community in India. Here he also differ in methodology in the process of Dalit community formation, because he would like completely to abolish the 'caste system', in order to deal with the 'Dalit brokenness' and for that he encouraged the 'new doctrinal basis' of their faith, he wanted them to bring changes in the fundamental notion of life by abolishing, first, 'sub-castes', to have inter-caste dining' and involve 'inter-caste marriage'.

As a Prototype Dalit Christian leaders, Dr. B.R Ambedkar's real views about the Dalit Christians, are found in his three reasons quoted above, when talks, why Dalit Christians have failed till now in raising any meaningful effective movement for their whole liberation. The first reason, he gave was a practical one dealing with the issue of leadership, which is needed for any movement and on the other hand about this issue he pointed out there is a 'complete absence of desire among the educated Christians' both non-Dalit as well as Dalit Christian. The second reason was both theological as well as psychological, which 'found in the mental make-up of Dalit

Christians' and the third, reason is a theological in nature according to which among the Dalits Christian there is an 'absence of any urge is due to the teaching of Christian Church. The teaching that full of humanity is due to his/her sin and reason why one must become Christian because in Christianity there is a promise of forgiveness of sin'. He further adds:

> Whatever may be the theological and evangelists, basis of these doctrine there is no doubt with disaster.... This is what exactly happened with the Dalit Christians. Instead of having taught that their fall was due to a wrong social and religious environment and that their improvement they must attack the environment, they were taught their fall was due to their sin. Consequently the Dalit Christians instead of having empowered to conquer their environmental context, conferred themselves with the belief that there no use of struggle for simple reason that their fall is due to the sin committed not by them by some remote ancestors of their called Adam and Eve.[4]

So as a Prototype Dalit Christian theologian Dr. B.R Ambedkar above gave a call for complete shift in doing theology in order to bring the change in the mental set up of both Dalit Christians as well as non-Dalit Christians. In the case of Ezra, Nehemiah and Tobit we find them in action to fight with the causes of their community's fall. Besides their re-building the central place of worship or temple and re-introducing their common festivals and religious rituals, they laid stress both in the right teachings of their faith, with required interpretation (commentaries) so the people just out of captivity can understand the theological meaning of their scripture (Nehemiah 8:8-9).

The same way the third work of 'Tobit' lay stress on the way and rules of practical life or what we call 'Christian ethic' (Tobit 1:3). God's justice for those who follow his righteous path, which include a right relationship with community members and others, is the running theme of Tobit. Both Tobit and his daughter-in-law are the Prototype models of such human beings, who at any cost follow the life journey leading to the wholistic liberation both at individual as well as family and community levels (Tobit 8-11).

Ezra, Nehemiah and Tobit, are the Prototype Dalit leaders, one a Dalit theologian, second a Dalit politician and third a Dalit spiritualist, lead their community in regaining their lost human dignity while in the captivity as well as in post-captivity.[5]

NOTES

1. See for detailed discussion *Dr. Babasaheb Ambedkar: Writings and Speeches*, vol. 3, Education Department, Government of Maharashtra, Bombay, 1987, pp. 27, 55, 57, 63, 67, 69, 77-8.
2. See *Dr. Babasaheb Ambedkar: Writings and Speeches*, vol. 5, Education Department, Government of Maharashtra, Bombay, 1989, pp. 475, 476.
3. See for details: *Dr. Babasaheb Ambedkar Writings and Speeches*, vol. 5, ibid., pp. 471-2.
4. See *Dr. Babasaheb Ambedkar, Writings and Speeches*, vol. 3, op. cit., p. 67.

CHAPTER 13

Biblical and Theological Response

13.1. A Case for a Dalit Study Centre

It is true the Dalit theologians for the last two decades have been involved in responding to the challenge of the caste based social order and they also have taken serious note of the second (or added) challenge of the process of globalization. The Centre for Dalit/Subaltern Studies, New Delhi right from its inception in 2001 has made efforts by bringing together Dalit and non-Dalit scholars for collective reflections. Two, concrete outcome of the Centre's efforts can be found in the two volumes namely *Globalization and its Impact on Dalits* and *Broken Among the Victims: Dalit Perspective at the World Social Forum 2004*.[2] The Centre is also working on 25 volumes of the Dalit Bible Commentary[3] and on a mega project related to the 'Dalit Heritage and Liberative Traditions'[4] at an all India level with the same purpose. The scope of this brief chapter will not permit us to go through the contents of these works and programmes, instead of that we will refer here to the Biblical teachings specially of Jesus Christ, which contains some of the basic principles and guidelines for those who would like to enter into the process of theologizing as part of their response to the major challenges, coming out from today's Dalit context.

13.2. Jesus' Nazareth Manifesto

Interestingly Jesus Christ's whole life mission was to deal with the context similar to the context of Dalits. This is clear from his teachings as well as his actions. He began his mission in his own small village (Nazareth), where he announced his mission agenda in the form of 'Nazareth Manifesto'. To spell out his mission agenda, he used the words of Prophet Isaiah, which reads: 'The Spirit of the

Lord is upon me, because he has anointed me to bring good news to the poor. He has sent me to proclaim release to the captives and recovery of sight to the blind, to let the oppressed go free, to proclaim the year of the Lord's favor' (Luke 4:18, 19). (*see also discussion in chapter 10, section 3.2 on Jesus' Nazareth Manifesto.*)

Jesus through this Manifesto made his agenda public, because he announced that he was going to begin his work with four groups of people. These four were the poor (*deen*), the captives (*bandi*), blind (*andhey*) and the oppressed (*dalit*). Jesus must have come face to face with these four segments of human society, which were the actual realities of people living in the region of Galilee at that time. Galilee was considered a socio-culturally backward region, and within its fold lay an even lesser known village called Nazareth, from where nothing good was ever supposed to have emerged. At least these were the views of average people of those days. But the words of the Nazareth Manifesto reveal Jesus' mission, with the contextual realities of Galilee as its cornerstone. But who are these four targeted groups of people of his mission?

The 'poor', the first target group of his mission, included not only the 'economically poor' but also poor in other ways too, i.e. physically weak, socially outcast and sinners in general (10:25-27, John 4:1-41, Matthew 20:1-16). This understanding of the 'poor' brings Jesus' concern closer to the Dalits in India, because they have faced these multiple poverties for more than 3500 years continuously.

After mentioning a specific group among the people (poor) to whom Jesus was going to reach out with the 'good news', he informs of the next two groups he was going to deal with during his mission; these were a mixed group of people, both rich and poor or dominant and dominated. These were 'captives' and 'blind'. The captives here are not referred to in the literal sense, but also meant those people who were captives of ideologies and of various kinds of structures. Such structural captivity included the captives of various systems pertaining to religious, cultural, economic, social and political spheres (Luke 4:1-5; 7:36-50; 11 20:19-26). Likewise, the third group, namely the 'blind', consisted not only of those afflicted with physical blindness, but also those whose mind and heart were closed to truth and values (Luke 4:37-45).

The fourth group of people referred to in the manifesto of Jesus are the 'oppressed', whom he said he would set free. For the expression 'oppressed', a Bible translator, Yesu Das Tiwari, used the Hindi word *'dalit'* in the Hindi New Testament, which was published by the Bible Society of India in 1967. At that time the Dalit movement, particularly among the Christians, was unknown. But the expression 'dalit' here is most suitable, because it covers all kinds of oppressions—religious, social, economic and political—that is being faced by the Dalits. Jesus intended to deal with these oppressions as part of the freedom offered to the Dalits.

The Nazareth Manifesto of Jesus envisions the transformation of the whole human society, which includes also the liberation for the dominant and oppressive group of people, who had become captive and blind to the various structures created by them, because of which the other groups, suffered too.

This is much about the mission agenda of Jesus, which supposed to be the agenda of his followers in future including the present Christian community in India. But to understand the spirit of Jesus' mission here we will give some examples of his teaching and works found in the first four of the New Testament in order to show how he rejected the various patterns of exclusion of people followed by the dominant groups of society of his time. One of the focal point of his teachings was that all persons are equal. Groups considered socially, economically and religiously low were his targets for empowerment. He challenged the dominant groups belonging to every areas of life and made them understand that their claims to consider themselves superior or higher than the other have no foundation and are contradictory to the divine will. The best examples, how Jesus tried to teach ordinary people and empower them through stories and by entering into a direct dialogue with them, we find in the Gospels. Here a few examples are given.

First example is from the parable of the Good Samaritan as told by St. Luke in his Gospel (Luke 10:25-37). According to St. Luke, this parable was told by Jesus to a teacher of religious law, who came to him to know about the way to receive eternal life. While entering into a dialogue with the teacher, Jesus asked him, as to what the Scripture says about it? The teacher in his answer gave the summary of Ten Commandants, which tells: '*Love the Lord your God with all your heart, with all your soul, with all your strength, and with your mind*'; and '*Love your neighbour as you love yourself.*' Jesus told the teacher your answer is right, so follow it and you will live. But the teacher of law asked Jesus, '*Who is my neighbour*'? It is in response to this question Jesus told him the parable of the Good Samaritan, according to which, a person was robbed and got seriously wounded by the robbers and was left on the road side. But then two persons belonging to two socially elevated groups (in our Indian language, the so-called high castes) priest and Levite came, but did not even look at the wounded person. But the third person belonging to a lowest considered socially group (in the Indian context, untouchable or today's Dalits), a Samaritan came on the same way, but when he saw the wounded, he took care of the person and saved his life. The point here Jesus made was that any person in need (who may belong to any faith or no faith) is our neighbour.

Again another story of a dialogue, which Jesus had with an untouchable woman (*in Indian context a Dalit*), who also happened to be a Samaritan. St. John narrated in detail the dialogue, which took place between Jesus and this woman, in his Gospel, chapter 4:1-41. In Jesus time, Jews used to consider Samaritans as untouchables upto the extent that even they will not use the same cups and bowls used by them (very close to the two tumblers practice in some parts of India which means one for the 'Untouchables' and other for the 'touchable'). Because of this social distinction, when Jesus asked drinking water from a woman of this untouchable community, she instead of giving him water raised a question by saying: 'How is it that you, a Jew, ask a drink of me, a women of Samaria'? (John 4:7-9). Also in Jesus' time no religious teacher would talk to a woman. This was the reason, when his disciples saw him '*they were greatly surprised to find him talking with a woman*' (John 4:27). But the whole point of this actual story is that Jesus showed his disciples, how there is need *to reverse the existing caste or race or gender based social order.*

The third example from Jesus' teaching, we can refer to the parable of the labourers in a Vineyard as recorded by St. Matthew in his Gospel, chapter 20:1-16. Here according to the parable, which Jesus told in order to explain the meaning of the Kingdom of heaven or God, the owner of the Vineyard hired some labourers at different times during the day. But when at the end of the day he asked his manager to pay all the labourers equal wages, the labourers who were hired first and worked for longer hours, objected to this action of the owner of the Vineyard, but he did not change his decision of equal payment to all labourers. Here we see Jesus introducing an alternative economic order, but radical in nature based not only on the principle of equal opportunity of employment, but also equal wages to all.

The final example, which is narrated by St. Luke 19:1-10 of a rich tax collector, Zacchaeus who was very keen to see Jesus, but could not see him, because of his being short in stature. But Jesus reached out to him and offered to visit his house. Zacchaeus welcomed Jesus to his house. But others grumbled and said: 'He has gone to be the guest of one who is a sinner.' But a real change came in the life of Zacchaeus and he said to the Jesus: 'look, half of my possession, Lord, I will give to the poor; and if I have defrauded anyone of anything, I will pay back four times as much'. Jesus in return said to him: 'to-day salvation has come to this house.' Here we see a rich sinner changing through Jesus' approach, based upon the principles of love, humility, faith, hope and critical thinking. *Because true education is the only way of bringing about a change or transformation.*

13.3. Conclusion

In conclusion I want to stress that Dalit-theology has to adopt the holistic mission approach as the final goal, which will not merely be restricted to the spiritual aspect of life, it has to include in it economic, social and political empowerment of the Dalits. It will also not be restricted only to Dalit Christians, but to all the Dalits belonging to all faiths or no faith. Even it has to address the non-Dalits the so called dominant caste groups as they equally have lost their original divinely created humanity.

So the mission agenda has to include (as was the case of Jesus' mission agenda) on one side to raise the Dalit awareness that they are remnant of casteless community based on divinely established principle of equality in contrast to the divisive caste system created by human beings; and on the other side the Dalit theology also has to create the possibility of fuller liberation or salvation, based on the Christ-event of redemption, which will not only stop with freeing the Dalits from the oppressive structures, but will go further to achieve the salvation for the whole people of God, including their oppressors. And this way the Dalit will enable the Dalits as well as others together to become an instrument of establishing a 'just society'.

The Dalits must rather free themselves and free their oppressors and participate in creating a new human being, one who is neither oppressor nor oppressed, on the contrary, a person in the process of liberation. Here comes a demand for the paradigm shift in a mission agenda for those who would like to engage themselves (including Christian Community) in the process of 'mission in context'.

NOTES

1. James Massey (ed.), *Globalisation and its Impact on Dalits: A Theological Response*, CDS, New Delhi, 2004.
2. T.K. John (ed.), *Broken Among the Victims: Dalit Presence at the World Social Forum 2004*, CDS, New Delhi, 2004.
3. See for full commentary on 'Jesus' Mission Agenda', in James Massey, *The Gospel According to Luke, New Testament*, vol. 3, *Dalit Bible Commentary*, CDS, New Delhi, 2007, pp. 69-73.
4. A mega project on 'Dalit Heritage and Liberation Traditions' is being carried on, which to be completed by the end of 2014.

PART 6

DALIT LIBERATION THEOLOGY

CHAPTER 14

Dalit Theology: Vision, Nature and Role

14.1. Introducing Dalit Theology

The doers of Dalit theology, beside placing it, in the past historical as well as present Dalit context also work on an assumption that the existing theologies, which include, old missionary theology and the present Indian Christian theology are irrelevant for the Dalits, because these are neither based on their life experiences nor do they fulfil the needs of their life. These according to them, also do not address the issues faced by the Dalits in their daily life.[1] Therefore, when the Dalit theologians refer to Dalit theology, they are, in fact, making an affirmation about the need of a theological expression, which will address and help them in search of their daily bread, to overcome their life situation of oppression, poverty, suffering, injustice, illiteracy and denial of their human identity or dignity. So these realities of Dalit life, form the reason(s) for the formulation of Dalit theology, which actually is a response to the context of the Dalits.

Here one other important point to be noted is that the expression 'Dalit', when added as a prefix to 'theology', serves as a pointer to the role of this theological expression or Dalit theology. The term 'Dalit' refers to the 'state' into which the people, who address themselves with this name are living. This is an oppressive state, into which they have been forced to live for centuries, by their opponents or oppressors by using the instrument of caste. Those Dalits of today, who have realized their personal as well as community state of oppression, to this realized state they have named as 'Dalit'.[2] The main factor behind this realization is their history, because it is their history, which has helped them to know about their past lost identity, which their opponents had deliberately tried to destroy. It is from the past history, the Dalits have also learned, how systematically their oneness has been destroyed by introducing among them hundreds of human division by naming them on the basis of their assigned names according to various low level jobs assigned to them.[3] This realization of the Dalits have forced them to engage themselves in the quest of 'solidarity' in order to once again regain their oneness. But it is Dalit theology, which helps them in placing the various actions of the past and the present in the theological context, as an assurance of what they have done or are doing is right in the eyes of God. These are the reasons why two themes: Dalit history and Dalit solidarity have been the major concern for some of the Dalit theologians. But beside these two themes, other questions, which we will deal in our remaining reflection will be: what relationship Dalit theology has with the existing and various liberation theologies, and also who will really do Dalit theology? At the end we will conclude with a brief description of the role of Dalit theology.

14.2. Importance of Dalit History

In India there are a number of leaders, both among the Christians and others, who say, 'We should not talk about the past.' In other words what they are saying is that we should forget our history. Thinkers belonging to other faiths, who hold such opinions include political ideologists, who belong to power-blocks of either so-called upper castes or classes, because they are afraid of losing their power or power structures. On the other hand, the Christian leaders or thinkers include those who hold power within the Church structures by virtue of being converts from the so-called upper castes. But along with these two categories of Christian groups opposed to the idea of, recognizing or acknowledging the past are a number of Christian leaders, who themselves are having Dalit origin, because of the fear that they or their forbears would be exposed. Of course, they are also influenced by the old missionary theological thinking that everything that we had, whether religious beliefs, or ideologies, or practices are evil or contrary to the Christian faith. Such groups of people also ask why should we remind ourselves of our past, because it means going back to where we started.

There are many other arguments which can be offered on behalf of those who oppose the idea of referring to the past. But we must understand that it is only our past history which can tell us about our present identity. This is particularly true of those members of Dalit communities, who are not only living a degraded life of poverty today, but have also lost their very humanity. A section of Dalits today are educated and are not living a life of poverty, which is true, but a majority of these people are mentally poor or their attitudes towards their own self is not fully human. Such cases clearly prove that mere economic upliftment or just formal education is not enough for regaining a full human dignity. In dealing with the situation of the Dalits, however, the efforts of Christian churches, the Indian government and most Non-Government Organizations have been limited mostly to these areas of life. Since these efforts are not enough to re-establish the full humanity of Dalit, it is imperative that attention should be given to their historical background, because the knowledge of the past alone could reveal that once Dalits were also full human beings, enjoying all the benefits of a normal human being, which include land, property, human dignity, natural resources and human freedom. And again this will not be possible until Dalit history is written from Dalit point of view that is 'the view from below'. Till now the views, which exist whether concerning history or theology or ideology, are from 'above', that is, they are either produced by the so called upper caste historians or others or from the background of European (mostly) representing the same 'view from above'. Therefore for Dalit history from their point of view, that is 'from below', an attempt is made to re-construct it, which have become part of the present work (chapters 1-5), because this is the first step towards re-constructing Dalit theology, which is to be the basis for recovering their lost human dignity about which we have come to know from their history.

On the question of the past history of a 'slave nation', to whom God gave liberation and made a 'nation', the words of the Bible are very eloquent—the same God commanded through Moses that they have to tell their past history of slavery and freedom to their children from generation to generation:

> When your children ask you, in time to come, 'What is the meaning of the decrees and the statutes and the ordinances that the Lord our God has commanded you?' Then you shall say to your children, 'We were Pharaoh's slaves in Egypt, but the Lord brought us out of Egypt with a mighty hand....

If we diligently observe this entire commandment before the Lord our God, as he has commanded us, we will be in right' (Deuteronomy 6:20-25).

The Bible also tells that whenever this nation ignored this commandment, God sent them back to a life of slavery and whenever they realized their mistake, He liberated them. In this sense, Indian Christians, particularly the Dalit Christians have not begun their history, because generally speaking they have continuously denied their past. In the New Testament St. Paul reminds also the Dalit Christians that they should always remember their past, and by doing so how God, out of nothing, has made them 'something' or a 'people' (I Corinthians 1:26-28). Enough said about the importance of Dalit history, so now we move to our next section on the 'Dalit.[4]

14.3. Importance of Solidarity

The expression 'solidarity', here is used in place of 'historical praxis',[5] because 'solidarity' is the most suitable expression, which can help Dalits to re-discover the core message of Christian faith from their perspective.[6] Also it is the solidarity which can help in bridging the divisions created by the caste people among the Dalits. But what actually we mean from this expression 'solidarity'? The answer to this question, we find in Divine solidarity, a story of which we find in the Bible. Because to begin God himself first has shown His solidarity with the human beings in history. The Bible writers, in order to concretize God's action of solidarity, picked up a case history of a nation namely Israelite, who with the time became a slave nation in Egypt. But God saw their suffering and oppression, which they had from the hands of their oppressors, Pharaohs of Egypt and He decided to help them through Moses (Exodus 1:8-14, 2:23-25). While commissioning Moses, he said 'I have witnessed the misery of my people in Egypt and have heard them crying out because of their oppressors. I know they are suffering and have come down to rescue them from the power of the Egyptians...' (Exodus 3:7, 8). Here we see God not only offering His solidarity with the oppressed in words or in ideas, but in actions also shows that He 'came down to rescue them', which means He became a part of their struggle. His action also shows that He took a definite side of the oppressed against the oppressors, which was not a religious action, but it was more of a political act, which included even economic and social dimensions also. Then of course we read in Exodus how God fought against the Egyptians on behalf of the Israelites through Moses till they did not receive complete liberation.

The climax of God's solidarity with the human beings, particularly with the oppressed people of this world can be seen in His incarnational act. The summary of this act of God we find in John 1:14. Here we find that through the act of incarnation, God not only Himself identified with human beings by becoming a human being, he also fully became a part of human history. A concrete picture of God's solidarity with human beings can be seen in Luke 2:1-7. Here we find a human child 'wrapped...in swaddling clothes, laid... in a manager' (Luke 2:7). With this, two of the Old Testament prophecies also got fulfilled, which many hundred of years earlier were predicted by a prophet about God's participation in human history. It was prophet Isaiah who prophesied 'A young woman... will give birth to a son', who will be called 'Emmanuel' which means 'God with us' (Isaiah 7:14) and the same prophet said God as a human being will have 'no form or comeliness' (Isaiah 53:4). So here (as part of the fulfilment of these prophecies) in the act of incarnation, we do meet God in full solidarity with human beings, not just as any human being, but one who became the poorest of the poor (in real sense a Dalit), who lost His other worldly identity completely for human beings' sake. This is what the expression 'solidarity' means and which we find in the historical incarnational act of God, which indeed challenges the Dalit Christians to follow it, so that their common experiences (along with the Dalit in general) should become the basis of an authentic Dalit theology.

14.4. The Particularity of Dalit Theology

Concerning Dalit theology, the one most important thing we should remember is that like its other sister liberation theologies, it is a theological expression, which has taken birth on one side from the historical experience of oppressed people, who address themselves by the name 'Dalit', and on the other side their encounter with the God of the Bible, who has always been biased towards the oppressed and historically poor. It is also based upon the Dalit assumption that they themselves are the makers of their history, which means that they are the subject of their history, not an object, which the histories written by their opponents have tried to show throughout the ages. This of course is the first step towards the Dalit liberation, because in real truth it is they (today's Dalits) of Indian Society, who represent the divinely undivided humanity of the created world. This is the original state of their lives, which Dalit theology is supposed to enable them to recover. Upto the realization of their original state, of course is, which Dalit history has revealed to them, because the 'divinely undivided humanity' is the one which their opponents have tried to destroy intentionally.

The concrete results of their opponents' onslaught upon their very humanity, resulted into the loss of their basic rights, which included educational, social, economic, cultural, political, spiritual and religious as seen in chapters 2, 3, 4, and 5 of this work. The recovery of all these now depend upon their solidarity. Because it is their commitment to their solidarity, which can generate power among themselves to face the challenge of their opponents. This solidarity is again two sided, a commitment to God on one side and a commitment to their fellow Dalits (who may belong to any religion, creed, ideology) on the other side. Now this dual commitment to solidarity, is in real sense the subject of the Dalit theology.

Dalit theology, as understood by some is not a counter-theology as compared to the traditional theologies, which include the European constructed missionary theology or the present Indian Christian theology. Because these theologies were neither intentionally formulated as enabling theological expressions to deal with the life issues of the Dalits nor these were based upon the experiences of the Dalits.

In the same way, Dalit theology cannot be replaced with any of the liberation theologies. It is particularly true with the South American born 'Liberation theology'. It is true that Dalit theology has commonality with 'Liberation theology' on the question of history as well as in the general goal, i.e. 'the whole liberation of the whole people,' but on the question of the actual history, context, racial elements, ideological basis, almost all the liberation theologies are different. For example our African brothers and sisters in North America were brought in by force, they never came with their choice.[7] On the other hand South Americans who have gone through a kind of economic oppression in Europe and later on gave birth to today's 'Liberation theology' were racially from the same stock as their oppressors. The theology in South America is based upon the economic based class system, whereas in North America, it is colour, culture, social and slave-master relationship based oppression, which becomes the basis of 'Black theology'. In the same way, the Korean based 'Minjung theology' is the outcome of ordinary people's pain, their frustrations, their agonies and their sufferings, along with their hopes, aspirations and struggle.[8]

But when we talk about Dalit theology or Dalit people's experiences, the situation changes immediately. Here the Dalits, unlike their sister communities of different countries, have lost everything. Dalit story of oppression is also too long as compared to any other group of the world. Also in the case of the Dalits, they lost almost everything, including their land, culture, language, colour, religion and political/social rights. For them everything has to begin new. Here their opponents, who as colonizers came at different stages of history, have today become the owners or masters of not only the resource material that belonged to the Dalits, they even became the owner of the Dalits. So the enslavement of the Dalits is multifaceted, which even the Dalits today themselves have accepted as reality. So in this way the historical context is enough to show that Dalit theology cannot be clubbed with any other theology/theologies either traditional or liberation.

14.5. Who is to do Dalit Theology?

Now about the question: 'Who is to do Dalit theology?' There is no doubt these have to be the Dalits themselves, who have to do this theology. Because it emerges from their pains, suffering, exploitation, sorrow, bitterness, anger and hatred, which they have been carrying on for generation to generation, for centuries, in their inner being. This truth actually brings us to one of the basic questions of epistemology. Because it is the theology of the Dalits, which emerges from their struggle based experience. Of course the committed non-Dalits, who genuinely are concerned with Dalit liberation can also do such a theology, but that actually will be a theology about the Dalits, and not of the Dalits.

But is there a difference between 'a theology of the Dalits' and 'a theology about the Dalits?' Yes, there is a difference, because the first emerges from the experiential knowledge of the Dalits and the later is the outcome of a intellectually acquired knowledge of the non-Dalits. Here in this process of theologizing, the roles of hermeneutics and epistemology are very important. It is the hermeneutics, which tells us that there is nothing which can be taken as neutral or objective point of view. Hermeneutics also accepts the subjective point of view and in the process of Dalit theology, the later view is the view of the oppressed Dalits. After the hermeneutics, the question of epistemology comes first before one enters into the process of theologizing, because any acquired knowledge will have its own implications as compared to the experiential knowledge. This also makes one other point clear that Dalit theology or even any true theology, cannot emerge only through academic exercises. A genuine Dalit theology will emerge from the Dalit-praxis for liberation and by the theologians involved in their struggle. Here we must add that both the content and form of Dalit theology are a corporate contribution of the Dalits engaged in the struggle for their liberation.

But while accepting the above position, we must also remember that it does not mean that we reject or even lessen the role of the non-Dalits who are committed to the cause of the Dalit liberation. We are only trying to differentiate between the 'emotional identity' (of the Dalits) and the 'solidarity in action' (of the non-Dalits). Here the difference is being made between the experience of the pain of the victims (Dalits) and those who do not have the experience of that pain (non-Dalits). Because non-Dalits' experience is about the dalithood, not of the dalithood.

What is being said is true in general, but here one who believes in God's solidarity with the oppressed Dalits in His incarnational act, has to accept the truth that a non-Dalit by following the model of incarnational solidarity can authentically identify with the oppressed Dalits' faith-experience and work with the struggle of the Dalits for their liberation. Personally I believe every baptized Christian is supposed to have that experience (means of death and resurrection) by which that person becomes, genuinely a part of Dalit struggle. If this is true then the whole universal Church or Christian community can be a part of the Dalit struggle. So finally what is our answer to the question: 'Who is to do Dalit theology?' Our answer is both Dalits and non-Dalits, though the theology based on the experiential experience of the Dalits will be a theology of the Dalits and the theology based on the gained experience will a theology about the Dalits. Yet both these will have an indispensable, complementary role to play in conscientizing and creating solidarity among the Dalits and non-Dalits in the struggle for the Dalits' liberation, which actually will become a means for bringing in a structural change in the society and will lead towards a just and humane society.

14.6. Role of Dalit Theology

About the role of Dalit theology, we have to say: *First*, it has to address to the Dalits themselves about their state and the consciousness. It can help in raising the consciousness of the Dalits to the fact that they are remnants of a casteless community, based upon a divinely established principle of equality (as against the caste based divided communities, which is the handiwork of human beings). Dalit theology also has to raise their consciousness to the fact, that their assigned inferiour status is neither of their own creation, nor a divinely ordained reality, but is imposed on them by a man-made system. Therefore Dalit theology has to prepare the Dalits to reject the old caste based religious order which have perpetuated their captivity, because this will pave a way toward their full liberation.

Second, Dalit theology has also to address the non Dalits, both within the Christian community (Church) as well as outside. Because the opponents or the oppressors of the Dalits have equally lost their original divinely created humanity. The role of Dalit theology with regard to this will make them conscious about the suffering and pain of the Dalits and also about their own non-humanity, which allows them to treat the Dalits oppressively. Again Dalit theology will help them in regaining their humanity.

Third, Dalit theology has to play a role in raising the conscience of the Church/Christian Community as a whole. The current traditional theologies have been playing a role which has forced the Church to maintain the status quo or existing orders of political, economic, social, religious, cultural, including caste based divisions, not only outside, but within the Church life also. So it is Dalit theology which can challenge the Church to change her stand, with regard to all these structures. In this way Dalit theology will help the Church to become an instrument of change.

Fourth, Dalit theology has to enable the ordinary Christians to take active part in the struggle of the Dalits. At present even the ordinary members of the Christian community in India are convinced that it is against the teaching of Christian faith to join any struggle or movement. But as seen in the section on 'Dalit solidarity', our Lord Himself in His incarnational act of solidarity has shown the way to us for such a situation.

Fifth, Dalit theology has to create the possibility of full liberation or salvation, basing upon the Christ event of redemption, which will not stop only with freeing the Dalits from the oppressive structures, but will go further to achieve the salvation for the whole people of God including their oppressors. And in this way, Dalit theology will enable the Dalits to become an instrument of establishing a just society in which all will enjoy the equal human dignity.

NOTES

1. T.K. Oommen, *Protest and Change: Studies in Social Movements*, Sage, New Delhi, 1996, pp. 120-6.
2. See for detailed discussion and the use of the term 'dalit' in the Indian context: James Massey, *Towards Dalit Hermeneutics*, CDS Pamphlet no. 4, New Delhi, 2001, pp. 18-22.
3. See for detailed discussion on Dalit History: James Massey, *Roots: Concise History of Dalits*, CDS Pamphlet no. 3, New Delhi, 2001, pp. 20-46.
4. See for detailed information on the importance of history and analysis of data available in Indian Church History: Massey, *Towards Dalit Hermeneutics*, op. cit., pp. 23-44.
5. Gustavo Gutierrez, A *Theology of Liberation: History, Politics and Salvation*, Orbis Books, Maryknoll, New York, 1973, p. 7.
6. See for the meaning of solidarity in the Gospel sense: Pope John Paul II: *Sollicitudo Rei Social* (On Social Concern, Encyclical Letter), St. Pauls, Bombay, 1988, p. 74.
7. Basil Moore (ed.), *Black Theology: The South African Voice*, C. Hurt & Co., London, 1973, pp. 49, 52.
8. Kim Yong-Bock, *Messiah and Minjung: Christ's Solidarity with the People for New Life*, Christian Conference of Asia, Hong Kong, 1992, p. 5.

CHAPTER 15

Paradigm Shift in Theological Education

15.1. From Advocacy to Solidarity

The advocacy approach in social, development and theological circles, now is in use for more than three decades. To begin with, it was used by the social activists and development proponents in the second half of the 1960s. They used it in the Greek sense (*parakletos*, 'one called to stand someone')[1] in order to show their special concern for the oppressed and the poor. They instead of taking a neutral stand between the rich and the poor, the oppressor and the oppressed, took sides with the latter groups. With this stand, the social activists started speaking on their behalf against the structures and systems, especially related to the workers' rights. This approach continued to be in use till the end of the 1980s and also had played a positive role in raising the conscience of the various oppressed groups all over the world including in South Asian countries.

Another important point also should be made here. The advocacy approach also had the mandate from the Scripture and particularly from the life and teaching of Jesus Christ because his Nazareth manifesto (through which he announced the good news to the poor, freedom to the captives, sight to the blind and liberty to the oppressed) had direct bearing on the formation of this approach (Luke 4:18). Here we must remember the advocacy approach has a prerequisite, i.e. commitment to the cause.[2]

The advocacy approach in the sense stated here is part of the concern of the early liberation theologies. The reason behind this may be that many of them do not belong to the poor or the oppressed groups themselves, but they have made the cause of the oppressed their own. This is an important point to note, because if we accept it, then the liberation theologies like Black theology, Feminist theology, Dalit theology or any local context based theology, will have to adopt a different approach in their undertaking. Of course advocacy elements will also be part of their concern, but along with that, there will always be extra elements based on their special historical contexts and needs. It is particularly true with Dalit theology, and possibly with other theological expressions too, which are formulated in South Asian local contexts. As far as I am concerned, I can perhaps speak about Dalit theology more truthfully, because of my own background as a Dalit. For the Dalits, the most important thing, which they need is 'solidarity'. Since, advocacy approach is the one, which others till now have used on their behalf, it has failed, because it lacked comprehensive approach to the issue. Therefore most of the Dalits have moved from an 'advocacy' to 'solidarity' approach.

But why this shift? A brief answer to this question is given here.

First, we need to remember that the advocacy approach is limited to certain issues and it is more used as a method either for or against someone. This is not true with the solidarity approach, as it is a comprehensive concept in its content and commitment. Even advocacy becomes part of it. About this shift, social activists and development proponents (who actually introduced this approach) have also voiced their assent. For example Bishop George Ninan in one of his talks pointed out that:

> In a country like India, it was easy a few years ago to identify the capitalist class to give it a face, a name and a location. But today it is not confined to any single country or industry or family. The owners have become nameless, a faceless, multi-national corporation that transcends geographical boundaries. So we find that the poor and marginalised and exploited are in the first world as well as in the third world.... Under these circumstances, who is going to advocate whose cause?... Hence the time has come for yet another shift in approach. For the 21st century the approach must move from advocacy to solidarity, a solidarity in which the oppressed and marginalised of the world will stand together shoulder to shoulder, along with all the traditional victims of society—women, the so-called lower castes, adivasis, children—to fight for a world in which it, will he possible for this vast number of people to find rooms to grow into fuller of life.[3]

Bishop Ninan is right, because the time has possibly come, when the poor and the oppressed themselves have to enter into a 'solidarity', which will be their power base and will help them in shaping their present economic, social and political existence.[4] It is this reality which also will help them in destroying the oppressor's hold on them. In this process, the role of theology will become vital in showing that the actions taken as part of the liberation process are right in the eyes of God. The document has laid stress in the broader meaning of the solidarity, about which we have also discussed in our last chapter in Dalit theology. This document *Sollicitudo Rei Social's* (on Social Concern) is given as 'solidarity that is...a commitment to the good of one's neighbour with the readiness, in the Gospel sense to lose one-self for the sake of the other'.[5] Solidarity in this sense is also our response to God as an expression of our faith in Him.

Having discussed about the advocacy approach and reasons; behind our proposal to move from advocacy to solidarity, we will now turn to the theological education in India and South Asia.

15.2. Present State of Theological Education

If we look at the situation of theological education, around the globe including in South Asia region, from the point of view of the advocacy or solidarity approach, we certainly will find it not very encouraging. Serious concern shown about this situation has been expressed by Christian leaders as well as theologians. For example at a consultation held in Oslo, Norway during August 1996 on the theme 'Viability of Theological Education', it was expressed,

> We acknowledge that some patterns of theological education have not assisted the churches to move forward, to respond to hurting peoples, to relate holistically to the earth, or to be people—focused and Christ-centred. We confess and grieve that we have sometimes ignored crucial insights about life and God in our work as theological educators.[6]

An Indian theologian Gnana Robinson has pointed to another weakness of our theological education: 'Theological Education, instead of liberating people, seem to enslave people, enslave them to the feelings of bitterness, anger and hostility on the basis of caste, race, colour and creed; instead of uniting and empowering them, it tends to divide and weaken them.'[7] Another Indian theologian K.C. Abraham while speaking on 'Theological Education', pointed out another side of the problem of our theological education when he said, 'Imagination and passion are two essential components of an 'empowering-others-for-mission'. Such an education model is rarely operative in many of our colleges. Instead, many of our present programmes are characterized by a concern for a cool, dispassionate, neutral and objective—whatever it means—scholarship.[8]

These views agree that there is a serious problem with the whole system or approach which is being followed presently by our South Asian theologians and theological educators. One of the major factors responsible for this state of our theological education, at least in India, is due to the very nature of the two of our traditional theological expressions which include the missionary theology and the Indian Christian theology, upon which we have been, till now, dependent. The first expression reached us with the arrival of European missionaries, and the second expression was born with the efforts made by some of the so-called upper caste converts as their response to their faith. Both these theological expressions had a particular understanding of human history, which we need to take note of seriously. Because of this factor, these two expressions have made theology irrelevant and ineffective in the contexts of the majority of the peoples in South Asia including India.

As both these theological expressions centred around the study of God or *Brahman*, having in their mind the Greek connotation of the expression 'theology', as the science of Pure Being or God,[9] these systems have very little to do directly with human history. In the case of the first, there are two histories, namely sacred and human (profane), and the emphasis in theology has been basically on the sacred aspect of history. This is specially true of the theology, which reached us through the missionaries. It lacked depth and understanding of the human context particularly the Indian or South Asian. This weakness of the inherited theology makes it ineffective in our context. On the other hand, in the case of the second, history has no meaning. Because, according to the Indian classical Hindu religion, history is cyclic, which moves on, from one great age or *yuga* to another, until at last the wheel turns full circle and returns to the beginning. According to this view, history has no concept of either a purpose or progress.[10]

As noted earlier in our discussion, the 'inherited theology' as well as the current 'Indian Christian theology' do not have a real place for human history in their basic concerns. These have not taken into consideration the various local contexts. Because, their basic concern is God, not human being. Their efforts are to reach God as a human being. These expressions do not bring God to human history or human beings. On the other hand we agree with James H. Cone, when he says:

> Theology is human beings reflecting on the meaning of God in the world.... It is incumbent upon every person of faith to talk about, to reflect upon, and to interpret the meaning of God in their lives, in the life and struggle of their communities. No one else can do that for them. Now, since theology is something of a telling of a story of God's presence in the world, every person has to tell that story. Europeans cannot do that for African Americans and African Americans can't do that for Dalits people. Each theology is therefore a particular theology.[11]

Now if we agree with Cone, then till now while following and teaching these two traditional theological expressions in the Indian seminaries and colleges, we have left the vast majority of Christians and others from the purview of theological education, particularly women, Dalits and tribals, which form between 80 to 90 per cent of the Christian membership in India (which also apply to other South Asian countries). Whatever we have been teaching, it was not their 'story' about 'God's presence in the world'. About this truth some years ago, in one of my articles, 'Ingredients for a Dalit Theology', I pointed out:

> We must remember that these thinkers and their experiences ... were very different from an average Christian's in India because all of them came either from a high caste or their families were rich. So after they became Christians, their immediate concerns were not the same as thousands of those who became Christians, who were both poor and belonged to the lower strata of our society. These high caste converts' immediate concern was how they should relate or interpret their new faith or experiences in Indian thought forms, i.e., based on the Brahminic religion and culture in which they had grown up. Their major preoccupation was searching for an indigenous expression of Christianity, which forms an important element in Indian Christian theology.[12]

Thus their theology did not address itself to or reflect the issues, which the majority of Christians faced either before or after they became Christians. Now these Christians' concern has not been to search for an Indian expression of their new faith. In fact in this they are more indigenous than any of the urbanized Christians. What these poor village Christians are searching for even today is how to earn their daily bread, how to overcome their life situation of oppression, poverty, suffering, injustice, illiteracy and denial of identity. Indian Christian theology and other theologies have failed, and continue to ignore these basic issues of life, which for the majority of Christians, and for most of the Indians, are questions of survival.[13]

In brief, this is what we can possibly say about the present state of theological education in our country, which indeed is not very comfortable. But then what possibly can we do in this situation? To look for an answer for this question, let us now move to the next section of this paper.

15.3. Solidarity in Theological Education

The distinction between 'advocacy approach' and 'solidarity approach' has been discussed earlier in detail. From our discussion it has become clear that the advocacy approach has been used on behalf of others. But on the other hand when we say 'in solidarity with some one' it means either one takes the place of the other person or one 'becomes' someone. But how this idea of solidarity can take a form of an action? Part of the answer to this question we find in the following words of Paulo Freire:

> In fact, thinking about intellectuals and their role, their practical action as part of wider practical action, i.e. social practical action, leads in necessarily to reflect on their vision of the future.... Action to translate the vision into reality, in its turn, begins to require, as I understand, virtues or qualities on the part of intellectuals in their words and their actions should convince as closely as possible.... And to translate, or attempt to translate, the vision into reality in such conditions is to act on and not with the people. In that case, in other words, if I work on and not with the people, I contradict my revolutionary words about the creation of a just society.... If I work simply for the people and not with them, I become more and more elitist.... That is not, of course, my approach. When I ask a company with whom I shall translate the vision into reality, I reply with the dominated social classes, with the popular masses, and with those who, although of a different social class from the workers attempt ... to commit 'class-suicide'. Hence the intellectuals who hold to this vision of the future must confirm it by passing over into the world of people.[14]

In order to apply these thoughts of Freire to our theological education, we have to replace in the above statement, 'intellectuals' with 'theologians' or 'theological educators'. The future vision about which Freire has spoken is 'the creation of a just society' which is also the vision of any theological expression. At present the problem is not with the vision, the problem is with the translation of this vision into a reality. This, of course, will not be possible as long as our theological educators will continue to work for God's people. They ought to work not with them, but out there in the world. But before that they have to go through the experience of what Freire calls a 'class-suicide' and what I said in 1994 about a 'caste-suicide', while describing 'A Vision of a Dalit'. A question I at that time raised was, can the so-called upper caste people play any role in the struggle of the Dalits? Part of my answer was:

> ...it is also true that the members of the so called upper class can play a constructive role in the struggle of the Dalits as well as their own, provided, they firstly put their full trust in the abilities of the Dalits and stop giving them a paternalistic treatment; secondly, they should be ready to enter into a Dalit situation, fully, which is the only way of identifying with their struggle, and thirdly, they should be ready to commit 'caste-suicide', which means wholly reject the system they belong to and fully enter into the struggle of the Dalits in order to work with them, not for them.[15]

Here again, 'the so called upper caste' can be replaced with 'theologians' or 'theological educators'. What is being said about the Dalits in this statement is equally applicable to the tribals, women, various backward classes, religious minorities and other weaker sections of our South Asian societies. But the main point of the above two statements lies in these two expressions, 'work with the people' and 'enter into Dalit situation'. We find the way to do this in the 'incarnational act' of God about which we have already discussed in this paper. According to our discussion, 'God not only identified himself with human beings by becoming a human being ... in the act of incarnation, we do meet God in full solidarity with us, not just as any human being; but one who becomes the poorest of the poor (in real sense a Dalit), who lost his other-worldly identity completely for the sake of human beings'. Here the expression 'lost his other-worldly identity completely' means He went through the process of what Freire, a 'class-suicide' or what I called, a 'caste-suicide' in the Indian or South Asian context.

Now the question is: Are our theologians or theological educators willing to go through this suicidal experience in order to implement the new paradigm of theological education? For example two of the Indian theologians, to whom I have already referred earlier, K.C. Abraham and Gnana Robinson have helped to articulate this new paradigm. K.C. Abraham while talking about the 'Paradigm Shift in Contemporary Theological Thinking' has talked actually about the need and basis of the formulation of a new theology in these words:

A Paradigm-shift in theology, a new way of understanding and interpreting Christian faith, a new way of theologising is evident in the theologies that are emerging from the marginalised in India, in our continuing effort to support the challenges of religious plurality and poverty we need to affirm this change and reformulate our theology.[16]

On the other hand, Gnana Robinson actually has proposed a new paradigm for theological education, which he has summed up in these words:

In brief, the new paradigm for theological education should be a life-centred paradigm, aiming at preparing people in all contexts to opt for life and, in solidarity with those whose life is threatened, the marginalised and oppressed, to struggle for their liberation, through working towards creating a New Humanity in Christ.[17]

Finally if we have to translate this new vision and the paradigm, we need to introduce radical changes in our theological education system, in its structure, content and teaching methodology in terms of the solidarity approach. For such radical changes, the initiative has to come from the Spirit and from the people of God. It's hoped they will hear such a divine call and will also continue to respond to the same.

NOTES

1. *The New Bible Dictionary*, IVP, London, 1968. p. 16.
2. Gustavo Gutierrez, A *Theology of Liberation: History Politics and Salvation*, Orbis Books, Maryknoll, New York, 1973, p. IV.
3. This quotation is taken from a note prepared by Bishop George Ninan based upon his informal talk in a Church of North India meeting recently.

4. See for a detailed treatment, 'Dalit Solidarity and Theology', in James Massey, *Downtrodden: The Struggle of India's Dalits for Identity, Solidarity and Liberation*, WCC, Geneva, 1997, pp. 59-65.
5. John Paul II, Encyclical Letter, *Sollicitudo Rei Socialis* (On Social Concern), Bombay, 1999, pp. 74, 78.
6. *Ministerial Formation*, World Council of Churches, Unit I: Unity and Renewal Ecumenical Theological Education, April 1997, WCC, Geneva, p. 38.
7. *Affirming Faith in Indian Context*: A *New Mandate for the New Century* (A Report of the National Consultation on Theological Education 1995), ed. D.S Satyaranjan, Senate of Serampore College, 1996, p. 124.
8. Gnana Robinson, 'Theological Education in India Today: Problems and Challenges', in *National Council of Churches Review*, vol. CXV no. 4, April 1995, p. 291.
9. N.P. William, 'What is Theology?', in *The Study of Theology* prepared under the direction of Kenneth E. Erik, London, 1939, p. 3.
10. R.H.S. Boyd, *An Introduction to Indian Christian Theology, ISPCK*, Delhi, 1991, p. 186.
11. 'Theology, Ideology and the Dalits: An Interview with James H. Cone', in *Dalit International Newsletter*, vol. 3, no. 1, February 1998, p. 6.
12. James Massey, 'Ingredients for a Dalit Theology', in *Towards a Dalit Theology*, ed. M.E. Prabhakar, ISPCK, Delhi, 1989, pp. 58.
13. Ibid., p. 59.
14. Paulo Freire and Antonio Faundez, *Learning to Question*: A *Pedagogy of Liberation*, WCC Publications, Geneva, 1989. pp. 54-6.
15. James Massey, 'Vision of a Dalit', in *National Council of Churches Review*, vol. CXIV, no. 7, August 1994, p. 576.
16. K.C. Abraham, 'Paradigm Shift in Contemporary Theological Thinking', in *Bangalore Theological Forum*, vol. XXIV, nos. 3 & 4, September & December 1992, United Theological College, Bangalore, p. 61.
17. Gnana Robinson, 'In Solidarity with New Humanity and New Creation in Christ: A Task of Theological Education in India', in D.S. Satyaranjan (ed.), op. cit., p. 58.

CHAPTER 16

Spirituality of Combat Leads to Whole Salvation

16.1. Myths and Stories of Oppression (Examples)

(a) When they divided *Purusa* (creator god Brahma),
How many portions did they make?
What do they call his mouth, his arms?
What do they call his thighs and feet?
The *Brahman* (priest) was his mouth,
of both arms was *Rajana* (Kshatriya warrior) made.
His thighs became *Vaisya* (trader),
From his feet the *Sudra* (serving caste) was produced.[1]

(b) From the arm of Vena, thus rubbed, sprang a celebrated monarch name Prithu, by whom, in olden times the earth was milked for the advantage of mankind…when he (Vena) was inaugurated, by the Rishis or sages, a monarch of the earth, he caused it to be everywhere proclaimed, that no worship should be performed…no gifts bestowed upon the Brahmans. 'I, the King, said he, am the Lord of sacrifice…' then those pious Munis (brahman sages) were filled with wrath, and cried out to each other: 'Let this wicked wretch be slain'…and they fell upon the King…slew him….And the people…said 'Now that the Kingdom is without a King…' The sages, hearing this consulted, and together rubbed the thigh of the King, who had left no offspring, to produce a son. From the thigh, thus rubbed, came forth a being of the complexion of charred stake, with flattened features…a dwarfish stature….His descendants, the inhabitants of the Vindhya mountains….By this is means the wickedness of the Vena was expelled; those *Nishadas* (a title for Dalits or indigenous) being born of his sins, and carrying them away….The Brahmans proceeded to rub the right arm of the king, from which friction was engendered the illustrious son of Vena, named Prithu… And thus was born the mighty Prithu…the Lord of the earth…was the first ruler to whom the title of Raja (King) was ascribed….[2]

(c) The Kshatriya reads the Veda and learns it, but does not teach it (this right is only with Brahmans)...such as saying prayers, the recitation of the Veda, ...is forbidden to him (*sudra*)...a Sudra or a Vaisya is proved to have recited the Veda, he is accused by the Brahmans before the ruler; and the latter will order his tongue to be cut off....In the days of King Rama, human life was very long-always of a well-defined and well-known length. Thus a child never died before its father. Then, however, it happened that the son of a Brahman died while the father was till alive. Now the Brahman brought his child to the door of the King and spoke to him....Then Rama began to inquire into the cause of this, and finally they pointed out to him a *Candala* (a Dalit) who took the greatest pains in performing worship and in self-torment. The King rode to him and found him on the banks of the *Ganges* (a river considered holy) hanging on something with his head downward. The King bent his bow, shot at him, ...Then he spoke: 'That is it! I kill thee on account of a good action which thou art not allowed to do.' When he returned to him he found the son of the Brahman alive.[3]

(d) However, Chokhamela (died AD 1338) and Kanaka, the untouchable (Dalit) saints were not allowed to enter the temple of Vithal at Pandharpur and the temple of Krishna at Udipi respectively. Thus they had tried to assert their right of spirituality and equality, but in vain.[4]

16.2. Current Spirituality

Current Indian spirituality is drawn from the religious traditions of the Vedas, Upanishads, the two epics—*Ramayana* and *Mahabharata* and the *Manusmriti*. These reflect the views of the Aryans who were the first colonizers of the Dalits. The Aryans who in time came to address themselves as upper castes successfully crushed (*dal*) the spirituality of the Dalits. The three examples (a, b, c) taken from the *Rigveda* (earliest written source in India), *Vishnu Purana* (Brahmanical written sources) and from an account of Al-Beruni (written about AD 1030) a Muslim of Iranian origin (b. AD 973 and d. AD 1048-9) respectively, confirm that serious attempts were made to crush the spirituality of the Dalits. Example (d) drawn indicates that the attempts to crush the spiritual rights of the Dalits, continue even during later periods including today.

The *Rigveda*, bears testimony to the fact that the Dalits had their own laws to govern their spiritual and religious life, which as expected, the Aryans regarded as 'Alien laws' (10.22.8). However, we do find remnants of Dalit spirituality in their religious traditions. Traditional scholars of religion have labelled the religious traditions of the Dalits as 'little traditions' and those of their opponents, the Aryans as 'great traditions'. This division of religious practices, assigns a secondary place to Dalit spirituality. The roots of Dalit spirituality lie in their worship of nature, earth, water, trees and animals, etc. In contrast to Aryans who worship in a temple or a building, the Dalits practise corporate worship in an open place. For instance, in my own village, the Dalits worship a humanly-made dome-shaped mound of earth, called *Bala Shah*. This mound faces eastwards and is placed under a tree or in an open spot with an earthen lamp (*divya*) burning over it. On an auspicious day, the devotees worship here with their offerings.

Another point of contrast is that Dalit spirituality is liberative in nature because of its inclusiveness. On the contrary, traditional Aryan spirituality is oppressive in nature because of its exclusiveness.

The content of Dalit spirituality is mostly found in the narrative stories, folklores and songs.

16.3. Dalit Responses (Examples)

16.3.1. *Dalit Marathi Poets and a Story Writer*

(a) Their inhuman atrocities have carved caves
in the rock of my heart
I must tread this forest with wary steps
eyes fixed on the changing times
The tables have turned now
Protests spark
now here
now there
I have been silent all these days
listening to the voice of right and wrong
But now I will fan the flames
For human rights.
How did we ever get to this place
this land which was never mother to us?
Which never gave us even
the life of cats and dogs?
I hold their unpardonable sins as witness

and turn, here and now,
a rebel.[5]

(b) I do not ask
for the sun and moon from your sky
your farm, your land,
your high houses or your mansions
I do not ask for gods or rituals
    Castes or sects
Or even for your mother, sisters, daughters.
I ask for
my rights as a man…
My rights: contagious caste riots
festering city by city, village by village,
man by man
For that's what my rights are
Sealed off, outcast, road-blocked, exiled.
I want my rights, give me my rights.
Will you deny this incendiary sate of things?
I'll uproot the scriptures like railway tracks.
Burn like a city bus your lawless laws
my friends!
My rights are rising like the sun.
Will you deny this sunrise?[6]

(c) On roads laid out according to the plan
Breaths thwarted till yesterday, crawled and sped
along
And with each swing of these orphaned breaths
my mute existence was moved
and swayed as a pendulum.
The unscrupulous pundits awaken desire
In the stillborn womb of civilization,
flaunted overhead, naked placards,
with slogans of purity and holiness
their metaphysical gymnastics trampled and
scattered my life, unbalanced already,
the life of the Dalits crushed
by tyrant stones of grinding inequality….[7]

(d) Come harvest time with its operations of winnowing and sifting, … That day, as usual, Grandpa Yetalya took me with him as he went out looking for a job of winnowing and treading out the corn at the threshing floor.... We stopped at a threshing floor. There, tidying a pile of dishevelled ears of corn, was Bapu Patil. Grandpa approached Patil and saluted him with a *johar*. Acknowledging Grandpa's salute like a swaggering maharaja, Bapu Patil said, 'Hey, what brings you here at such an early hour? Hope you haven't come here with your mind set on evil. For don't they say, an encounter with a Mahar in the morning, and you're doomed for good'. '...Why do you say that, Anna? I am your slave. I have come to you on purpose on hearing of the operations at your threshing floor. My lord is our bread-giver and we find it a privilege to beg for our share of corn, master. I am your begging Mahar and feel proud to be so....' 'Don't give me that line, you're no longer the Mahar-Mangs (names of two Dalit communities) of the good old days, to beg for your share of the corn. You are now Harijans! You've even started claiming equality, ... Come on, don't you know that the rain-god got enraged because you—because you—the Mahars and Mangs—have profaned religion, ...

And mind you, even if a Mahar or Mang gets educated no one will ever call him a Brahmin. A Mahar is a Mahar even if he passes L.L.B. and becomes a barrister. You should know the story of Chokhamela. Was he let into the temple by Vithoba of Pandharpur?...' The next moment I set to work with my head bent low, moving the grubbing-hoe in the heap of corn. Somehow I managed to suppress my anger. Bapu Patil was standing close by, watching us for some time. After a while he left but not before warning us: 'Finish the job before I return from breakfast. We'll yoke the bullocks for the winnowing in the evening. Hurry up. Don't you know you have to work hard if you want your share of corn?'...

But after we had toiled throughout the day Bapu Patil did not given Grandpa even a few measures of jowar. Grandpa was crestfallen. As we dejectedly left the threshing floor, however, Grandpa could not fail to notice the pen where stale, rancid pieces of bread lay scattered on the ground in front of the oxen. It's rightly said that as the Chamar has his eye on the *chappal*, so does the Mahar on stale bread. Flies were swarming over the mouldering crumbs which had turned green and foul.

Grandpa begged Bapu Patil for those crumbs. The oxen seemed to have refused to eat them....He walked in silence for a few moments. He looked as if he were lost in deep thought. Suddenly he stopped and turning to me, asked, 'How will the Mahars survive if they abandon the land-right? Thanks to it we can at least get these stale crumbs. On this way can I approach the landlord and beg for bread as my right. But if that too is gone, what are we left with?...We Mahars have been misled by the false notion of land-right, taking it as a rightful favour to beg for bread as long as we live. We forget all the while that the crumbs they give us make us slaves....' At night everyone at home greedily hogged the stuff. What with the heavy meal, we feel asleep immediately after supper. But the next morning we woke up to the sound of Grandpa writhing in agony like a poisoned dog. He was vomiting an purging too...I was sitting by Grandpa's bed...Sitting by the side of his bed, shedding tears, I felt benumbed and dispondent. My mind was wailing in agony. When shall the meek and humble people of my community be uplifted? And when shall they be treated like human beings...When? In the mean time my maternal uncle had brought a doctor....Examining Grandpa, the doctor asked, What did he eat last night? I went into the kitchen and brought the earthen pot in which the rancid crumbs of bread mixed with dulli had been...the doctor looked surprised as he said, 'That's it! The mould in the stuff created toxin. The toxin must have caused his dysentery. It's a serious case....' Grandpa showed great amazement as he lay in bed: 'What? You say the crumbs had turned to poison? It was in fact poison? Poisoned bread...?' ... None of the medicines suggested by the doctor proved effective and were became helpless. Mustering all his strength and with tremendous will power Grandpa finally succeeded in articulating a few words: 'Mhadeva, don't weep, my boy. I'm an old thing now. And being so old, I may stop breathing any moment. What can I say to you now? I can only say: never depend on the age-old bread associated with our caste. Get as much education as you can. Take away this accursed bread from the mouths of the Mahars. This poisonous bread will finally kill the very humanness of man...' Then he stopped abruptly, turned his face away and closed his eyes for ever.[8]

16.4. Dalit Spirituality

In Panjabi there is a saying, '*Jis tan lage, soi jane*' (the real pain is known by the victim). The seven responses given above reflect the harsh truths of Dalit spirituality and the anguish felt by saints and poets as Dalits.

The poetry passages used to express this pain are translated from Hindi, Panjabi, Telugu, Marathi. In set (A) the Dalit Muslim saint, Kabir has boldly declared that all human beings are spiritually equal as they share one source of origin (*Light*). He questioned, 'who is noble? or who is inferior?'

The next poetry passage under set A is quoted from the Sikh scripture *Guru Granth Sahib*, and is written by the fourteenth century poet saint Namdev. A Sudra by birth, he vehemently condemns the maltreatment given to him on his first visit to a Hindu temple. When the upper caste devotees realized he was a low caste washerman they pushed him out from the temple. Pained by this treatment, he retired to the courtyard behind the temple and there he had an intimate spiritual experience with God, as a result of which the door of the temple turned towards him.

Passage (c) of set A, represents the testimony of a Dalit conscience in the middle ages; that of Ravidas whose spirituality even the Brahmins respected. His poetry clearly shows that the Brahmins respected him and therefore attempted to elevate his status in the hierarchy though on their own terms. This is reflected in the line: 'Yet upper caste Brahmins to me make obeisance.' The reason for this was because Ravidas' relationship with God had been set right.

The extracts of set B are taken from the writings of Dalit Marathi authors who are Buddhists by faith. The four examples vividly show that Dalit consciousness made them revel and they no longer want to be the objects in upper castes' writing but have chosen to be the 'subjects' of their own writings. As Lanjewar clearly states, 'I have been silent all these days listening to the voice of right and wrong. But not I will fan the flame for humble rights.'

Limbale vehemently demands his rights as a 'human being' when he says, 'I do not ask gods or rituals, castes or sects… I ask rights as a man…my rights: contagious caste riots, festering city by city, village by village, man by man. For that's what my rights are—sealed off, outcast, road-blocked, exiled. I want my right, give me my rights… My rights are like the rising sun will you deny this sunrise.' 'The sunrise' symbolizes the new spirituality—a spirituality which had till now been crushed (*Dal*) and broken but which had risen in revolt to protest and demand a fuller Dalit liberation.

Contrary to the Bhakti Dalit saints who struggled only for a religious equality,[9] the Dalit Marathi poets demand a full human liberating spirituality which will lead to a total change.

Bandhumadhav's story, titled 'Poisoned Bread' states that the poisoned bread is an instrument which kills the very humanness of man, in other words, it destroys the inner spirituality of the Dalits as it is given to them by the upper castes as part of the services rendered. 'This bread' became the cause of Grandpa's death; and the latter warns his grandson saying, 'Mhadeva…never depend on the age old bread associated with our caste. Get as much education as you can. Thake away this accursed bead from the mouths of the Manars (a Dalit community of Western India). This poisonous bread will finally kill the very humannes of man….'

16.5. Dalit Christian's Response (examples)

Jashuva Kavi[10]

(a) I have heard that four sons
Were born to Old Brahma
But tell me, O Savithri, who is this
Panchama (fifth) who is worse than faeces?

(b) In this fatted, arrogant world,
Who are friends and relatives to the poor
Except, worms and creatures of anthills?

or

Who will walk to the low, except
A bird or a bat or a rat?

(c) Having waved farewell to the setting sun
He sat down to eat his meagre meal of gruel.
At the end of a long day's back-breaking toil
And stretched on a cot, resting his weary limbs.
Welcome Queen of Bats, resident in sacred Shrines,
Enjoying honour we lowly men can't have,
Convey our greetings to your kinsfolk too
Meditating head down in the awnings of
temple towers.

(d) Crying I told her of the incident,
Hugging me to her breast and kissing me
She said, 'Son, this is an awful country,
But don't complain of caste discrimination;
You'll lose your food, as a Panchama
You have no claim to human rights or your life.
These gods here won't grant their favours
They will not accept a Panchama's worship
The Lord Jesus Christ is your refuge,

Adore Him, He'll be merciful.'
(e) Justice has never been a coward
Truth cannot be put to death
There is no need of fear for
A creature to speak to the Creator.
(f) Equality and friendship are mere words,
Rules and regulations are only slippery knots
Mercy and kindness are but crocodile tears
I condemn these strange ways of religion.
Jesus sacrificed Himself, For the good of the world
How come the divisive doctrines and denominations
Caste factions, communal problems and troubles
Preaching words without doing good works is not Salvation.
(g) You have demonstrated to all equality,
Eating with the poor and despised tax-collectors
You have shown to the world, your humility
Washing and wiping your disciples' feet...
Come to my house too, great teacher.

16.6. Dalit Christian Spirituality

Jashuva, questioned the authority of the *Rigveda* on the mythical explanation given for the caste structure. In doing so, he raised a question of the very 'Root of Dalit Spirituality' when he asked: 'I have heard that four sons were born to Old Brahma. But tell me, O Savithri who is this Panchama who is worse than faeces?' The title for Dalits is *Panchama*, and means the fifth. Jashuva questioned the identity of the Dalits who according to Brahmanical Hindu traditions were a 'no people' or non-existent. The Creator had nothing to do with the Dalits and they were therefore non-spiritual.

Jashuva Kavi compares a Dalit with a Bat, the latter is neither an animal nor a bird. This is precisely the reason why Kavi chooses the Bat as a symbol of his messenger to God. He asks the Bats (who unlike Dalits, have access to sacred shrines) to extend the greetings of the Dalits to other kinsfolk, who are 'Meditating head down in the awnings of temple towers'. This also reflects Jashuva's inner thirst for spirituality.

Jashuva's mother was spiritually rich and she laid the roots of spirituality in him in his childhood. When he was alienated by his upper caste mates she was his companion. She told him, 'as a

Panchama' he had 'no claim to human rights'. Since a Dalit has no place in the religious and social system of the country, therefore he has to look for an alternate spirituality. She told him, 'The Lord Jesus Christ is your refuge. Adore him, he'll be merciful' for only Jesus Christ demonstrated to all-equality including 'the poor and despised tax collectors.'

Like the Old Testament prophets, Jashuva had complete faith in divine justice. Every creature can speak without fear to the Creator and no one can put Truth to death. He questioned the structure of the Christian Church, and the preaching of the pastors as he felt that they did not practice what they loudly preached. His spirituality was deeply rooted in his Dalit experience and life and it was this that gave him that courage to question the existing religious and social structures. He also raised a question by saying, 'How come the doctrines and denominations?' Earlier than him, in one of his essays, Dr. B.R. Ambedkar commented about the same question of Christian denominations and the way these had affected their life negatively. He said: 'On the contrary their religion which is their only cement is infected with denominational differences. The result is that the Indian Christians are too disjointed to have common aim, to have common endeavour....'

The story of first Panjabi Dalit convert Ditt portrays a powerful case of Dalit spirituality, because it also talks about the folly of the established Christian practices. It seems as if the Christian teaching that he imbibed from Nattu (a local Panjabi preacher) were entirely indigenous in character therefore bereft of European cultural and social values. This was perhaps the reason why the Rev. S. Martin (a missionary) was hesitant to accept him for baptism.

Furthermore, Ditt questioned the established practice of 'a new convert staying with a missionary for more instruction and protection', when he insisted on returning to his village. It seems that the Spirit which was behind his conversion forced him to go back to his people. This returning to his people led to the beginning of the 'Spirit or Christian Movement' among the Dalits of Panjab. The missionaries found it difficult to accept this truth, therefore they call it a 'Mass movement' instead of 'Spirit movement'. Similar Spirit led movement began with the conversion of Vethamanikam of Travancore. (*See chapter 5, section 5.1 for details.*)

16.7. Dalit Combat Spirituality

It is clear from the records of Hindu Brahmanical literature that the opponents of the Dalits and Tribals (Adivasi) made a concerted effort to crush their spirituality. The mythical verse in the *Rigveda* 10:97:11, 12 concerning the creation of human beings leaves out the Dalits and Adivasi completely outside the purview of a divine relationship. This clearly means to show the absence of spirituality in the life of these communities.

It is important, however, to recall the efforts of the saints of the Bhakti movement to preach the spiritual equality of all human beings. But their efforts were confined to the religious sphere all along. The real voices demanding a total change in the life of the Dalits and the existing social structures can be heard in the poetry of the Dalit Marathi poets, the examples which because of the scope of this paper are not given here. But still it should be added that these poets influenced Dr. Babasaheb Ambedkar who rejected the Hindu religion, which upheld the caste system and embraced Buddhism as an alternative. These poets represent a spirituality that leads to a total change, acquiring total liberation with full human rights. This spirituality of liberation encourages them to fight for freedom, justice and human dignity.

The early Dalit converts like Vethamanikam from south India and that of Ditt from the north, add a new dimension to the spirituality of liberation or to the 'whole salvation'. These reflect on a liberation from the Christian perspective, rejecting the two basic traditional form of spiritualities practiced by the Church/Christian community in India (supported by the missionaries) namely, 'the spirituality of relief' and 'the spirituality of reform'. In Ditt's example, in his rejection of missionary protection and instruction after his baptism, we find elements of both these spiritualities. He instead depended on the power of the Spirit.

The case of Jashuva Kavi, brings out the story of liberation more vividly. From childhood his mother made it clear that gods like 'Brahma' will not show them any favour and even 'they will not accept a Panchama's worship'. Thus, he was motivated to search for an alternative spirituality which could offer him full 'human rights'. This alternative spirituality according to his mother was to be found in Christ, 'The Lord Jesus Christ is your refuge. Adore him, he'll be merciful.' Jashuva's response to Christ was, 'You have displayed the essence of love by embracing the world, so let me embrace you too'.

Jashuva's commitment to Christ brings him closer to the Old Testament prophetic spirituality (and also to the biblical model, which is the incarnational model: John 1:14, Luke 2:1-7, Isaiah 53:4) which compels a person to fight, denounce, struggle, combat in order to bring about a radical change in the set up of human existence and relationships. This was the only way for all including Dalits and Tribals to lead a fuller life, experience a finer humanity and a new earth.

The spirituality of the Dalits (also of Adivasi)—is a spirituality of liberation as offered to them as well as their oppressors. The unique feature of this is—liberation can flow only from the oppressed as it is their need. The liberation of the Dalits and Adivasis will destroy the system built by the oppressors for survival of their own structures and status. The power generated by their struggle will liberate both the oppressed as well as their oppressors.

Dalits and Adivasi can become the channel of this liberation or salvation as they carry within them the hidden seeds of that humanity which the Creator made on the principle of equality (Genesis 1:27). Thus, they are the only section of society, which represent the undivided humanity of the created world as the rest of the Indian society is divided. It is in this hidden relationship of the Dalits and Adivasi with the Divine, lie the roots of their spirituality of combat, which leads to the 'whole salvation'.

NOTES

1. *Rigveda* (c. 1500-1000 BC) 10:97:11, 12.
2. The *Vishnu Purana* (AD 1045), Book 1:13.
3. *Al-Beruni's India* (AD 1030), ed. E.C. Sachau, Atlantic Publishers, New Delhi, rpt. 1989, p. 56.
4. R.K. Kshirsagar, *Dalit Movement in India and its Leaders*, MD Publications, New Delhi, 1994, p. 32.
5. Jyoti Lanjewar, trans. Shanta Gokhale in *Poisoned Bread*, translations from Modern Marathi Dalit Literature, ed. Arjun Dangle, Orient Longman, Bombay, 1992, p. 22.
6. Sharankumar Limbale, translated by Priya Adarkar in *Poisoned Bread*, Translations from Modren Marathi Dalit Literature, ed. Arjun Dangle, Orient Longman, Bombay, 1992, pp. 64, 65.

7. Yusoja, translated by Charudutta Bhagwat in *Poisoned Bread*, translations from Marathi Literature, ed. Arjun Dangle, Orient Longman Ltd, Bombay, 1992, p. 67.
8. Bandhumadhav, translated by Ramesh Dnyate in *Poisoned Bread*, translations from Modern Marathi Literature, ed. Arjun Dangle, Orient Longman, Bombay, 1992, pp. 147-9, 151-3.
9. See for details on Dalit Bhakti Saints on page 151.
10. Swarnalata P. Ranjan, 'Christian Dalit Aspirations as Expressed by Jashuva Kavi in Gabbilam (The Bat)', in *Indigenous People: Dalits; Dalit Issues in Today's Theological Debate*, ed. James Massey, ISPCK, Delhi, 1994, pp. 324, 327-9.

Bibliography

(1) Primary Sources

Adi Sri Guru Granth Sahib Ji (in Punjabi), Sri Damadami Bir, Pana 1430, Parkasak Bhai Javahar Singh Kirpal Singh and Kampani, Amritsar, n.d.

Acharya, Shriram Sharma (ed.), *Rigveda* (in Sanskrit with meaning in Hindi), 4 vols., Sanskrit Sansthan, Bareilly, 1985.

Burnell, Arthur Coke (tr.), *The Ordinances of Manu*, Motilal Banarsidass, Delhi, 1971.

Goyandaka, Jayadyal (ed.), *Sukhipat Mahabhrat* (Hindi), Gorakhpur, n.d.

Griffith, Ralph T.H. (tr.), *The Hymns of the Rigveda*, Motilal Banarsidass, Delhi, 1986, rpt.

Hume, Robert Ernest (tr.), *The Thirteen Principal Upanishads*, Oxford University Press, Delhi, 1992.

Sen, Makhan Lal (tr.), *Ramayana*, Rupa & Co., Calcutta, 1989.

Swami Vireswaranda (tr.), *Srimad Bhagvadagita*, Sri Ramakrishna Math, Publication Department, Madras, 1987.

The Vishnu Purana (AT). 1045, Book 1.13.

Green, Jay P. (tr.), *The Interliner Bible, Hebrew-Greek-English*, Hendrickson Publishers, London, 1986.

The New Testament (Hindi), The Bible Society of India, Bangalore, 1967.

The Harper Collins Study Bible (New Revised Standard Version), Harper Collins, London, 1993.

Nai Hindi Bible, The Bible Society of India, Bangalore, 1985.

Pavitra Bible: Naya Niyam (in Hindi), India Bible Publishers, New Delhi, 1978, 1982.

(2) Earliest Publications by the Missionaries and Others

Anderson, William B. and Charles R. Watson, *Far North in India*, Presbyterian Church of North America, Philadelphia, 1909.

Andrews, C.F., *North India*, A.R. Mowbray & Co. Ltd., London, 1908.

Clark, The Revd. Robert, *A Brief Account of Thirty Years of Missionary Work of the Church Missionary Society in Panjab and Sindh, 1852-1882*, Mission Press, Lahore, 1883.

Gordon, The Rev. Andrew, *Our India Mission, 1855-1885*, Andrew Gordon: Philadelphia, 1888.

Jenks, David, *Six Great Missionaries of the Sixteenth-Seventeenth Century*. A.R. Mowbray, London, 1930.

Kaye, John William, *Christianity in India: An Historical Narrative*, Missions Publisher, London, 1859.

Newton, John, *Historical Sketches of the Indian Missions of the Presbyterian Church in The United States of America*, The Allahabad Mission Press, Allahabad, 1886.

Possehl, Gregory L. (ed.), *Ancient Cities of the Indus*, Vikas Publishing House, New Delhi, 1979 (contains original essays written between 1924-1979).

Taylor, H.F. Lechmene, *In the Land of the Five Rivers: A Sketch of the Work of the Church of Scotland in the Panjab*, R. & R. Clark, London, 1906.

(3) Government Original Documents and Reports

The Constitution of India (As on the 1st July, 1999), Government of India, New Delhi, 2000. *Census of India*, 1991, Series 1, India, Paper 1 of 1992, Final Population Totals, New Delhi, 1993.

Karnataka Backward Classes Commission (Constituted under the Commissions of Inquiry Act, 1952), Report, vol. I, pt. I, Bangalore, 1975.

Report of the Backward Classes Commission, vols. I & II, pt. I, Government of India, New Delhi, 1980.

Report of the Commissioner for Scheduled Castes and Scheduled Tribes (April 1985-March 1986). Eighth Report, Government of India, New Delhi.

Scheduled Castes and Scheduled Tribes (Prevention of Atrocities) Act, 1989 and *Protection of Civil Rights Act*, 1955 and *Protection of Civil Rights Rules*, 1977 with short notes, 4th edn. 1993, Eastern Book Company, Lucknow.

Shrikant. L.M., *Report of the Commissioner for Scheduled Castes and Scheduled Tribes for the period ending 31st December*, 1951 Government of India, New Delhi, 1961.

Singh, K.S., *The Scheduled Castes, People of India*, National Series Volume II, Anthropological Survey of India, Delhi, 1993.

National Commission for Scheduled Castes and Scheduled Tribes, Special Report January 1998, New Delhi.

The Scheduled Caste and Scheduled Tribes (Prevention of Atrocities Act, 1989 (no. 33 of 1989) and The Protection of Civil Rights Act 1955 (72 of 1955) with short notes, Lucknow, 1990.

Report of the Commissioner for Scheduled Castes and Scheduled Tribes, Twenty-Eight Report 1986-87, Government of India, New Delhi, 1988.

National Commission for Scheduled Castes and Scheduled Tribes, Fourth Report 1996-97-1997-98, vol. 1, Government of India, New Delhi, 1998.

(4) Dictionaries and Other Sources

Apte, Vaman Shivram, *The Practical Sanskrit-English Dictionary*, Motilal Banarsidass, Delhi, 1989.

Brown, Francis, *Hebrew and English Lexicon of the Old Testament*, Clarendon Press, Oxford, 1957.

Kautzsch, E., *Gesenius, Hebrew Grammar*, translated into English by A.E. Cowley, Clarendon Press, Oxford, 1910 (rpt. 1946 and 1949).

Macdonell, Arthur Anthony and Arthur Berriedall Keith, *Vedic Index of Names and Subjects*, vol. 1, Murray, London, 1912.

Monier Williams, Sir M., A *Sanskrit-English Dictionary*, Motilal Banarsidass, Delhi, 1988.

The Interpreter's Dictionary of the Bible: An Illustrated Encyclopedia, vol. 3, Abingdon Press, Nashville, Sixteenth Print, 1996.

Ryder, E.T., 'The Language of the Old testament', in Peake's *Commentary on the Bible*, ed. Mathew Black, Thomas Nelson and Sons, London, 1963.

Webster's Encyclopedic Unabridged Dictionary of the Engligh, Gramercy Books, New York/Avenel, 1994. *The New Bible Dictionary*, Inter-Varsity Press, London, 1968.

Dr. Ramsankar Sukal Rasal, *Bhasa-Sabad Kos* (in Hindi), Allahabad, 1971.

Bhai Kahan Singh, *Mahan Kosh* (in Panjabi), Bhasha Vibhag, Patiala, 1981 (rpt).

(5) UNDP Resolution

Human Development in South Asia 2001: Oxford University Press, Oxford, 2002.

India Development Report 1999-2000: Oxford University Press, New Delhi, 1999.

Development Report 1997, UNDP, Oxford University Press, New York.

(6) Dr. Babasaheb Ambedkar's Works

Ambedkar, Dr. Babasaheb, *Writings and Speeches*, vol. 3, Education Department, Government of Maharashtra, Bombay, 1987.

Ambedkar, B.R., The Untouchables, Who were they and How they become Untouchables in *Dr. Babasaheb Ambedkar: Writings and Speeches*, vol. 7, Education Department, Government of Maharashtra, Bombay. 1990.

Ambedkar, B.R., 'What Congress and Gandhi have Done to the Untouchable' and 'Mr. Gandhi and the Emancipation of the Untouchables' in *Dr. Babasaheb Ambedkar Writings and Speeches*, vol. 9, Education Department, Government of Maharashtra, Bombay, 1991.

Ambedkar, B.R., *Dr. Babasaheb Ambedkar, Writings and Speeches*, ed. Vasant Moon, Government of Maharashtra, vol. 5, Bombay, 1989.

Moon, Vasant (ed.), *Dr Babasaheb Ambedkar's Writings and Speeches*, vol. 7, Education Department, Government of Maharashtra, Bombay, 1990, reprint of '*Who are the Shudras*' and (reprint of *The Untouchables*).

(7) Secondary Sources

Ahmad, Imtiaz, *Caste and. Social Stratification among Muslims in India*, Manohar, Delhi, 1978.

Aixala, J., *Jesuit Formation and Inculturation in India Today*, Gujarat Sahitya, Anand, 1978.

Al-Beruni's India (AD 1030) ed. E.C. Sachau, Atlantic Publishers, Delhi, rpt. 1989.

———, *An Introduction to the Study of Indian History*, Popular Prakashan, Bombay, 1991.

Baago, Kaj, *Pioneers of Indigenous Christianity*, CLS, Madras, 1969.

Banks, Marcus, *Organizing Jainism in India and England*, Clarendon Press, Oxford, 1992.

Beteille, Andre, *Society and Politics in India*, Oxford University Press, Delhi, 1992.

Baxi, Upendra, *Political Justice, Legislative, Reservation for Scheduled Castes and Social Change* (Dr. Ambedkar Memorial Lectures-1978), Madras, University of Madras.

Bhattacharyya, Haridas (ed.), *The Cultural Heritage of India, Evaluation of Religio-Philosophic Culture in India*, vol. IV, *The Religions*, Ramakrishna Mission, Institute of Culture, Calcutta, 1983.

Bhattacharyya, N.N., *Ancient Indian History and Civilization, Trends and Perspectives*, Manohar, Delhi, 1988.

Birth, Cyril Bruce, *An Introduction to Indian Church History*, CLS, Madras, 1981.

Boyd, R.H.S., *An Introduction to Indian Christian Theology*, ISPCK, Delhi, 1991.

Banerjea, Rev. K.M., *The Arian Witness or the Testimony of Arian Scripture in Corroboration of Biblical History and the Rudiments of Christian Doctrine including Dissertation on the Original and Easy Adventure of Indo-Arians*, Asiatic Society of Bengal, Calcutta, 1875.

Boyd, R.H.S., *An introduction to Indian Christian Theology*, ISPCK, Delhi, 1991.

Chanda, Ramaprasad, *The Indo-Aryan Races: A Study of the Origin of Indo-Aryan People and Institutions*, Varendra Research Society, Calcutta, 1875.

Chatterji, Suniti Kumar, *Indo-Aryan and Hindi*, Firma K.L. Mukhopadhyaya, Calcutta, 1969.

Chattopadhyaya, K.P., *The Indian Culture Contacts and Migrations*, Sanskrit College, Calcutta, 1970.

Chaudhuri, Nirad C., *The Continent of Circe*, Jaico Publishing House, Bombay, 1983 (rpt.).

______, *Constitutional Provisions for the Scheduled Caste*, Indian Social Institute, New Delhi, 1974.

Dangle, Arjun, *Poisoned Bread* (translations from Modern Marathi Dalit Literature), Orient Longman, Bombay, 1992.

Desika Char, S.V., *Caste, Religion and Country*, Orient Longman, Delhi, 1993.

Divekar, V.D., *Social Reform Movements in India*, Popular Prakashan, Bombay, 1991.

Dumont, Louis; *Homo Hierarchicus: The Indian Caste System and its Implications*, The University of Chicago Press, Chicago, 1990.

Dutt, N.K., *Origin and Growth of Caste in India*, South Asia Books, Calcutta, 1986.

Drèze, Jean and Amartya Sen; *India: Development and Participation*, Oxford University Press, Delhi, 2002.

Elst, Koenraad, *Indigenous Indians: Agastya to Ambedkar*, Voice of India Publication, Delhi, 1993.

Fernandes, Walter (ed.), *Inequalities, Its Bases and Search for Solutions*, Indian Social Institute, Delhi, 1986.

Forrester, Duncan B., *Caste and Christianity*, Curzon Press, London, 1979.

Frederick, E. Stock and Margert A. Stock, *People Movements in Panjab*, GLS, Bombay, 1978.

Freeman, James M., *Untouchable: An Indian Life History*, Stanford University Press, London, 1979.

Fuchs, Stephen, *The Aboriginal Tribes of India*, The MacMillan Press, London, 1977.

Fuchs, Stephen, *At the Bottom of Indian Society*, Munshiram Manoharlal, Delhi, 1981.

Friere, Paulo and Antonio Foundez, *Learning to Question: A Pedagogy of Liberation*, WCC Publications, Geneva, 1989.

Galanter, Marc, *Competing Equalities, Law and the Backward Classes in India*, Oxford University Press, Bombay, 1984.

Ghurye, G.S., *Caste and Race in India*, Popular Prakashan, Bombay, 1979.

Gokhale, Jayashree, *From Concessions to Confrontation: The Politics of an Indian Untouchable Community*, Popular Prakashan, Bombay, 1993.

Gore, M.S., *The Social Context of Ideology, Political and Social Thought*, Sage, Delhi, 1993.

Grant, John Webster, *God's People in India*, CLS, Madras, 1965.

Grewal, J.S., *Guru Nanak in History*, Publication Bureau, Panjab University, Chandigarh, 1979 (rpt.).

Gupta, Dipankar (ed.), *Social Stratification*, Oxford University Press, Delhi, 1993.

Gupta, S.K., *The Scheduled Castes in Modem Indian Politics, Their Emergence as a Political Power*, Munshiram Manoharlal, Delhi, 1985.

Gutierrez, Gustavo, *A Theology of Liberation: History, Politics and Salvation*, Orbis Books, Maryknoll, New York, 1973.

Heick, Otto W., A *History of Christian Thought*, vol. II, Fortress Press, Philadelphia, 1966.

Hutton, J.H., *Caste in India*, Cambridge University Press, Cambridge, 1946.

Henry O. Thompson (ed.), *Voices from World Religions: Peace in Our Time*, ISPCK, Delhi, 1993.

Haridas Bhattacharyya (ed.), *The Culture Heritage of India*, vol. IV, *The Religions*, The Ramakrishna Mission, Institute of Culture, Calcutta, 1983 (rpt.).

Irudayaraj, Xavier (ed.), *Emerging Dalit Theology*, Jesuit Theological Secretariat, Madurai, 1990.

Isaacs, Harold R., *India's Ex-Untouchables*, Asian Publishing House, Bombay, 1965.

———, *Interpreting Early India*, Oxford University Press, Delhi, 1992.

Ilaiah, Kanclia, 'Dalitism Vs Brahmanism: The Epistemological Conflict in History' in *Dalit Identity and Politics*, ed. Ghan Shyam Shah, Sage, Delhi, 2001.

Job, G.V. et al., *Rethinking Christianity in India*, Published by A.N. Sudarisanan, Madras, 1938.

Joshi, Barbara R. (ed.), *Untouchable! Voice of the Dalits Liberation Movement*, Select Service Syndicate, Delhi, 1986.

Juergenesmeyer, Mark, *Religion as Social Vision—The Movement Against Untouchabitity in 20th Century Punjab*, University of California Press, Berkeley, 1982.

John, T.K. (ed.), *Broken among the Victims: Dalit Presence at the World Social Forum 2004*, CDS, New Delhi, 2004.

Kananaikil, Jose, *Scheduled Caste Converts in Search of Justice, Constitution (Scheduled Castes)*, Indian Social Institute, New Delhi, 1982.

Khan, Agha and Hussain Bin Talat (Co-chairman), *Indigenous Peoples: A Global Quest for Justice, a Report for the Independent Commission on International Humanitarian Issues*, Zed Books, London, 1987.

Kiyoshige, Naohiro, 'Old Testament Lessons on Peace', in *Called to be Peacemakers*', ed. Saguru Matsuki and David L. Swain, Japan Ecumenical Books, Tokyo, 1989.

Khan, Mumtaz Ali, *Mass-Conversion of Meenakthipuram: A Sociological Enquiry*, CLS, Madras, 1983.

Khare, R.S., *The Untouchables as Himself: Ideology, Identity, and Pragmatism among the Lucknow Chamars*, University Press Cambridge, Cambridge, 1984.

Kosambi, D.D., *The Culture and Civilisation of Ancient India in Historical Outline*, Vikas Publishing House, Delhi, 1992.

Kulkc, Eckehard, *The Parsees in India*, Vikas Publishing House, Delhi, 1993.

Kulke, Hermann and Dietmar Rothermund, *A History of India*, Routledge, New Delhi, 1991.

Kurimdkar, Narhar, *Manusmriti: Contemporary Thoughts*, Popular Prakashan, Bombay, 1993.

Khapde, D.K., *Mahatma Jyotiba Phule* (in Hindi), D.K. Khaparde Memorial Trust, Delhi, 1990.

______, *Kristadvaita*, *A Theology for India*, CLS, Madras, 1977.

Lokhande, G.S., *Bhimrao Ramji Ambedkar*, Intellectual Publishing House, Delhi, 1982.

Mackay, Ernest, *Early Indus Civilization* (Second Edition Revised and Enlarged by Dorothy Mackay), Eastern Book House, Patna, 1989.

Majumdar, R.C. and A.D. Pusalkar (eds.), *The History and Culture of the Indian People, The Vedic Age*, University Press, London, 1951.

______, *The History and Culture of the Indian People: The Vedic Age*, University Press, London, 1951.

Mandelbaum, David G., *Society in India*, Popular Prakashan, Bombay, 1990 (rpt.).

Massey, James, *Downtrodden: The Struggle of India's Dalits for Identity, Solidarity and Liberation*, WCC, Geneva, 1997.

———, *The Gospel According to Luke, New Testament*, vol. 3, *Dalit Bible Commentary*, CDS, New Delhi, 2007.

———, *Towards Dalit Hermeneutics*, CDS Pamphlet no. 4, New Delhi, 2001.

———, *Dalits: Issues and Concerns, India's 50 Years of Independence: 1947-97, Status, Growth & Development*, vol. 20, B.R. Publishing Corporation, Delhi, 1998.

———, *Dalits in India: Religion as a Sources of Bondage or Liberation with Special Reference to Christians*, Manohar, Delhi, 1995.

Massey, James (ed), *Indigenous People: Dalits; Dalit Issues in Today's Theological Debate*, ISPCK, Delhi, 1994.

Mathew, C.P. and M.M. Thomas, *The Indian Churches of Saint Thomas*, ISPCK, Delhi, 1967.

Mishra. R.B., *Caste and Caste Conflicts in Rural Society*, Commonwealth Publishers, Delhi, 1989.

Moore, Basil (ed.), *Black Theology: The South African Voice*, C. Hurt & Co., London, 1973.

Mukherjee, Prabhati, *Beyond the Four Varnas: The Untouchables in India*, Motilal Banarsidass, Delhi, 1988.

Mullick, S. Basu (ed.), *Cultural Chotanagpur: Unity in Diversity*, Uppal, Delhi, 1991.

Murgkar, Lata, *Dalit Panther Movement in Maharashtra*, Popular Prakashan, Bombay, 1991.

Narasu, P. Lakshmi, *The Essence of Buddhism*, Thacker &. Co., Bombay, 1948.

O'Hanlon, Rosalind, *Caste, Conflict, and Ideology: Mahatma Jotirao Phule and Low Caste Protest in Nineteenth Century Western India*, Cambridge University Press, Cambridge, 1985.

Oddie, G.A., *Social Protest in India*, South Asia Books, Columbia and Manohar, Delhi, 1978.

——— (ed.), *Religion in South Asia: Religious Conversion and Revival Movements in South Asia in Medieval and Modern Times*, Manohar, Delhi, 1991.

Oommen, T.K., *Protest and Change: Studies in Social Movements*, Sage, Delhi, 1990.

Ouwerkerk, Louise, *The Untouchables of India*, Oxford University Press, London, 1945.

Presler, Henry H, *Primitive Religion in India*, CLS, Madras, 1971.

Patil, Sharad, *Dasa-Sudra Slavery*, Sugawa Prakashan, Pune, 1991.

Paul, Rajaiah D., *The Cross Over India*, SCM Press, London, 1952.

Phule, Jyotirao Govindrao, 'Slavery' in *Collected Works of Mahatma Jotirao Phule*, tr. Prof. P.G. Patil, Government of Maharashtra, Bombay, 1991.

Picket, J. Waskom, *Christian Mass Movements in India*, The Abingdon Press, New York, 1933.

Prabhakar, M.E. (ed.)., *Towards a Dalit Theology*, ISPCK, Delhi, 1988.

Pope John Paul II, *Sollicitudo Rei Social* (On Social Concern, Encyclical Letter), St. Pauls, Bombay, 1988.

Rajaram, Navaratna S., *Aryan Invasion of India: The Myth and the Truth*, Voice of India, New Delhi, 1993.

Rajasekhriah, A.M., *B.R. Ambedkar: The Quest for Social Justice*, Uppal, Delhi, 1989.

Rao, Kande Prasada, *Freedom of Religion for Harijans in India*, Vijaya Printers, Ongole, 1990.

Rao, R. Sangeetha, *Caste System in India: Myth and Reality*, India Publishers and Distributors, Delhi, 1989.

Robb, Peter (ed), *Dalit Movements and the Meanings of Labour in India*, Oxford University Press, Delhi, 1993.

R.K. Kshirsagar, *Dalit Movement in India and its Leaders*, MD Publications, New Delhi, 1994.

Raj, M.C., *Dalitology: The Book of the Dalit People*, Rural Education for Development Society, Shantinagar, Turnkur, 2001.

Roach, Colleen, 'Information and Culture in War and Peace-Overview', in *Communication and Culture in War and Peace*, ed. Colleen Roach, Sage, Newbury Park, 1993.

Senn, Frank C. (ed.), 'Pietism': *Protestant Spiritual Traditions*, Paulist Press, New York, 1986.

Sethna, K.D., *The Problem of Aryan Origins: From an Indian Point of View*, Aditya Prakashan, Delhi, 1992.

Singh, Ram and Nancy Singh (eds.), *The Sugar in the Milk: The Parsis in India*, ISPCK, Delhi, 1986.

Smith, George, *The Life of Alexander Duff*, Hodder and Stoughton, Lonodn, 1881.

Smith, Vincent A, *The Oxford History of India*, Clarendon Press, Oxford, 1958.

Srivastava, Suresh Narain, *Harijans in Indian Society*, The Upper India Publishing House, Lucknow, 1980.

Stevenson, Margaret Sinclair, *Without the Pale: The Life Story of an Outcaste*, Association Press (YMCA), Calcutta, 1930.

Swami Dharma Teertha, *History of Hindu Imperialism*, Dalit Educational Literature Centre, Madras, 1992.

Singh, K.S., *The Scheduled Castes*, Anthropological Survey of India, Oxford University Press, Delhi, 1993.

Singh, K. Suresh (ed.), *The Tribal Situation in India*, Indian Institute of Advance Study, Shimla, 1986 (rpt.).

Thomsen, Vernoika Bennholdt et al. (eds.), *There is an Alternative: Subsistence and Worldwide Resistance to Corporate Globalization*, Zed Books, London, 2001.

The Scheduled Castes: People of India, National Series Volume II, Anthropological Survey of India, Delhi, 1993.

Talagari, Shrikant G., *Aryan Invasion Theory and Indian Nationalism*, Voice of India, Delhi, 1993.

Thapar, Romila, *From Lineage to State*, Oxford University Press, Bombay, 1990.

Tamez, Elsa, *Bible of the Oppressed*, Orbis Books, Maryknoll, New York, 1982.

Thekkedath, Joseph, *History of Christianity in India*, vol. II, Church History Association, Bangalore, 1967.

Trevaskis, Hugh Kennedy, *The Land of the Five Rivers*, Oxford University Press, Oxford, 1928.

Tyndale-Briscoe, Cecil, (of Kashmir), *An Autobiography*, Seeley Service & Co., London, 1946.

Vakil, A.K., *Gandhi-Ambedkar Dispute*, Ashish Publishing House, New Delhi, 1991.

Veeramani, K. and P.R. Kuppuswamy, *According to Law We Are still Shudras—But How?*, Emerald Publishers, Madras, 1989 (rpt.).

Webster, John C.B., *The Christian Community and Change in Nineteenth Century North India*, Macmillan, Delhi, 1976.

______, *The Dalit Christians: A History*, ISPCK, Delhi, 1992.

Wheeler, Sir Mortimer, *The Cambridge History of India, Supplementary Volume: The Indus Civilization*, Cambridge University Press, Cambridge, 1953.

Wilson, K., *The Twice Alienated: Culture of Dalit Christians*, Books Links Cooperations, Hyderabad, 1982.

Weil, Shalva, 'Symmetry between Christians and Jews in India: The Cananite Christians and the Cochin Jews of Kerala', *Indian Sociology*, ed. Louis Dummont, vol. 16, no. 2. Paris, 1982.

Weborg, John, 'Pietisma: The Fire of God Which Flames in the Heart of Germany', in *Protestant Spiritual Traditions*, ed. Frank C. Sen, Paulist Press, New York, 1986.

Yong-Bock, Kim, *Messiah and Minjung: Christ's Solidarity with the People for New Life*, Christian Conference of Asia, Hong Kong, 1992.

Zacharias (Fr.), *An Outline of Hinduism*, St. Joseph's Apostolic Seminary, Alwaye, 1956.

Zelliot, Eleanor, *From Untouchable to Dalit: Essays on Ambedkar Movement*, Manohar, Delhi, 1992.

Index